Willa Cather Remembered

Willa Cather Remembered

COMPILED BY L. BRENT BOHLKE
AND SHARON HOOVER

EDITED BY SHARON HOOVER

University of Nebraska Press, Lincoln and London

Acknowledgments for the use
of previously published material appear on pages 207–10,
which constitute an extension
of the copyright page.
© 2002 by the University of
Nebraska Press
Library of Congress Catalog-
ing-in-Publication Data
Willa Cather remembered /
compiled by L. Brent Bohlke
and Sharon Hoover ; edited by
Sharon Hoover. p. cm.
Includes bibliographical
references. ISBN 0-8032-2395-1
(cloth : alk. paper)—ISBN 0-
8032-7333-9 (pbk. : alk. paper)
1. Cather Willa, 1873–1947.
2. Novelists, American–20th
century—Biography.
3. Cather, Willa, 1873–1947—
Friends and associates.
I. Bohlke, L. Brent, 1942–1989
II. Hoover, Sharon.
PS3505.A87 Z93825 2002
813'.52—dc21
2002018111

"N"

This book is dedicated to the memories
of Bernice Slote and L. Brent Bohlke.

Contents

ILLUSTRATIONS

Preface

"You'll never believe what I've found," Brent, my late husband, would say as he came through the front door of our Lincoln home. His briefcase was loaded to the brim from a day of scouring the Nebraska State Historical Society for new information and insights into the personality of Willa Cather. He would lay his most recent discovery on the kitchen table, and while holding one daughter on his knee (I holding the other), he would share with the excitement of a boy on a quest of finding buried treasure a new bit of information that he hoped could be used in the progressive writing of his book, *Willa Cather in Person*. After accepting the position of chaplain and professor of English at Bard College in Annandale-on-Hudson, New York, we boxed these treasures of carefully researched information, and they traveled with us as we made our way from Nebraska to our new home in New York. It was here that the actual writing and completion of *Willa Cather in Person* took place. Upon the advice of Willis G. Regier, then the director of the University of Nebraska Press, it was decided that the information was too much to be used in one book and should be made into two, the second being titled *Willa Cather Remembered*.

Brent died before the first printing of *Willa Cather in Person* was finished. Because of his tireless efforts even during his illness, his delight in discussing Willa Cather with other scholars, students, or any interested person, and the infectious enthusiasm Brent shared with me, I held on to all scraps of paper, nearly illegible notes, newspaper clippings and writings that he had planned to use in the yet-to-be-finished *Willa Cather Remembered*. I boxed the unfinished work and moved it along with my two daughters back to

Nebraska, always hoping somehow the book he had planned to finish would be published.

Now that it has been completed, my daughters and I would like to acknowledge Susan Rosowski, with our deepest gratitude, for her advice and for introducing us to Sharon Hoover as the person to finish Brent's work. We want to express our gratitude to Sharon Hoover for her sensitivity, patience, and skill in organizing and editing and contributing so generously her time, talent, and energy to the completion of *Willa Cather Remembered*. Without their help, this book would be in the form of notes, papers, and numerous articles still waiting in a box.

Beverly A. Bohlke
Saraugh Bohlke
Susannah Bohlke

Acknowledgments

This book is a community work.

Bernice Slote and L. Brent Bohlke did the major compiling of the selections and developed the vision of the volume.

Susan Rosowski and Beverly Bohlke introduced me to the project, and they and Saraugh and Susanne Bohlke made me feel comfortable in taking it on.

Participants of the Willa Cather conferences and symposiums and members of the Willa Cather Seminar group at University of Nebraska–Lincoln supported the work.

The librarians and archivists at Alfred University, University of Nebraska–Lincoln, Nebraska State Historical Society, and Willa Cather Pioneer Memorial and Educational Foundation in Red Cloud all gave graciously to this volume. Special thanks go to Pam Lakin of Herrick Library for indexing.

Research assistants have given the book much of its accuracy in documentation by helping to verify information. I owe special thanks to Jennifer Buttaro, Michael Cadwallader, Jason Chilson-Cline, and Heather Yanda.

The editors and readers at the University of Nebraska Press provided important suggestions and showed great patience.

The National Endowment for the Humanities provided support for preparing the manuscript, and Alfred University provided a sabbatical in which I could sort the Bohlke papers and begin to plan the volume, now in your hands, while enjoying the landscape of the Great Plains.

Finally, there is the personal support that makes the academic work possible: neighbors Barbara Bennett, Lisa Wood, and Cindy York, friendly computer experts Javier Morales and Nadine Hoover, secretary Pat Sweeney, discriminating and tactful colleagues Carol Burdick and Michael Mc-Donough.

Special thanks go to James Woodress and Susan Rosowski for reading the first draft of the manuscript.

To my family and friends, I am always indebted. With all the support this book has had, there should be no errors. However, there will be, and those belong to me.

Sharon Hoover

Introduction

A local historian characterized Willa Cather's great-grandfather James Cather as "Above the average farmer in intellect. Possessed with rare physical strength and wonderful energy, these qualities gave him an advantage over weaker men. Always informed on the current topics of the day, his conversational abilities were admirable. Young men were always benefited by having him as a friend" (Woodress 14).[1] Like her great-grandfather, Willa Cather had qualities that helped her to move adroitly among numerous social circles. The reminiscences in this volume often conjure a worthy descendant of James Cather. His great-granddaughter was called "brilliant" and was said to be "endowed with wonderful vitality." As a journalist, then an editor at *McClure's Magazine*, she was highly informed on the topics of the day and never settled for easy answers. Reportedly, she could converse "unstintedly," yet, on the other hand, "in a half an hour's conversation" could "reveal" to a younger artist the "need of that activating force in art, the creative spark of desire." As she became older, Cather lost some of her earlier zest, but as a hearty young and middle-aged woman, she was known for her curiosity, energy, and "robust laughter."

Cather's personal qualities allowed her to move easily in cultural circles wherever she went. At fourteen, she wrote a letter to a woman who was away from Red Cloud, giving her extensive news of who had moved away, who had come, who had had picnics, and who was in love, all in lightly drawn, graceful, and lively language. Cather continued her letter by telling her older correspondent about making rounds with the local doctor, stuffing birds, and having an office with a library in her father's publishing endeavor, the *Red Cloud Republican*.[2] Cather appeared to know everyone in Red Cloud as well as much of its business and politics. At the University of Nebraska–Lincoln, Cather quickly made friends with the daughter of the university's president, Dorothy Canfield (Fisher), who was also a student in Cather's preparatory class. Although Canfield Fisher was several years younger than Cather, as it is often with bright children, the age difference was less important than the intellectual sympathies. Fisher, too, later became an important writer. As Cather began to publish and to study journalism, she became acquainted with the family of Charles Gere, the publisher and editor of the *Journal*, and with Will Owen Jones, the *Journal*'s managing editor, and his talented musician wife.[3] She also became friends with Louise Pound, later the first woman president of the Modern Language Association. Some friendships were temporary, some lasted over decades, and some waxed and waned and waxed again. Throughout her lifetime, Cather had a knack for making friends who helped her to grow socially, intellectually, and professionally. Many supported her faithfully until their deaths, even after being stung in some way by Cather's sometimes reckless conduct toward friends.

After she moved to Pittsburgh, just as she had in Red Cloud and Lincoln, Cather eagerly visited with active professionals and like-minded, aspiring writers and artists as well as with the affluent and genteel. Almost immediately, she struck up a friendship with the George Seibel family, in whose home she regularly enjoyed German suppers and the translation of French novels. She enjoyed attending musical evenings in the wealthy suburb of Edgewood, in such homes as that of John C. Slack, president of the Union Fidelity Insurance Company (Byrne and Snyder 27–28). After two years of living in boarding houses, she moved in with Judge Samuel A. McClung's family on Squirrel Hill. Their house was a stately, well-appointed, and well-cared-for home and a frequent gathering place for people interested in music, drama, and literature. Isabelle McClung became a close lifelong friend providing a gracious, supportive space for Cather to write not only in Pittsburgh but also later in France, although Cather never found the latter as conducive to work. One or more of Cather's friends probably brought a high school teaching position to Cather's attention and may have helped her to obtain it. Teaching, she thought, would allow her more freedom for her own writing. Her first year of teaching was exhausting, but as she became more at ease in her new role, she began publishing stories on a regular basis. She appeared to make no lifelong friends among the other teachers. Some, it is reported, openly disliked her, especially her way of making friends with brighter students, several of whom became writers. While teaching, she also gathered material for one of her best-known short stories, "Paul's Case."

Cather moved easily among people who could and would further her interests and career. While still in Pittsburgh in 1905, she was among the select dinner guests for Mark Twain's seventieth birthday. After moving to New York City to join the staff at *McClure's Magazine* and being sent to Boston to check facts on a series of articles on Mary Baker Eddy, Cather became friends with Mrs. Annie Fields of Boston, widow of the longtime publisher of Tichnor and Fields. Cather had seen the Tichnor and Fields imprint since childhood on books by such writers as Emerson, Hawthorne, and Longfellow. At Mrs. Fields's, Cather met Sarah Orne Jewett, who became for Cather an important mentor.

Cather helped others along too. As she became able, she helped family members further their education. She took young Dorothy Canfield Fisher under her wing in Lincoln, remained a lifelong correspondent of several of her students in Pittsburgh, encouraged Fanny Butcher in New York City, taught at Bread Loaf one summer, and read Shakespeare with the Menuhin children.

The Willa Cather experienced by her friends and acquaintances has not always been well known to late-twentieth-century readers. Bourgeois and Midwestern, Cather was not a member of a social register society like Edith Wharton, nor of avant-garde or expatriate circles as were Gertrude Stein and the somewhat younger H. D., nor was she a member of the "lost generation" of the even younger F. Scott Fitzgerald and Ernest Hemingway, although both apparently read her work. In a letter Fitzgerald wrote to Cather after he had written *The Great Gatsby*, he tells Cather that he hopes she does not think he has plagiarized her description of Marian Forrester in *A Lost Lady* for a description he has written for Daisy (Bruccoli 171–78). In the "roaring twenties," when the "lost generation" was in its twenties, however, Cather turned fifty and was intent on fully developing her talent, writing six major novels during the decade. She conceived narrative structures that would allow her, with precisely chosen words and artful but simple sentences, to write novels of drama and romance that eluded nineteenth-century sentimentality and ornateness: "The higher processes of art are all processes of simplification," she wrote (*On Writing* 40). Comparisons of Cather with the early-twentieth-century American writers, who were well known for being transcontinental in their behaviors and experimental in their writings and about whom much was written, have had the effect of making Cather appear aloof from her cultural peers and a difficult person to know. She could be difficult, as even Mildred Bennett, the driving force of the Willa Cather Pioneer Memorial for many years, admitted. Cather was often impatient, even intolerant, toward people whose opinions or talents did not match her own. She was ambitious and not above using others, even her friends, to further her own purposes. In addition, she did not crave publicity or the extra dollars from subsidiary rights, so her works and life existed for many years in the shadows.

To further dull our sense of Cather as a clear, often memorable personality, the conditions of her will have meant that her letters are relatively unavailable and, except for the few published in her lifetime, may not be quoted. Although large batches of letters were destroyed by Cather or by her friends, many remaining letters are located in collections as geographically diverse as Connecticut, Illinois, Nebraska, California, Texas, and Virginia. As a result, few people ever hear Cather's voice as a vibrant correspondent who maintained a lively, continual conversation with people in letters when she could not do so in person. The letters introduce us to a woman who wrote sparkling thank-yous, compassionate condolences, sensitive letters of advice, and moving letters expressing her own needs for help and comfort. They also document Cather's sometimes less tactful and stubborn choices, such as presenting a recognizable acquaintance in an unflattering fictional portrait (Madigan 13). At the same time, however, they document her energetic gregariousness throughout much of her life and her remarkable generosity to old friends.[4]

By presenting in one place the lesser-known recollections of Cather by people who knew her over the years of her professional life, which began when she was a student, the current volume should assist readers in knowing the Cather who sparked one classmate at the University of Nebraska to say, "I don't know if I like Willie, but she's never dull" (Bennett, "Willa Cather" 64). Leon Edel, one of Cather's early biographers and an astute reader of American literature, has appropriately pointed out "the problem with the reliability of eyewitnesses," and readers are reminded that each kind of source has its own validity (17–18). Cather, in 1922, writing a letter about the evolution of her volume on Mary Baker Eddy, points out the problem of the legends that grow up around an important figure, fuelled by people who suffer from envy.[5] The most important sources for a study of Cather's *oeuvre* are her novels, short stories, essays, and a single early book of poems. Secondly, a Cather student should consult the biographies. The most noteworthy is James Woodress's *Willa Cather: A Literary Life*, a comprehensive and reliable source for searching dates, places, and names. There are also Sharon O'Brien's provocative *Willa Cather: The Emerging Voice*; Hermione Lee's distanced reading of Cather, *Double Lives*; and Joan

Acocella's *Willa Cather and the Politics of Criticism*, a stimulating analysis of Cather's position in the ever shifting politics of twentieth-century American literary criticism. Greater access to and interest in the letters should permit them to become more important as basic documents to inform our readings of Cather's works.

There are other books, too, that any student of Cather's work must read: Bernice Slote's *The Kingdom of Art*, a conscientious and sensitive study of the development of Cather's aesthetic sympathies; William M. Curtin's *The World and the Parish*, a two-volume collection of newspaper articles Cather wrote from 1891 to 1902; and L. Brent Bohlke's *Willa Cather in Person*, a collection of interviews, speeches, and letters published in Cather's lifetime. Slote's and Curtin's books provide readers with invaluable insight into Cather's artistic prejudices, especially as a young woman, and Bohlke's volume documents interactions Cather had with the public until late in her life. Kathleen Byrne and Richard Snyder's *Chrysalis: Willa Cather in Pittsburgh 1896–1906* contains many details about Cather's Pittsburgh years not found in other Cather biographies. Several memoirs also provide indispensable sources of information about Cather as a writer and a woman, albeit overly colored at times by friendship and sympathy: Edith Lewis's *Willa Cather Living*, Marion Marsh Brown and Ruth Crone's *Only One Point of the Compass: Cather in the Northeast*, and Elizabeth Shepley Sergeant's *Willa Cather: A Memoir*.

The current volume does not duplicate any of the standard works but instead collects in one place a selection of less accessible reminiscences and articles that reflects more on Cather as a person than as a writer, although the two are often inextricably mixed. The materials were drawn from newspapers and journals, portions of books, and previously unpublished letters or reflections in which the authors talk about knowing Cather personally. Many of these writers knew Cather for many years, others knew her at a particular time and place, and a few saw her only in passing, but it seems worthwhile to note that she could sometimes leave a powerful impression on a person she knew only briefly.

The memories of Cather in this book are written by persons who reflect dominant interests in her life: journalists, literary people, librarians, students, pastoral advisors, and personal friends from Red Cloud's farm country to the world's recital stages. Some were celebrities—for example, Truman Capote creates a lovely vignette of an encounter he supposedly had with Cather over a cup of cocoa. Most reminiscences are written by lesser-known but important persons, such as Henry Seidel Canby, editor of the

Saturday Review of Literature, and Fanny Butcher, editor of the *Chicago Tribune* book section. A few of the writers are unabashed admirers; some disliked her. All, however, present Cather as a memorable character with an unmistakable presence.

Organizing the reminiscences presented particular problems. Arranging them strictly by date of publication creates a helter-skelter scenario of articles, useful to scholars because of its lack of editorial manipulation but not helpful for the more general but interested reader. To appeal to both kinds of readers, a dynamic of Cather's novels, I chose to organize the selections in what appeared to be three obvious groupings:

1. Journalists were the first to write about Cather, and they continued to write about her growing reputation throughout her life. Students who had Cather as a high school teacher and who later became professional writers were included in this section because the teaching along with the journalism and early professional attempts at creative writing formed an important, extended period in the development of Cather's art.

2. The center of the book presents reminiscences by literary people. Some of these articles are closely related to reviews; however, they are written primarily as personality profiles and present Cather as an individual first and a writer secondarily.

3. The last section collects memories of Cather by those who knew her in more informal relationships throughout her life. Because of that, the third section covers the most chronological ground, beginning with an interview about Cather with Carrie Sherwood Miner, on the occasion of Miner's hundredth birthday. Miner, who lived down the street from Cather in Red Cloud and became a lifelong friend, recalls their early years in Nebraska. Other selections in this section reflect memories of some whose lives were touched more briefly by Cather, yet they recall a particular aspect of her life that was significant to them.

Cather has been characterized as having sought success, then rebuffing the public role that follows. This conclusion seems to oversimplify the choices she made concerning her time, energies, and attention. As she grew away from young womanhood, she often limited her activities so that she could devote her greatest energies to her writing. Throughout her life, Cather made fast friends with people of like mind and curiosity, some of whom she alienated along the way but many of whom helped her on her path many times—professionally, psychologically, and even monetarily in her years of apprenticeship. After she had achieved her goal to become a writer who broke new ground in a literary tradition, however, she did not forget them. She wrote to them to congratulate them on successes, to console them in losses, to encourage them during hard times, and, again and again, to express her love for them. Only those who have access to the letters see Cather's attentions to and calls for friendship expressed in her own inimitable style, but the reflection of their essence appears in these reminiscences. A few of the selections in this volume reflect a deep resentment of Cather or provide a harsh critique of some of her personal or journalistic choices. For the most part, however, they reflect respect for a strong woman with clear prejudices, especially about writing, a gift for finding like-minded friends wherever she went, and a passion for life on her own terms.

Willa Cather Remembered

A Lively Apprenticeship

1

At fifteen, Willa Cather became a newspaper writer and editor. Her father, Charles Cather, was running the *Red Cloud Republican*. In late August 1889, on her father's letterhead, "C. F. Cather Real Estate and Loan Broker Officer," she writes enthusiastically to Mrs. Stowell that she is a staff reporter for the *Republican*, under the editorship of Doctor McKeeby.[1] She reminds Mrs. Stowell that she is adept at knowing all the business in town; therefore, she guarantees the paper's "newsiness."[2] The letter is filled with quick, well-drawn word pictures, graceful language, and realism with a light touch. The writing in the *Red Cloud Republican* is also lively, especially in its local news and humor sections. Some of the paper's ideas and its layout are then echoed in the *Hesperian*, the student newspaper at the University of Nebraska, when Cather becomes an editor on its staff.

The story of Cather's writing career began in earnest when she attended the university in Lincoln: a freshman college essay was published in the *Lincoln State Journal* without her foreknowledge, submitted by her professor Ebenezer Hunt; she and Louise Pound were involved in beginning a newspaper, the *Lasso*; Cather joined the staff of the yearbook, the *Sombrero*, which she and Mariel Gere edited for a year; Cather became a contributor and editor of the *Hesperian*; and she began to write for the city newspapers. In her junior and senior years, she wrote thousands of words of newscopy a week in addition to her classwork.[3]

Within a year of her graduation from college, Cather moved to Pittsburgh to be editor of the *Home Monthly*, a magazine for women designed to rival *Ladies' Home Journal*. She continued to send copy to the Lincoln newspapers, wrote a great deal to fill the *Home Monthly*, and submitted stories and poems to other publications. Meanwhile, she worked as wire editor for the *Pittsburgh Leader*, then taught in the Pittsburgh public schools. Placing stories in *McClure's Magazine* led her to New York City, where she worked in-house for S. S. McClure until 1912, when finally she felt she could support herself by writing only what she wanted to write.

Cather's itinerary on her way to a writer's life led her through the journalistic world of Lincoln as the city developed from a country town into a major cultural center, into the heart of Pittsburgh as it grew rapidly in culture and industry, and on to New York City and into the offices of what was considered one of the finest magazines of the early twentieth century. Cather continued to write both for *McClure's Magazine* and for "herself," even as she worked as a managing editor for McClure. As an editor, she met creative people and traveled throughout the United States and Europe to search for writers and stories. In a 1908 letter to Sarah Orne Jewett, Cather confesses that she feels split between wanting to save herself for her own writing and enjoying the perks of working in McClure's office.[4] Later, in a 1916 letter to Dorothy Canfield Fisher, Cather admits that she has always liked the verve and energy of the theatrical in history, on stage, and in life, and now that she has withdrawn from the show, she misses the energy such experiences induced in her.[5]

The following remembrances trace the development of the responses Cather elicited from those who worked with her or observed her in her work as she progressed from student and novice journalist to editor, teacher, and well-known powerbroker at one of America's foremost magazines.

A Writer's Beginnings

The publication of Cather's freshman essay on Thomas Carlyle in the *Nebraska State Journal* apparently turned her thoughts about the future from science to the humanities. By becoming a newspaper columnist and drama critic, she found a way to indulge in drama, music productions, and books and to publish her opinions about them. As the depression of the 1890s affected her family, she could also earn the money necessary to stay at the university. James Woodress estimates that during her final year of college, she published an average of more than four pieces a week for the *Journal* in addition to the writing she did for her extracurricular activities and for her classes.

Another advantage she reaped from her journalistic life was numerous professional and personal friends. Will Owen Jones was managing editor of the *Journal* when it published Cather's essay on Carlyle. In the spring of 1893, she took a class in journalism from him, and the following summer she served as one of his two assistants for a journalism course he taught for the annual Nebraska Chautauqua Assembly. His family fostered Cather's musical and social education too. Mrs. Jones (Edith Doolittle), a graduate of the New England Conservatory, consistently received rave reviews for her concerts. In May 1895, for instance, Cather's senior spring, three hundred people gathered in the courtyard in the home of Mr. and Mrs. L. C. Richards for a recital by Mrs. Jones, whose playing the *Boston Home Journal* said was marked by an "extremely fine technique," which was "delicately and accurately rendered."[1] Cather moved easily among the society that gathered around Mr. and Mrs. Jones, and she later moved with the same ease into the society in Pittsburgh. More valuable, however, than simply being accepted

Willa Cather and the *Hesperian* staff. Courtesy of the Nebraska State Historical
Society, Willa Cather Pioneer Memorial Collection.

in society, Cather seemed to find those of kindred spirit in each place she
moved, and she gathered a core of reliable and sensitive friends around her
who recognized her talent early, supported it steadily, and later, on occasion,
defended it.

ELIA W. PEATTIE

Elia Peattie (1862–1935) was the first "girl reporter" on the *Chicago Tribune*.[1]
Although her travels took her away from Chicago, she continued to review books
for the *Tribune* until her death. Like Cather, Peattie was obviously a talented young
writer and a woman of great energy and presence. When her husband became
editor of the *Omaha Daily Herald*, she wrote daily columns for the *Omaha World
Herald* and was active in community and professional affairs. In addition, she wrote
poems, essays, stories, and books. Unlike Cather, however, she soon found herself

with an ailing husband and four children. Hence, she was often burdened with producing a quantity of work to support her family. Peattie felt that her steady book reviewing—critiquing others' creative work—led to unevenness in the quality of her own more creative work, some of which is excellent and some less so.

The article Peattie wrote about Nebraska women journalists first appeared in 1895, the same year Cather graduated from the university and the year that Will Owen Jones proposed to the newspaper representatives association a resolution that a women's auxiliary be formed. The following year, the women became full members of the association. Each of the nine female journalists in Peattie's article was a writer; many were, in addition, accomplished business people, expert typesetters, and publishers. Whatever her specific responsibility, each woman successfully forged new frontiers in Nebraska for journalism and for women.

At the time the article was written, Cather was writing for the *Courier*, "a weekly paper devoted to society, literature, art and the polite world in general," in Peattie's words. Cather was Peattie's last subject in the article and received her highest praise.

Newspaper Women of Nebraska

Working with Miss Harris [Sarah Butler Harris of the *Lincoln Courier*] is Miss Willa Cather, a graduate of the University also, and a young woman with a genius for literary expression. Although not an editor in the correct sense of the word, yet her work is editorial and it has made the *Courier* the brightest paper in Nebraska, regarded from a literary point of view. Her criticisms, both literary and dramatic are clever, original and generally just. But above all they are clever and full of "ginger," as Mr. Hoyt, the playwright, would say. She has, as Miss Harris, a deep love of books, and an elegant style of writing. She keeps in touch with whatever is newest in the literary work the world over, and writes her opinions freely and one may say—gaily. If there is a woman in Nebraska newspaper work who is destined to win a reputation for herself, that woman is Willa Cather. She has great capacity for study, and is sure to grow from year to year in knowledge of her work and in felicity of style. Indeed, without flattery, it can be said that honest workmanship already distinguishes her columns. She was born in Winchester, Virginia, but moved with her parents to Red Cloud, Nebraska, in 1885. When she was fifteen years old her father came into possession of a newspaper—*The Red Cloud Republican*, and he installed his bright daughter as editor and business manager. After six months work on the paper she entered the state university from which she graduated in 1895. During her years at the "U of N," she was literary editor of the *Hesperian*, a semi-monthly magazine, for one year. The succeeding year she was managing editor of the same paper. For the last two years she has been dramatic critic on the *State Journal*, and is now, as mentioned before, associate editor of the *Courier*.

In *History of the Nebraska Press Association*, ed. Henry Allen Brainerd, Book 2, 23–32. Lincoln: N.p., 1923. First published in *Beaver City Nebraska Editor*. 1895.

WILL OWEN JONES

Will Owen Jones (1862–1928) graduated from the University of Nebraska–Lincoln in 1886 and became city editor of the *Nebraska State Journal*. From 1892, during Cather's college career, until his sudden death, which left Cather stunned, he was its managing editor. Jones was well known throughout Nebraska as a writer and speaker and recognized beyond the state for his personal and professional standards. President Theodore Roosevelt appointed him to the Board of Visitors of the U.S. Naval Academy in 1907, and the Carnegie Peace Foundation selected him as one of forty U.S. editors to tour Europe on a fact-finding mission in 1927.[1]

The novel Jones refers to at the end of his article is *One of Ours*, which had won the Pulitzer Prize, certainly a justification for his hiring Cather at the *Journal* when she was merely a student. Jones was one of Cather's first dedicated friends and supporters in the writing business.

More or Less Personal

The Lincoln friends of Miss Willa Cather regret that she does not feel strong enough to endure any public manifestation of the regard they feel for her and their appreciation of her accomplishments in the world of writers. Miss Cather, it will be remembered, began her career as a writer on the *Journal* while she was still a student in the university. For several years she wrote dramatic criticisms of such biting frankness that she became famous among actors from coast to coast.

That was in the days when the theater flourished here, not having yet been killed by the movies. Many an actor of national reputation wondered on coming to Lincoln what would appear the next morning from the pen of that meatax young girl of whom all of them had heard. Miss Cather didn't stand in awe of the greatest actors, but set each one in his place with all of the authority of a veteran metropolitan critic. Her admirers believe that she would have exceeded the reputation of the late James Huneker and other leaders in the profession if she had devoted her talents to criticism instead of fiction. She graduated from the university in 1895, and soon after that went on a home publication in Pittsburgh. From that rather mild occupation she passed over to the *Pittsburgh Leader*. About twenty years ago an agent of S. S. McClure, scouting in the west for new writers, asked the *Journal* office for the names of any Nebraskans who might be able to produce something for the magazine. Miss Cather's name was suggested. He called on her at Pittsburgh, and as a result she went to a new job and was associate editor of *McClure's* magazine from 1906–1912. Since then she has produced a work of fiction almost every year. Her newest novel is now ready for distribution.

Nebraska State Journal, 1 Nov. 1921, 6.

LOUISE POUND

Louise Pound (1872–1958), a university junior when Cather was still in preparatory school, belonged to a distinguished pioneer family in Lincoln, dressed in elegant clothes, and was socially adept and highly intellectual—she took a Ph.D. at Heidelberg. Nevertheless, these two young women became collaborators and close friends. In *Shakespeare Up to Date*, a satirical play that featured the heroines of Shakespeare after they were married, Louise played Juliet, her sister, Olivia Pound, played Ophelia, and Cather played Lady Macbeth. Lady Macbeth insists that Shakespeare has libeled them. She warns them "to beware; they vow vengeance against him, and the curtain falls while Lady Macbeth calls upon the powers that be to aid her."[1]

In a way characteristic of her energetic, intense youth, Cather appears to have been infatuated with Pound, but after being welcomed into the Pound home for two years, Cather was refused its hospitality when her zest for satire ran ahead of her social tact. After Cather wrote a scathing and identifiable portrait of Louise's brother, Roscoe Pound, who had returned from Harvard to teach at the University of Nebraska–Lincoln, the two women were never close again (Bennett, "Friends" 5–7). The rift healed somewhat, however, so that the two had occasional friendly interactions as they became older.

Pound had a distinguished scholarly career. She taught at the University of Nebraska–Lincoln and was elected to such positions as vice-president of the American Dialect Society and of the Linguistic Society of America, and she was the first woman president of the Modern Language Association. She was co-founder and senior editor of *American Speech*. She was also the first woman to be inducted into the Nebraska Sports Hall of Fame.[2]

Pound is not the author of the following unsigned piece, but it is telling that thirty-five years later, as a college professor, when she reaches for an example of the

Willa Cather and Louise Pound. Courtesy of the Nebraska State Historical Society, Willa Cather Pioneer Memorial Collection.

kind of young woman she would like to teach, she recalls her "spirited" student-friend Cather.

Modern Coed Lacks Fire, Laments Louise Pound

The modern college girl lacks fire and spirit, in the opinion of Dr. Louise Pound, professor of English language at Nebraska University and sister of Roscoe Pound, former dean of the Harvard law school.

Dr. Pound recalled the days when coeds always were fighting or plotting something. Today's maidens, she says, tend to be disinterested in everything.

"It is most discouraging," she said, "to have that young lady in my front row applying lipstick the entire period during my class. In reading some beautiful poem, when I am trying to keep myself from being moved to tears, or am trying to move my audience to tears, I find it a fascinating distraction to watch this girl smearing her mouth, oblivious."

Dr. Pound pointed to Willa Cather, noted novelist, who attended Nebraska University, as an example of the spirited coed.

Besides being quite outspoken, Miss Cather wrote telling portraits of her professors and leading lights generally, Dr. Pound recalled. At one time, she included Roscoe Pound in a sketch using material gained when a guest in the Pound household. This breach of etiquet Mother Pound and Sister Olivia found unforgivable.

When someone suggested to Dr. Pound the modern coed is "too busy trying hard to be sophisticated," she replied:

"The faculty is busy trying hard to be sophisticated, too."

Omaha World-Herald, 19 May 1937, 2.

MARIEL GERE

Mariel Gere (1874–1960) and her sisters, Frances and Ellen, were friends of Cather's from her earliest days at the university. Their grandfather was the son of a Nebraska pioneer who founded the *Nebraska State Journal* in 1867, and their father was Charles H. Gere, editor-in-chief of the *Journal* until his death in 1904. Letters to Mr. Gere from Cather show that she depended on his help in landing the job on the *Home Monthly* in Pittsburgh. Cather later credited Mrs. Gere with convincing her to let her hair grow and to dress in more feminine fashion. All her life, Cather trustingly confided in Mariel Gere, as evidenced by the many letters which went back and forth between them as they became lifelong correspondents.[1]

Although Mariel Gere majored in the sciences and later taught high school and wrote chemistry textbooks, she also wrote occasional articles for her father's newspaper. The following article was provoked by a review of James R. Shively's book *Writings from Willa Cather's Campus Years*. The book contained some examples of Cather's collegiate work and, in addition, letters Shively had solicited from Cather's former college classmates. Well aware of Cather's antipathy for public display of her private life, many of Cather's friends boycotted Shively's requests. On the other hand, some former colleagues seemed to enjoy the opportunity to bring her public reputation more in line with their more negative opinions of her. Not everyone in Lincoln had thought highly of Cather's talents or enjoyed her company, most notably her college classmate E. C. Ames, whose allegations that Cather lacked friends and talent Mariel Gere refutes.

Friends of Willa Cather's Campus Years

Friends of Willa Cather—and she had many friends—were astonished and most indignant when they read some of the things quoted in Sunday's review ("More or Less Personal") from the little book put out by the University of Nebraska Press, called *Writings from Willa Cather's Campus Years*.

The letter written by the gentleman (E. C. Ames) "who was in the university at the same time as Billy Cather" contains some statements that in my opinion are far from correct. For example, "Miss Cather had no friends, and wanted none," is a most astonishing statement.

I can name at least four faculty members who were unquestionably her friends and who appreciated her ability. Professor E. Hunt, Professor Herbert Bates, Professor James T. Lees, and Professor Clara Conklin. Chancellor Canfield, and Miss Mary Jones (the university librarian) should be included in this group.

Among university students who were her very real friends were Miss Katherine Weston, Miss Flora Bullock, Misses Mariel, Ellen, and Frances Gere, Miss Althea Roberts, Miss Maysie Ames, and Miss Katherine Melick. Also Will Westermann. There were unquestionably others, that I cannot think of at the moment.

Among newspaper writers, Mr. Charles H. Gere and Mr. Will Owen Jones were good friends of Miss Cather's and admirers of her work, as was Mrs. Sarah Harris Dorris (then Miss Sarah Harris). Mr. and Mrs. Max Westerman and Mrs. C. H. Gere were also close friends of this gifted young woman.

While Dorothy Canfield was too young to be a freshman in the university (I believe she took some art work there), she collaborated with Miss Cather in writing an article printed in the '95 yearbook called the *Sombrero*, and all through the years she has been a sincere friend.

Another statement in the (Ames) letter that is not quite correct is "Miss Cather contributed a column to the *Daily Nebraskan*." But the *Daily Nebraskan* was not published until 1901. However, there was a paper called *The Nebraskan* founded in 1894, which is probably the paper he referred to.

In saying that she wore short hair and dressed like a man, the writer of that letter is eminently correct, as far as the first two or three years of her sojourn in the university are concerned. It was not true, however, of her last two years, as she had let her hair grow long and wore distinctly feminine clothes, as I can prove by photographs of her that are in my possession, one of them in a ball dress that was decidedly up to date.

In regard to her thinking so well of herself, this may be the impression she gave to people who did not know her intimately, but her closest friends were aware that she was far from so sure of herself as he seems to think. I have letters from her which show surprising modesty for a young person of her ability.

One seems to draw the conclusion from the selections included in *Writings from Willa Cather's Campus Years* that her writing showed little or no literary ability. Yet Professor Hunt, who was one of the ablest English teachers the university ever had, and Professor Bates, whose literary taste and ability were most unusual, both believed those campus writings showed that she was remarkably gifted.

In fact, an essay she wrote for a freshman English class on Thomas Carlyle struck Professor Hunt as so superior to essays written by other students, that he showed it to Will Owen Jones, who forthwith published it in the *Journal*, he thought it so remarkable. Up to the time she read her essay in the paper Willa Cather had intended to study medicine. She changed her mind then and there and decided to devote herself to writing.

Before long, Mr. Jones asked her to write a column for the *Journal*, and I think the author of "Little Book" (James R. Shively) is mistaken when he says that she only wrote occasionally and that she was not paid for it.

In a letter to Mr. Jones which I have in my possession, she says, "a few years after this" (this being the time her Carlyle essay was published) "I began to write regularly for the *Journal*, you remember, and I was paid ———" (and she mentions the amount).

Lincoln Evening Journal, 28 Feb. 1950, 6.

GEORGE SEIBEL

George Seibel (1872–1958) and Cather met soon after she moved to Pittsburgh. Over his lifetime, he was a poet and fiction writer, newspaperman and editor, teacher and librarian, lecturer and local judge, a respected citizen. He read and wrote professionally in German, and in the following article portrays the tenor and content of the evenings he and Cather read French together at the Seibel home. Mrs. Seibel, who also participated in the evening reading, and their daughter were favorites of Cather's too, making the relationship between Seibel and Cather familylike. When Dorothy Canfield Fisher came to visit Cather in Pittsburgh during Cather's first Christmas away from home, Cather took her friend to the Seibel home. Seibel's gentle, self-mocking sense of humor gives readers well-delineated pictures both of a young, energetic, hungry-for-life Cather and an older Cather who protected her energy for her writing.

Miss Willa Cather from Nebraska

When Willa Cather died no one arose to pour forth reminiscences, anecdotes and personal gossip, because few people knew this artist who listened at the door of life and set down in sensitive prose the whispers she overheard.

She was so shy as to become almost a recluse; trashy publicity was her pet abomination; tea and brioches did not tempt her palate.

It was my happy fortune to know her very well in the earliest of her formative years, spent in Pittsburgh, before she became an ingrown genius.

Around the last *fin de siecle* Axtell, Orr & Co. were publishing the *National Stockman and Farmer* in Pittsburgh, devoted to articles on how to build a silo, and decorated with portraits of prize pigs. Just as other printers had been lured by the mirage of the *Youth's Companion,* so Axtell and Orr had heard of the fabulous millions pouring upon Cyrus H. K. Curtis and Edward Bok from the *Ladies' Home Journal.* That was how the *Home Monthly* came to be started. It would not have caused a ripple in the sea of printer's ink but for one thing. They imported an editor from Nebraska, and her name was Willa Cather.

Another chapter of accidents brought me one day to the office of the *Home Monthly.* A year earlier I had compiled a Souvenir Book for a *Saenger-fest.* My associate was a German pastor, the Reverend Heinrich Baehr, a musician and scholar who looked as if he had lived on an exclusive diet of potato pancakes.

Herr Pastor Baehr had once been employed as a tutor by Richard Wagner in Villa Wahnfried, at Bayreuth, and he told me many amazing anecdotes of the Master, Frau Cosima, and little Siegfried. He even offered to teach me the trade secrets of the "Meister," so that I'd be able to turn out music just as good as the *Waldweben* or the Bridal Chorus; but I declined this golden opportunity, and Wagner is still upon his pedestal.

The anecdotes told by the Herr Pastor were more in my line, so I dropped in at the office of the *Home Monthly,* and offered to write an article on "Richard Wagner's Wild Pranks."

The editor, Willa Cather, looked about eighteen; she was plump and dimpled, with dreamy eyes and an eager mind. She took that article, others about Christmas and Easter legends, translations of Heine, heaven knows what not. My stories and her editorial excursions were not nearly so interesting as the silos and prize pigs, or it may be that Voltaire was right when he said the bulk of the human race always were and always will be imbeciles. The *Home Journal* did not dethrone Bok and Curtis.

But through the *Home Journal* and Richard Wagner was established an understanding by which Willa Cather came to the Seibel home once or twice a week to "read French." Our reading covered a vast territory. The first book we took up was Alphonse Daudet's *Femmes d'Artistes,* short stories bubbling with malicious delight in feminine foibles. The second was Alfred de Musset's *Poesies Nouvelles*, in which we read "Rolla," the various "Nuits" of various months, the "Letter to Malibran," and other hits of melodious melancholia.

Time in between we spent in despising Marie Corelli and Hall Caine. We felt that if we could descend to such writing, we could easily coin a million apiece. But the mere thought of such a sum was philistine, bourgeois, blasphemous. The thought perished.

We read uproarious trifles like Edmond About's *Roi des Montagnes*, pathetic romance like Pierre Loti's *Pêcheur d'Islande*. If sometimes we touched pleasant pastry like Emile Souvestre's *Philosophe sous les Toits*, we indulged oftener in devil's food like Anatole France's *Le Lys Rouge*. We plunged into vats of color like Theophile Gautier's *Une Nuit de Cléopâtre*, and scaled towers of alexandrines in Victor Hugo's *Hernani*. Verlaine and Baudelaire were among the poets we discovered, Bourget and Huysmans among the novelists.

I had a faculty for instantaneous rough-and-ready translation. Each of us held a copy of the French text. I read aloud—in English. If anybody dissented, or knew better, I was interrupted. Sometimes there was a "what-the-hell-does-that-mean" pause.

Such pauses came frequently when we ploughed through our adored Flaubert. *Madame Bovary* wasn't so hard, but *La Tentation de Saint Antoine* and *Salammbô* proved most refractory until I discovered that a Latin lexicon and classical dictionary were more help than Littré.

While drilling through *Salammbô* an odd incident almost made me believe in unconscious cerebration, special revelation, or somnambulism. Somewhere in the chapter about Tanit and the Zaimph I stumbled over an obscure passage.

What did it mean? Nobody knew.

We turned the passage inside out and upside down, but could not shake any meaning out of it. It was segregated for future solution, and the problem haunted me for several days.

One day a friend came to inspect the Seibels' recently acquired baby—Erna, age three months, religiously put to bed at seven o'clock every evening. This friend was Leonard J. Hohl, a railroad and mining engineer, born a Swiss, and he had a ready command of three or four languages. After the infant had been inspected and approved, she was put through her gurgles and coos, and dumped into her crib. Then I thought of the difficult passage in *Salammbô*. But John Hohl, as he was known, also gave it up.

After we had gone to bed, I know not how many hours of sleep passed.

Sometime between one and four A.M. the infant cried, according to the nocturnal custom first observed by Alfred Tennyson. My wife poked a monitory digit between my fourth and fifth ribs.

"The baby is crying."

I woke with a sudden start, and said:

"Now I know the meaning of that sentence in *Salammbô*."

Evidently my mind had worked on the problem after I fell asleep, and solved it just as the baby woke. Maybe the baby's mind was also busy with Flaubert's phrase, and woke up to tell us.

A day or two after that baby was born, Willa Cather had looked her over and exclaimed:

"Oh, look at George Seibel's hands!"

Those hands are an inheritance: for generations the Seibels have been pianists or pickpockets. No, I do not play.

When Willa came to those French soirées, we usually first had a simple supper. It was before the days of calories or vitamins. Noodle soup, plebeian but nourishing, potato salad, larded with delicious slices of cucumber, cookies of crisp and crackling texture, left a pleasant taste. As the baby grew bigger, there were four at the supper table. The infant was often permitted to linger until someone would say: "It's time to put the k-i-d to b-e-d." One night she piped up and said: "The k-i-d doesn't want to go to b-e-d." Education was progressing; children learned to spell in those days.

A few years later, as the baby became mischievous and eloquent, at one memorable supper Erna ate her berries, then said: "Look, Wee-you" (her pronunciation of Willa), and raised the berry-dish to her lips, draining the juice before a horrified mother could invoke the sacred laws of table etiquette.

That phrase, "Look, Wee-you," became a family motto as a special litany of unconventional defiance, whenever any departure from the social Decalogue had to be condoned.

But our Christmas festivity was the rubric of the calendar. Willa always helped to trim the tree on Christmas Eve. Somewhere she had acquired a peculiar taste for eating the needles of the fir or pine. Perhaps a perverse sect of vegetarians among her Virginia ancestors! She crunched her share of anise cakes and *pfeffernüsse*, but the evergreen racemes were the dessert of her delight.

"I wish I could eat all the needles," she used to say, "and curl up under the tree like a contented boa constrictor."

One Christmas Eve she brought a guest—a young girl, vivid and vivacious, full of sparkle and wit. Her name was Dorothy Canfield. A few years later she wrote a book on Corneille and Racine, but she is best known by *The Deepening Stream* and *The Brimming Cup*. I often used to wonder if Dorothy Canfield Fisher remembered how on that Christmas Eve I allowed her to stay up an hour later and drink an extra cup of coffee? I now know that she did and does, fifty years after, with details I have forgotten, including the verses of Heine about the Three Kings.

Another evening Willa brought a sheaf of manuscripts to read, some of her own poetry. Under the green student-lamp, which occasionally emitted an approving gurgle, she read the poems later collected in *April Twilights*. On the flyleaf of one copy of that thin volume, published by Richard G. Badger in 1903, she wrote:

To George Seibel,
the first and kindest critic
of these verses.
Willa Sibert Cather
July Fifth 1903

I can still remember the velvet cadence of her voice as she read "Winter at Delphi" and "Aftermath," two sugared sonnets which neither of us then realized were begotten by Swinburne and Rossetti. Other poems had a drop of absinthe from Verlaine, whom we had been reading, or wine-wet rose petals from FitzGerald's *Omar*, whom she had first imported into our home one Christmas in a green corrugated cardboard edition published by Dodge at San Francisco in 1896, at the prodigal price of 25 cents.

I wonder often what the Vintners buy
One half so precious as the stuff they sell.

We became amicable rivals in the accumulation of libraries. After she had acquired a red buckram set of Stevenson in Scribner's Thistle Edition, I got one in old gold which cost 50 cents more a volume. One Christmas she brought us a copy of Eugene Field's *Love Affairs of a Bibliomaniac*, one of my firsts with her autograph. Under the potent inspiration of Eugene Field I probably wrote "Book and Heart" a little later, accepted by Jeannette L. Gilder for the *Critic*, and the first poem I ever sold for solid shekels.

All this time Willa was writing, writing, writing. She was living at the home of Mrs. Marie Eyth, 6012 Harvard Street, East Liberty, and often would come home at two in the afternoon, "all smiles and animation," to work on stories. She had an arrangement with the landlady for a cup of strong black coffee, the virtues of which had been learned from Balzac. She always dropped a coin into a vase on the mantel, to repay the landlady for the extra trouble—that was the Nebraska conscience. Often she would bring home a bit of music for Mrs. Eyth to play—some new composition of a Sewickley friend named Ethelbert Nevin. In this humble lodging, with a screen to divide bed from workshop, Willa Cather wrote her first important things; later she moved to the home of Judge S. A. McClung, whose beautiful and stately daughter Isabelle she honored with the dedication of *The Troll Garden* and *The Song of The Lark*.

During this time, while Willa was heroically struggling to put the *Home Monthly* ahead of the *Ladies' Home Journal*, she met the usual trials and tribulations of an editor with patience and ingenuity. One day, on her way to see the young artist who was drawing cover designs for the *Home Monthly*, she stopped at our home and exhibited a photograph of a beautiful girl.

"Virginia makes beautiful pictures, but she can't draw a woman's face. She always gets the eyes too far apart. No matter how much I caution her, she puts the eyes almost below the ears. I'm giving her this picture to copy, so she can't go wrong."

A week later Willa got her cover design. Returning the photograph, the artist said:

"That was a beautiful model. But I had to change it a little. Her eyes are too close together."

Somewhat later when she became telegraph editor of the *Leader*, Willa's Nebraska conscience became less troublesome. She learned Salverte's axiom that "Man is credulous because he is naturally sincere," and the Psalmist's hasty remark that "all men are liars." Since not all can be journalists, some must be readers. I would not libel Willa's journalistic status by any insinuation that she was immune to all temptation to improvise. On at least one occasion she displayed the resourcefulness every newspaper worker finds his most useful asset.

My telephone rang one afternoon. I always hated the telephone. I imagined I could not hear as well as I should, though somehow I always managed to hear everything I wanted to hear. My telephone rang, and Willa was on the line.

"Will you talk about Friedrich Nietzsche for about five minutes, slowly and distinctly?"

"What sort of game is this?"

"Never mind, I'll tell you about it next time I see you. Now talk about Friedrich Nietzsche, slowly and distinctly, about five minutes."

So I talked about Nietzsche for five minutes—slowly and distinctly—*Zarathustra* in a nutshell, the Superman put through a nutmeg grater, everything I could misremember from an unforgettable lecture of two hours and forty minutes.

Next day I learned why the telephone had been subjected to this strain. Willa had gone to interview the pianist Harold Bauer for the *Leader*. He talked mainly about Nietzsche, so volubly and volcanically that she might as well have been listening to a thunderstorm on the Brocken.

I do not remember seeing the printed interview, but I am sure Bauer's views on Nietzsche were reported in a way that met his full approval.

Not only Nietzsche, but other new planets swam into Willa's ken during those years. Once she brought a little volume by a new poet—it was *A Shropshire Lad*, by A. E. Housman, whom she had looked up in London a year or two earlier. She found him "long and thin and gray," and not one modern book on the shelves of his study. At the time she went to Shropshire, few people had ever heard of a Housman.

Willa also became deeply interested in the then revolutionary music of Richard Strauss, though I quoted Moszkowski's epigram, "If Richard, give me Wagner; if Strauss, I prefer Johann." She wrote articles about both Housman and Strauss a year or two later, when I had become Sunday editor of the *Gazette Times*.

She developed the habit of bringing along new books by new men—there was *Differences*, a first novel by Hervey White, for whom we predicted great things which never came to pass. My copy was her Christmas gift, as is my copy of Sarah Orne Jewett's *Country of the Pointed Firs*. I was fonder of Mary E. Wilkins and her *New England Nun*, but Willa preferred the austere and unsentimental *Country Doctor*.

William James in one of his letters describes *The Country of the Pointed Firs* as a source of "exquisite pleasure," and such it was to Willa Cather, a devoted disciple of James in days before psychology became the happy hunting-ground of the erotic extrovert.

William's brother, the hieratic Henry James, was usually a bone of contention between us. I hated his style, or lack of it. Willa thought it was the last word—and I hoped it was. But we agreed that he was a great critic, and delved into all those Gallic writers of *Partial Portraits* and *French Poets and Novelists*—Balzac, Sand, Mérimée, Maupassant—with occasional excursions into Dumas fils, Edouard Rod, intoxicating whiffs of Baudelaire and Richepin, deep draughts of young Rostand's ruby wine. Henry James was the guide whose hand held ours, and his critical standard was our polestar on those voyages.

More than in books, Willa was interested in the study of human nature. She was avid of the world, always wondering, always questing, always digging, a prospector in the deep and quiet lodes of the soul. For her the proper study of mankind was man. She expressed her own philosophy of life and authorship in the words: "No man can give himself heart and soul to one thing while in the back of his mind he cherishes a desire, a secret hope for something different."

Ellen Glasgow, when I met her many years later, told me she was impressed by Willa Cather's reticence, but reticence is a relative quality, the other side of expression. The reticent writer is listening, observing, taking notes, a flesh-and-blood dictograph.

Willa, like Goethe, had eyes in every pore. Expression never was easy for her; she had to toil for perfection like her idol Flaubert. Away from her writing-table she was ever absorbing life. Her perennial avidity accounts for the perfection of her pages. In January, 1911, while on a visit to Washington, she went four nights in succession to see Sarah Bernhardt. At the same time she was also beginning to cultivate the reticence that later made her almost a recluse. A few years ago she implored an instructor in Allegheny High School, where she had taught, as an act of "friendliness" not to name a literary society after her. From authentic hearsay I know her will is worded to keep any of her works forever out of Hollywood. But she was different on our Christmas Eves, and during her prentice years in Pittsburgh one of her dominant passions was seeking and grasping all sorts of opportunities to see things and learn more of humankind. One week we skipped a reading of our freshly imported *Cyrano de Bergerac* because she went to a picnic of the Glassblowers' Union with the labor editor of the *Leader*.

Many people have been under the impression, after reading *Death Comes for the Archbishop* and *Shadows on the Rock*, that Willa Cather was a Catholic. I once heard a priest in all honesty declare that she was. In all sincerity I asked him for the proof, and he was unable to find any. Over the radio symposium "Invitation to Learning," on C.B.S., the statement was made by one man that she was a convert to Catholicism, and the other members of the panel echoed the statement as if it were something well-known and undeniable. This time I wrote to Lyman Bryson, director of the symposium, for the evidence, and received an acknowledgment of error, with the information that she was Episcopalian, and they would correct the point the next

Sunday. I did not know what this statement was based upon, and did not inquire further, but I had heard Willa say that her family were originally Baptist, I had never heard her speak of being personally connected with any church, and in all her converse of a frank and friendly sort she always seemed to stand just where I stood. We both believed in Santa Claus and the Golden Rule.

Willa had a sense of quiet humor which found expression in many ways. When she had lent one of her books to a good friend, Miss Elisa May Willard, who was head of the catalogue department in the Carnegie Library, and the book did not return, Willa was "afraid it has been catalogued." When the green student lamp at our French soirées emitted its warning gurgle, like the lamp of Henry Ryecroft in the Gissing book, Willa would say in melo-dramatic tones, "The fatal moment has arrived," and I would rise to refill the reservoir from a grimy can of Elaine, a kerosene highly commended for midnight oil, now only a figure of speech. When our family cat, Hasenpfef-fer, would join our Christmas festivities by tinkling the little toy bell hung on the lowest branch of the tree, Willa would clap her hands in glee. Perhaps Dorothy Canfield Fisher remembers this too—she was there and must have met Hasenpfeffer.

After Willa had worked several years on the *Leader*, editing "flimsy" at the telegraph desk, she went to teach in the Pittsburgh High School—first Latin, then English. That was where she got the material for "Paul's Case," her first masterpiece. But she had done fine bits of fiction before—"Eric Hermann-son's Soul" in the *Cosmopolitan*, "Jackaboy" in the *Saturday Evening Post*.

A curious minor point in "Paul's Case" came out after I read the story and insisted that the Paul of the first pages would not act like the Paul of the closing pages. Paul was not drawn from one boy in her high school classes, but from two boys—hence the dualism I sensed and she later admitted.

About that time another forlorn hope of literature was launched.

When a young man known as "Chick"—his real name being Charles Clark—got $20,000 from some uncle or grandmother, the young man de-cided that Pittsburgh needed a literary journal like the *London Spectator*, only more so. He called it *The Library*, and imported an editor from the cultured East named Ewan Macpherson. Ewan discovered Willa Cather and George Seibel, whereupon we both began to produce masterpieces in ex-change for chunks of Chick's uncle's or grandma's coin.

First Ewan Macpherson discovered that my poems were in the vein of Sir John Suckling. I looked up Sir John, and promptly switched to the vein of Austin Dobson. I also discovered the beautiful Ohio River, good for $40, and satirized *Success* magazine to the tune of $15, while Willa wrote a scientific mystery story in the vein of H. G. Wells and glorified Lizzie Hudson Collier, our stock company's leading lady, as "One of Our Conquerors."

Willa wrote under a variety of *noms le plume*, as she had done for the *Home Monthly*. One I recall was Nickelmann, borrowed from a folklore figure in Gerhart Hauptmann's *Sunken Bell*, which we had read once as an interlude of our French program.

Chick's $20,000 was vanishing fast, the mortgage on my home was almost ready to be burnt, when S. S. McClure swooped down upon Pittsburgh to carry off Willa Cather for his magazine.

The rest is literary history. That too is a ghost of Christmas past. Our sick age is surfeited with sin, incarnadined with carnage. The crucified lions of Flaubert would not even interest the Humane Society. Thais and Cleopatra are insects gone with the wind or imbedded in cheap amber. The novelist of nowadays is an unskilled surgeon who dissects a trollop and sniffs the aphrodisiac stenches.

Willa Cather always wrote English: she never invented a new jigsaw language like James Joyce. Her English was vigorous English, unlike the tepid and often stagnant current of Marcel Proust's French. Much of this literary virtue sprang from her training under McClure and was carefully nursed by Viola Roseboro. I did not see too much of her after her migration, but on my first visit to New England, after her exile from Pittsburgh, I learned she was in Boston, and spent an evening at her apartment on one of the literary cross-streets of Beacon Hill. She was getting Georgine Milmine's account of Mary Baker Eddy into shape for publication. The author had the facts, but they had to be verified and authenticated; the manuscript must be whipped into shape for McClure's magazine, in which it first appeared. Willa had spent weeks on the job, but was glad she would get back to New York next day. She liked Boston, and was very fond of its fish, but it was making her fat. After discussing science and health, with a dietetic undercurrent, I took my departure and came to my hotel to find I had forgotten my umbrella. Knowing she was to leave next morning, I telephoned. The umbrella was safe, and she would leave it at the boarding-house where such good fish were served. I called there next afternoon, and "Miss Cather did leave an umbrella, but it belongs to some one else." My assurance that I was the some one else made no impression upon the dour housekeeper. But I insisted on describing the umbrella, with my engraved monogram, established my identity, and recovered my property. Whether "some one else" fared as well, I never learned. The double moral of which is that if you own an umbrella, have your initials put on the handle if you intend to forget it somewhere.

The next time I saw her was in No. 5 Bank Street, for many years her home in Greenwich Village—and I had no umbrella. She had the same clarity of vision, a widened human sympathy, and a deepened artistic responsibility. She had moved away from Edith Wharton's blue-stocking world into a humbler and sweeter sphere of daily tragedy and triumph in humble lives. Scandinavia became her new fatherland.

I remember mentioning her name in the Gyldendal Boghandel of Copenhagen, and being received almost like an ambassador from an Empress.

But she was sanely Nordic—closer to Björnson and Hamsun than to Ibsen, and far removed from the strait-jacket of Strindberg.

Her books were never recondite nor in need of exegesis or apology. She wrote before Freud had popularized complexes and fixations, when authors still dealt with the feelings and foibles of everyday humanity. Only one of her books, *My Mortal Enemy*, stirred some teapot tempests. Who was Myra Henshawe's "mortal enemy"? After reading the novelette, I decided it was her husband, but most readers thought Myra was her own "mortal enemy." One lady of literary propensities argued with me loud and long, and would not be convinced. A little later a letter came from Willa about another matter, and at the close she said:

"I wanted your address this fall to send you a copy of *My Mortal Enemy*, which I had a premonition you would understand—and that most people wouldn't."

"You see," I told the lady, "the author says I would understand; so you are one of the 'most people who wouldn't.'"

"But she doesn't say who is the 'mortal enemy.' I stick to my theory."

When I answered Willa's letter I wrote that I thought I had understood, on the strength of a few passages, but must be wrong because a literary lady insisted she must be right.

Back came another note from Willa: "Of course, you are quite right. Please tell Mrs. B——, with my compliments, that I can't see much in this particular story unless one gets the point of it. There is not much to it *but* the point."

Did this convince the literary lady? She said to me:

"You are very clever, and *you* put that idea into her head."

Hudibras was right, as usually misquoted,

He that's convinced against his will,
Is of his own opinion still,

and doubly right if you change the gender.

GEORGE SWETNAM

George Swetnam (1904–1999) has been called "the foremost historian of western Pennsylvania," or "Pittsylvania" as he preferred to call it. During the 1930s, he earned a Ph.D. in Assyriology, then, like many other young men of the decade, became, as he called it, a hobo. After three years, he found a faculty position teaching English, then when layoffs hit colleges and universities during World War II, he found himself in journalism as a reporter, a copy editor, and a rewrite man (more stressful than being a hobo, he once said). After he began writing stories from history, he was given his favorite journalistic assignment, as a writer for a Sunday magazine. He loved the magazine writing and at times wrote most or all of the copy, using many pseudonyms. His many books range from *Guide to Western Pennsylvania* (co-authored with Helene Smith) to *The Carnegie Nobody Knows* and *Devils, Ghosts and Witches*. In his nineties, when asked, "How do you find things to write about?" he responded, "How could I help it, being alive?"[1]

Crawford Peffer (1867?–1961) is Swetnam's source for the following glimpse of Cather. Peffer was president of the Redpath Bureau, a major organization in the business of arranging itineraries for speakers and entertainers, an important business in the days of Chautauquas when thousands of people attended speeches and shows to keep informed about their world. Peffer's anecdote about Cather presents her, as if in a snapshot, in the *Pittsburgh Leader* office doing her job.

Bill Cather's Buddy

Crawford Peffer was only a youthful law student in those days, and Bill Cather was a rookie reporter for the old *Pittsburgh Leader*.

But Mr. Peffer still takes pleasure in the days when he used to argue for hours over nothing with the young woman who was soon to become one of America's leading authors.

That was back in the fall of 1897, when he was unconsciously preparing for his career as one of the greatest lyceum circuit operators of the palmiest period of the lyceum in America.

During Mr. Peffer's freshman year at Allegheny College he had become friendly with Edwin P. Couse. And by the time young Peffer was studying law, several years later, Mr. Couse was telegraph editor of the *Leader*.

"I often went to his office at the close of the day's work, about 4 P.M.," recalls Mr. Peffer. "One day I found a young lady with flashing blue eyes, sitting opposite him at his large flattop desk, whom he introduced to me as 'Miss Cather, my new assistant.' By way of further introduction, he said that she had graduated from the University of Nebraska, Class of 1895, and had recently come to work in Pittsburgh for the *Home Monthly*."

In such fashion one Pittsburgher first became conscious of Willa Cather, who later gained world-wide fame as an author.

Crawford Peffer was a native of North Mahoning Township, Indiana County, only six miles from Punxsutawney.

Willa Cather, born in Virginia, brought up in Nebraska, had come to Pittsburgh in 1896 to work for a small magazine published in the Heeren Building, Eighth and Penn, by Charles Axtell, whom she had met in Nebraska.

A year later the magazine changed hands, and Miss Cather moved over to the *Leader*, where she did some reporting, helped on the telegraph desk, and was drama critic for the next four years.

During this time she lived in the East End in the home of Judge Samuel. A. McClung, whose daughter, Isabelle, was her life-long friend. In 1901, Miss Cather began teaching English, first at old Central High School, later at Allegheny. And after five more years she joined the staff of *McClure's Magazine*, in New York, and went on to fame.

"I am probably the only one living who remembers Miss Cather in her first days of newspaper work," says Mr. Peffer.

"Miss Cather was unconventional in both dress and conversation. She wore skirts much too short for that day and mannish looking shirtwaists. Soon we were calling her 'Bill,' a name she seemed to like.

"Bill Cather was the most argumentative person I have ever met. She disputed on any subject that Couse or I brought up."

After her first year of teaching, Miss Cather went to Europe with Isabelle McClung, and Mr. Peffer did not see her again until years later, when she was editor of *McClure's Magazine*.

In the meantime, Mr. Peffer had given up law for Chautauqua and the lyceum field, in which he had always been interested.

At Covode Academy, near his home, and in Punxsutawney, he had attended lyceum lectures in his boyhood. Later he had worked at Chautauqua in summers and attended lyceum attractions in college.

In Pittsburgh the budding law student met H. J. Norman, district agent for the Redpath Bureau, who gave him an opportunity to go on the road, booking open dates.

Within a few years he became one of the five owners of the far-flung operations of the Redpath Bureau circuits. He and Keith Vawter, who entered at the same time, held a majority interest.

After more than sixty years of connection with Redpath, Mr. Peffer is now retired, living in Portland, Maine, with a daughter, a Girl Scout executive.

During his years of lyceum interest and work he met most of the big names of the field. He knew Russell H. Conwell, Bishop John H. Vincent, Henry Waterson, Bill Nye, Will Carleton. He played baseball with William Lyon Phelps, and once rescued James Whitcomb Riley from being swamped by a crowd of female admirers.

His work kept him in touch with such men as the Rev. T. DeWitt Talmage, Albert Bushnell Hart, and William Rainey Harper.

But none does he remember with more pleasure than a cub reporter for the old *Pittsburgh Leader,* whom he used to call "Bill."

Pittsburgh Post-Gazette, 3 July 1960, 3.

A Nebraska Legend Grows

After the publication of *My Ántonia* in 1918, and throughout the 1920s and 1930s, Nebraskan journalists kept Cather's name before the public. Winning the Pulitzer Prize in 1923 for *One of Ours* confirmed her friends' and supporters' belief in her talent, of course, and further raised her public stature so that her travels, reviews of her books, and celebrations of Nebraska settlement all were occasions for articles about her. The following articles show Nebraskans working her into the story of their heritage. Her life, as they told it, was that of a Nebraska hero, and it became the Willa Cather thousands of Americans imagined throughout most of the twentieth century.

ELLA FLEISHMAN

When Cather was traveling, she often stopped in Omaha to see friends and would agree to speak to public groups. She became so well known in Omaha society that citizens of the city raised funds to commission her portrait for the Omaha Public Library.

Ella Fleishman does not admit to knowing Cather herself, and this article, like many others of its time, perpetuates the error that Cather's birth was in 1875, when the records show that she was born in 1873.[1] Fleishman's interviewees, however, knew Cather familiarly. Evaline Rolofson Newbranch, a college friend of Cather's, became the wife of Harvey Newbranch, an editor for the *Omaha World-Herald*. Keene Abbott's brother Ned was on the *Hesperian* staff with Cather. Dr. H. A. Senter, a leading Omaha resident, was president of the undergraduate University Union Literary Society when Cather was its secretary.

Willa Cather working at the *Nebraska State Journal.* Courtesy of the Nebraska State Historical Society, Willa Cather Pioneer Memorial Collection.

Willa Cather, Former Nebraska Girl, Puts Prairie in Literature

Nebraska prairies have a place in literature; Willa Sibert Cather, whose girlhood was passed in this state, has put them there. Her *My Ántonia, O Pioneers!* and *The Song of the Lark* have done for this prairie country what Bret Harte did for the far west, what Cable did for New Orleans, and what a dozen writers have done for New England.

"Miss Cather's description of life on Nebraska prairies and in the prairie towns about 1895, is worth more than a dozen historical records," testifies Grant M. Overton in his *Women Who Make Our Novels.*

"A scant paragraph sets you out on the plains, and the breath of the wind that billows the long grass never leaves your face," wrote another critic of the three novels of the west which place the former Nebraska girl in the front rank of present day women writers.

Miss Cather's name is strongly linked with that other successful woman novelist, Dorothy Canfield, who, curiously enough, attended the University of Nebraska at the same time with Miss Cather, the two having collaborated in the prize serial story, "The Fear that Walks by Noon Day," published in the school paper, *The Sombrero,* in 1895. Miss Canfield's father was chancellor of the university that year.

Numbered among the writer's Omaha friends and old schoolmates are Mr. and Mrs. Harvey Newbranch (nee Evaline Rolofson), Keene Abbott, and Dr. H. A. Senter.

Naturally enough it is the woman who gives the most adequate description of the "Billy" Cather of those days—short, heavy-set, square-faced, and bobbed-off hair (yes, even then!), and the one bit of feminine weakness, perhaps the mark of genius of the brilliant girl who has since risen to literary fame.

"A whack on the back, so startling I nearly fell out of the window through which I was looking, when 'Billy' Cather came up behind me, is my most vivid remembrance," Mrs. Newbranch confessed.

"While thoroughly unconventional, an out-of-doors girl if there ever was one, Willa Cather had one unexpected quirk—she always dressed up in the most formal fashion to attend the theater, contrary to the custom of most of the university girls. With her, long white kid gloves was the first essential to attending the theater—she was dramatic critic for the *Lincoln State Journal* at the time. Without white gloves, she refused to review the drama."

"It's queer, you should have that one weakness," Mrs. Newbranch once commented.

"Well, I must have one, 'Rolly,'" she replied. Nicknames for her school friends was a habit with Miss Cather.

One September, "Billy" Cather appeared at the opening of school with hands calloused and chapped beyond any ladylike appearance. She had driven a lumber team on the prairies throughout the hot summer, on account of a shortage of field help.

"My, what a comfort you must be to your mother with your domestic tastes!" "Rolly" twitted caustically.

"I'm the disappointment of my mother's life. My only comfort is that my little sister, ten years old, is quite different from me and bears every indication of fulfilling my mother's desire for one lady in the family," she replied.

"Billy" Cather appeared mostly in sailor suits, much worn in those days, and looked especially beautiful in evening dress, Mrs. Newbranch recalls.

Dr. Senter remembers Miss Cather as a high-spirited, brilliant student, extremely popular in the student body. "She gave great promise in those days, was brilliant in her English classes, and active in the Union Literary society." In one of the stories spun by members of this society, Miss Cather and Mr. Newbranch sprang a "beetle-browed brute from Box Butte" on their unsuspecting listeners.

Keene Abbott, dramatic critic for the *World-Herald*, followed Miss Cather in writing dramatic reviews for the *State Journal*.

Once the managing editor, Will Owen Jones, called him on the carpet for a particularly scathing review he had written.

Mr. Abbott offered his defense. "It's no worse than those Willa Cather did," he stoutly maintained.

"Well, but that was Miss Cather!" replied the editor, indicating that even as early as her college days, Miss Cather's ability was recognized and appreciated.

Upon her graduation in 1895, Miss Cather went east to the *Pittsburgh Leader*, where she served as telegraph editor and later taught English in the Allegheny High school. Then came her chance on the staff of *McClure's*, where she presently rose to the position of editor. During that time, she gave Keene Abbott an assignment, when Mark Twain died, to visit the humorist's old home at Hannibal, Missouri, and write the story for *McClure's*.

Miss Cather was a great lover of Poe's works and wrote an essay on Poe for one of the college contests, according to Mr. Abbott.

Miss Cather came to Nebraska when she was nine years old, from Virginia, where she was born in 1875 [*sic*]. Her father settled on a ranch near

Red Cloud, in the heart of Bohemian and Scandinavian settlements, where the future novelist grew to know so well the characters she delineates. All her material was gathered before she was 20, Miss Cather stated, and she makes trips back west each summer to renew these old remembrances.

"I can thus recall old feelings of my youth. The west has for me something which excites me and gives me what I want and need to write a story."

Miss Cather wrote she would like to send a greeting to her Nebraska friends, only "Walt Whitman was the only man I ever heard of who greeted people by states, and I doubt whether people enjoy being greeted in such large masses."

Miss Cather's last summer trip was a long stay in Arizona and New Mexico, Mancos and Durango, Colorado, penetrating some of the many hardly accessible cliff dweller remains and remote mesa cities of the Pueblo Indians.

She is unmarried and lives at 5 Bank Street in Greenwich Village in New York.

Omaha World-Herald, 1 Feb. 1920, 1,2.

MARJORIE WYMAN

Marjorie Wyman, a young Omaha woman who came of age in the 1920s, uses the hook of the audacious styles of the flappers to write her Sunday feature about Cather.[1] By 1924, when Wyman's article appeared, Nebraskans could safely claim Cather as their own local celebrity and brag that she was thirty years ahead of her time, even when she was a co-ed at their own University of Nebraska–Lincoln.

Willa Cather, Novelist, Was Modern Flapper at Nebraska U Thirty Years Ago

"Judy O'Grady
And the Colonel's lady
Are sisters under the skin."

Even so was the co-ed of thirty years ago kin to the flapper of today. So was the student of three decades ago, closely related to the modern girl, with the patent-leather, slicked-down, short, straight close shingle. Thus indeed is the mannishly-dressed girl of the hour a sister indeed to the boyish schoolgirl of 1891—for that was the year in which there came to Lincoln from Red Cloud the first bobbed-haired University of Nebraska girl—Willa Cather.

"Billy Cather," who was graduated from the University in 1895, was even then a conspicuous figure among the girls of her class and year. Since then, she has become more than a talented schoolgirl; she is an authoress of no mean repute. Her novel, *One of Ours*, for which the material was drawn almost entirely—and quite recognizably—from Lincoln and the University of Nebraska, has brought recognition to the name of Willa Sibert Cather.

But those were the days when she came from her home in Red Cloud to enroll for the first time in an institution of higher learning. And instead of being the conservative authoress of today, thinking along serious lines, and reflecting in her modern age and the ideas of the people here today, she was a very young schoolgirl. She had always wanted to be a boy, and the next best thing was to dress as much as possible in the fashion adopted by the others.

Hair clipped short—the shingle of today—parted sometimes on one side, and worn sometimes in a pompadour, "Like a prizefighter," a box coat with mannish lapels, high collars fastened up under the chin, and a man's shirt in the days even before the advent of the "shirtwaist"—that was Willa Cather.

It was not a fad then. Golf for women had not yet become universal, and the excuse of the inconvenience of skirts and long hair on motor camping trips had not yet been invented. Small cloche-shaped hats were not the fashion then—photographs show the larger "merry widow" type. But Willa Cather wore instead a straw sailor after the type of a man's hat, or in winter, one in the same style, but of different material.

To Miss Cather, it was not the style, then, nor the fact that "everybody's doing it." For they weren't. No one else dreamed of doing anything of the sort. But she had always gone in for boys' sports—horseback, and the like—and she wanted to dress the part. It was a personal desire that prompted the introduction of such a style of dress.

"Willa followed her own inclinations, anyway," Miss Mariel Gere, a schoolmate of Miss Cather, says, "and she didn't care much what other folks said or thought. She was always a little eccentric, but as she grew and went on through school, her notions seemed to change, and she became more like other girls."

Miss Mable Lindly, also a schoolmate, tells of the garb which the authoress-to-be affected. "She was very masculine in her manner of dressing," Miss Lindley says, "from the time she first came here to school. It was just personal eccentricity, though, for she dressed as she did everything else, more with regard to what she wanted to do than with respect to the thing or what other girls did."

Miss Nellie J. Compton, who was graduated the year after Miss Cather, tells of her as she appeared on the campus, in the mannishly-cut clothes and the stiff hat, with her close-cropped hair just showing under the narrow brim.

Miss Louise Pound speaks of the hair cut which was Miss Cather's and says she was the only girl in school who had clipped her hair at that time. "Most girls would have been afraid of appearing conspicuous, being the only one to affect that style, but Willa had no fear of that. Of course, those were the days of originality, when students were not so ultra-organized, before the red tape of a large institution had cut off independence.

"During her senior year, she used to curl her hair, but until then she wore it straight. It was too short to curl, I think. She is sorry for it now, for she has become very conservative, since she has grown a little older."

Miss Lindley, too, mentioned the difference in Miss Cather's ideas. "I think she rather regrets it," she says in speaking of the episode in the writer's life, "for she is more in the public eye now, and is less daring."

Dr. J. H. Tyndale is another of the friends of Miss Cather who knew her in her younger days. When she came down from Red Cloud to school, she was extremely boyish, and told him too that she had always wanted to be a boy. But when she went to a party at a private home dressed in boys' clothing, that was the last straw, and he told her that she would have to be less conspicuous.

It was Dr. Tyndale who encouraged the young school girl in the writing she wanted to do. People "pooh-poohed" the work she did, he says, and time and again she would come to him to tell how she wanted to go home. Her fetish is correct English, after the manner of Henry James, and to lower the quality of her use of the mother tongue would be committing sacrilege, to her eyes. Imitation is her bogie, and as she said to her old friend, she "would not for anything copy the work of another, even unintentionally."

It was a twenty-two year struggle for the young Nebraska girl from the time of her discouraging school days, when things she wrote seemed "raw," she was told, to the later days when, after the writing of *My Ántonia* and *One of Ours*, she was awarded the Pulitzer prize, and the subsequent victory of *A Lost Lady*.

Even then, of course, Miss Cather was more or less of a personage. For that was the age of literary [societies] and the supremacy of the arts school. Willa Cather's stories, verses, and essays are spread over the pages of the *Hesperian Student*, a monthly pamphlet-form publication, and of *The Sombrero*, the annual of early days, the predecessor of *The Cornhusker*.

Greek was the principal study, and Miss Cather shone in the study of the ancient language. Miss Gere recalls her liking for the subject, and particularly her enjoyment of the courses she took under Professor James T. Lees, until recently professor of Greek in the university.

"Anacreon" is the name of a poem signed with her initials appearing in the old *Sombrero*:

> The Muses found young Love one day,
>   When mamma was not there
> They bound and carried him away
>   To serve the Graces fair.
> When Aphrodite found him gone,
>   She thought him rather young,
> And wrathfully she hastened on
>   To free her captive son.
> But when she cut the bonds of fate,
>   Ah! Sad the tale to tell.
> The laddie's mamma came too late,
>   He liked his job too well.

For she was writing even then in a sort of desultory fashion.

"Billy Cather" had a fondness for writing satire, and even, in ridiculing certain ones in university courses, wrote sarcastic parodies on famous works. Her "Count, Gismond!" and her "Count, Count, Count," as written to the meter of Hood's "Song of the Shirt," will be remembered by former students who read the publications of the day.

Her junior year found her managing editor of *The Hesperian Student*, a magazine made up of miscellanies, locals, and personals about students and faculty, a page of editorials, and given over largely to its literary department. The first semester, when she was literary editor, shows us some of her works, some of them signed with her initials, and some anonymous ones which might easily have been written by the editor of the department.

During the semester of the managing editorship of "W. Cather," as her name is used on the first sheet of each issue, a new page appeared. It was labeled, "Not to be Read," and was made up of jokes, humorous jingles, and an occasional hit on some faculty member or student. Near the end of the year appears a poem which may be a reflection of the masculinity of the staff—for girls were, except for Miss Cather, only literary editors—or may be a reflection of Miss Cather's humor. Perhaps, indeed, it is an accidental pun:

When you write a merry jest,
   Cut it short.
It will be too long at best.
   Cut it short.
Life is brief and full of care.
   Editors don't like to swear.
Treat your poem like your hair.
   Cut it short.

Lincoln Sunday Star, 29 June 1924, 6.

JOHN M. THOMPSON

John M. Thompson (?–1938) could boast of about thirty-six years of writing "the history of the events of the day" for the *Lincoln State Journal*, a time that included Cather's university years when she was in and out of the *Journal's* office. Clearly, the young Cather created a strong impression on the newspaper veteran; Thompson provides us with a distinct and sharply defined image of the somewhat unconventional young woman who also wrote for the *State Journal*. His recollections may be a bit short on accuracy at times: "I doubt that Miss Cather ever applied for membership in any literary society." However, his honest good humor spiced with irreverence makes the article a delightful bit of reading.

"Confessions" of a Reporter—Partial but Voluntary

Lincoln people in large numbers are able to boast of having known many of the nation's celebrities when these famous persons were more or less humble residents of the city. I never held membership in the "I Did It" club, but I have full membership in the "I Knew Him When" club.

There is Miss Willa Cather who in her student days was dramatic and music critic for the *State Journal*. It is now the proper thing to say that her talent was early recognized by everyone about the newspaper office where she was trying her wings. I remember the terrible scrawl which she made when using pen and ink, and there is a legend about the office that her spelling was not exactly up to date. Her spelling was all right for those who understood it. It was modeled somewhat after the orthography of the Shakespearean period and was never quite the same from day to day.

If Miss Cather was not up to date in spelling she was fully thirty years ahead of the times in setting the style now called bobbed hair. Now that this is the style I have no doubt Miss Cather shows her independence of thought by refusing to follow it.

I have "been told," as Doctor Brady would say, that a certain literary organization in Lincoln rejected Miss Cather for membership during her student days because of her independence of thought or for some other reason. I doubt if Miss Cather ever applied for membership in any literary society. I have not investigated the tale, but at any rate, Miss Cather later wrote some best sellers which members of that society no doubt read, and if the tale be true, the society is forever barred from claiming Miss Cather was "One of Ours."

In addition to wearing bobbed hair when bobbed hair was not the vogue, Miss Cather wore short, narrow skirts with a little cap and jacket and carried a cane about the university campus and was quite boyish in appearance. At the close of her college course she actually created a furor. She appeared in a ball dress, and for the first time her friends beheld her as girlish, youthful, and charming. I used that word "furor" years ago when telling about the effect of some action by Governor Shallenberger. His private secretary, W. J. Furse of Alma, said I had it all wrong, that I should have written it, "few roar."

Lincoln State Journal, 24 July 1927, F3.

JUNE PROVINES

June Provines (?–1983) was a Chicago journalist and radio show host. Over her lifetime, she wrote columns for the *Chicago Daily News,* the *Chicago Tribune,* and the *Chicago Sun,* using the scene around Chicago and the people in it as her subjects.[1] Chicago's great train station was a crossroads for people traveling east and west, a good place for a stopover, and since Cather had many friends there, she did often stop. By 1932, Provines could assume that Cather's fame was well known in the city among students and adults, so she treats the incident in which local students meet a person of renown in an anecdotal manner. This journalist's image of Cather has become that of an acknowledged celebrity, a person everyone can recognize.

This Gala World

It was probably the high point of the year for the three high-school juniors in Park Ridge. They are writing term papers on the works of Willa Cather. Learning that the novelist was to speak at the Chicago Woman's Club last Thursday, they went to hear her and came away elated, both at having seen and heard her "in the flesh" but also because of a good slant it would give their themes. As they were about to cross the street, walking away from the concert, they were stopped at the curb by traffic. Miss Cather's car, with Miss Cather inside, in maroon velvet and sensible brown suede oxfords, drew up in front of the girls, and the writer opened the door. The girls probably can't tell you exactly how it happened, but the first thing they knew they were chatting with her and she had dashed off her autograph for each of them—on hastily offered school paper, tangible evidence of a real adventure.

Chicago Daily News, 24 Oct. 1932, 13.

P. I. W.

Whoever P. I. W. was, she or he recognized the allure to newspaper readers of a legend in the making and helped to make Cather a part of the stuff of Nebraska legend.[1] By the late 1930s, however, legend often reflected stereotypes such as that of the young genius, the hardships of new settlers, and the nobility of a "favorite son"—or daughter—and errors began to take on the false ring of truth. For instance, the "home" referred to as "a big, white-painted frame structure," does not refer to the small house at Third and Cedar in which Cather spent her youth but to the house at Sixth and Seward Street where the Cathers moved in the 1920s. Also, when Cather first moved to Nebraska, she rode her pony only two or three miles for the mail. Some of the legendary embellishments over the years came from Cather herself and some from repeated stories of what one or more informants thought they remembered or had heard about her.

The Home on the Nebraska Prairie Which Always Recalls Willa Cather

Some towns base their claim to fame on historical landmarks, scenic wonders, or remarkable business enterprises. Red Cloud, Nebraska, has Willa Cather.

It is a pleasant experience to visit the prairie town where the great American woman writer spent her girlhood and where she still returns to rest and visit whenever she can get a brief release from her activities in the East. To Red Cloud she is "Willy." Everybody calls her by her first name with that peculiar localized pronunciation. And there is nothing which Miss Cather likes better than to be among the people who call her that and who hold her in a deep, almost family, affection.

More than four decades have passed since Willa Cather left Red Cloud to find international fame and fortune in the field of letters, but Red Cloud remains her home in more than a sentimental sense.

"Willy Cather? She hasn't been here since the winter of 1931, but we're looking for her any time now. Maybe this year. The old Cather home is up by the courthouse. Catty-corner across the street to the southwest, just below the Methodist church. You can't miss it."

Thus a filling station operator will direct you if you ask about Red Cloud's favorite daughter.

The home is there, a big, white-painted frame structure as imposing as any residence in Red Cloud. In it, Willa Cather spent her tomboy girlhood, getting acquainted with the people of the West, learning to know and love the great plains to such an extent that although she now lives in New York, in Europe, or wherever the fancy of the time or the exigency of her present literary enterprise dictates, she still retains her western accent and viewpoint and her characteristic ways.

There were seven children in the Cather family. All of them have left Red Cloud except Miss Elsie Cather, a younger sister, who owns the family home and spends her summers there. She teaches in a high school at Lincoln in the winter. Willa was the oldest, red-haired, blue-eyed, and venturesome.

Her father, Charles Cather, was a Virginian. He took his family to Nebraska when his daughter was eight years old and for a time farmed twenty miles from the city. Those were the days when Willa rode her pony twelve miles a day to get the family mail.

Mrs. Cather, Willa's mother, had been brought up in gentle surroundings in the East, and the lack of conveniences and comforts oppressed her. But it was really the difficulty of getting a physician when there was illness in the family which impelled the move to Red Cloud, old friends in the town say. Willa—named for her grandfather, William Cather—frequently was ill as a child. Her mother knew she had a remarkable daughter, and she induced the father to change his residence to the town.

There Willa grew to young womanhood. Her education was informal and yet remarkable. Schools were not what they should be, and the girl quickly outstripped her teachers in some subjects, while other subjects frankly bored her. Her mother's mother, Mrs. Boak, was a highly educated woman, and she undertook to teach this rebellious child of the prairies. Later the task was taken over by Uncle William Ducker—no relative, but so named by Willa. Mr. Ducker was a merchant and a graduate of Oxford University, England.

Under his tutelage, Willa acquired the literary background which was to serve her as a writer.

Willa attended high school only one year and entered the University of Nebraska in 1891, at fifteen [*sic*]. The university was a new world to her. For the first time she had a chance to write, and residents of Red Cloud saw her articles appearing in the *Sombrero*, which was the name of the student publication of the University of Nebraska. Later she became dramatic critic of the *Lincoln State Journal* and held that post until she was graduated in 1895.

Then Red Cloud heard of "Willy" through her work on the old *Railroad Courier*, edited by Sara Harris, and through frequent trips she made to her home to see her family and friends. Opportunity took her to Pittsburgh, Pennsylvania, and she worked there as a telegraph editor and dramatic critic.

Friends in Red Cloud still remember the proud day when Willa's first book appeared. It was a book of poems, called *April Twilights*, published in 1903. *The Troll Garden*, issued two years later, was a collection of short stories, and it earned Miss Cather an appointment to the staff of *McClure's Magazine*, of which she was managing editor from 1908 to 1912.

During this time Red Cloud saw "Willy" Cather nearly every year at vacation. In 1912, however, the writer visited the Southwest and fell in love with New Mexico. The southwestern scene was to figure in some of her most famous books, among them *Death Comes to the Archbishop* and *The Professor's House.*

There are many persona in Red Cloud and its vicinity who figure in Miss Cather's books, and they are all proud of it. One farmer, who had to go to a hospital for a serious illness, told the hospital attendants, "You'd better treat me right. I'm *My Ántonia*'s husband." The real prototype of *A Lost Lady* lived in Red Cloud. The town of Sweetwater, described in that charming story, is based upon Red Cloud and its neighborhood.

One interesting fact the visitor to Red Cloud learns is that Miss Cather herself assumes roles in some of her works, always as a subordinate character and usually disguised as a man. But the residents who know her recognize some of the episodes and particularly some of the mental attitudes she describes as being typically her own experience.

There are many little anecdotes concerning the famous author in Red Cloud, too. One of them concerns an incident of a visit at home one Christmas when she went with her sister, Elsie Cather, to one of the town's stores, in which there was a display of her books. An elderly farm couple appeared and began to discuss the books, trying to decide which one of them to purchase. Miss Cather, in the rear of the store, heard them talking and said to her sister, "I've got a notion to go up there and offer to autograph that book for those people."

Any collector of books knows the kind of a favor she was proposing. Her sister urged her to do so, so she approached the couple with her offer.

The farmer and his wife looked uncomfortable. Finally the wife replied: "We'd be glad to have you do it, Miss Cather, but you see we're going to give this book away."

Miss Cather's parents died comparatively recently, and her brothers and sisters have scattered. Her brothers, Roscoe, Douglass, James, and John, and her sister Jessie are all in California. Elsie divides her time between Lincoln and Red Cloud. But the town continues to look forward to "Willy's" visits. The people know she will return and call in neighborly fashion as she used to do.

She will be visiting Mrs. Walter Sherwood and Mrs. Mary Creighton with whom she keeps up an unbroken correspondence. Father Fitzgerald, the priest of the Catholic parish, who has known her for thirty years or more, will have a long talk with her, and she will spend hours with Miss Mollie Ferris, who was her mother's best friend. Moreover, Miss Cather will visit the old ranch and talk with Mrs. Charlotte Lambrecht, who was a neighbor of the days on the farm, a friend she has remembered with a Christmas greeting every year since she left that farm. There are dozens of others.

Kansas City Star, 10 July 1937, 12.

A Pittsburgh Teacher

In March 1901, Cather was hired to replace a Latin teacher at Central High School in Pittsburgh. The following fall she taught English. The school was "a dismal, grimy structure on a bluff looking down on the Union Station," according to one of her freshmen students, Norman Foerster (1887–1972), later a teacher and a critic (E. Brown 71–72). In 1903, she moved to a more pleasantly situated and better paying position at Allegheny High School, where she remained until S. S. McClure hired her to join his magazine staff. Mary Roberts Rinehart graduated from Allegheny High School in 1893. Many years later, she recalled a brief encounter with Cather:

> For four years I sent out material as I wrote it, only correcting the typed copy. Then one day I decided to rewrite a story which had come back from twelve different markets, a quiet story about the Spanish War. In its revised form I sent it to Scribner's and it was accepted. That taught me something. I still knew no writing people. Once indeed I had met Willa Cather, teaching in the high school which I had attended, and she told me she wrote a story and then laid it away, sometimes for months. After that she did it again. But I was too young and eager for that. Ideas were coming fast and strong. I had to get one out of the way to be ready for another. It was the Scribner experience from which I learned.(87)

In 1980, Kathleen D. Byrne and Richard C. Snyder's chapter titled "Miss Cather of Central and Allegheny High Schools," in their book *Chrysalis: Willa Cather in Pittsburgh*, presented a good summary of Cather's teaching years. Very little scholarly work followed, however, until Millanee Kvasnicka completed her dissertation, "Education in the Parish/Preparation for the World: The Educational Tradition in the Life and Works of Willa Cather," in 1997. Since then, Kvasnicka, herself a high school English teacher, has published several articles that introduce Cather the teacher to other teachers and scholars.

The following reminiscences—of several of Cather's former high school students—were recalled years after the fact; nevertheless, they provide a coherent glance into an important dimension of Cather's life.

ALEXANDER WOOLLCOTT

Alexander Woollcott (1887–1943), essayist and humorist, knew Cather personally, although that is not clear in his *New Yorker* column containing a letter from an unnamed former student of Cather's. Kathleen Byrne identifies the unnamed student as Margaret Doane Gilson, "a worshipful teenager at Central" who once asked Cather if she might submit an article to the *Literary Review* about Cather's teaching. In typical fashion, Cather refused, telling Gilson that she had been bothered enough with the teaching while she was doing it.

Shouts and Murmurs and Contents Noted

Some passing allusion to *Death Comes for the Archbishop* in a recent issue of this page was enough to bring me a note from a woman in Pittsburgh who writes, in part, as follows:

> Miss Cather taught me Freshman English in high school here in the early nineteen-hundreds, and I have forgotten very little that she said. In fact, it is all I know of any English course that I ever had. So vivid was her personality, so unforgettable her method of making us see the picture, that even yet I hear her voice when I read her books. We read "The Ancient Mariner" and "Lancelot and Elaine" in that course, and her comments are still with me. She stood before us in her rainy-day skirt, thumbs in belt or pocket, wavy brown hair, thin mobile lips, hazel eyes, *retroussé* nose, not very tall, not in the least a school teacher. But, to a group of us who worshipped at her shrine, hers was the one hour of the day which stood out as something of vital moment. It was the hour for which we lived. One of her stories, now in *Youth and the Bright Medusa*, is taken from those days; it is called "Paul's Case." How little that faculty knew there was an eagle among them, and how glad I am that I have one of its feathers!

I have put this letter aside as a reminder that some day I must attempt a similar sketch of Miss Sophie Rosenberger, who was my ideal in the days

Willa Cather during her Pittsburgh years. Courtesy of the Nebraska State Historical Society, Willa Cather Pioneer Memorial Collection.

when she presided over the second grade of the Franklin School at 14th and Washington, Kansas City, Missouri. Bless me, that was back in the fall of 1893. She has recently honored me by registering her bulldog at the kennels under the name of Alexander Woollcott. I was much gratified by this gesture, but the neighbors report to me that my namesake is thus addressed in full only when he has been simply unbearable.

What interests me further in the excerpt quoted above is its fresh evidence of the infallible judgment so many readers display for just those oddments of information which would tickle this old fancy. Apropos of nothing, for instance, here is a report from one who, up in Provincetown, appears to have been poring over the lists of New England freemen prior to 1650. One of these rude, musket-toting pioneers who built him a cabin and took pot-shots at the red brothers was named—to the frank delight of my informant—Marmaduke Ravensdale. And to my delight, too. Marmaduke Ravensdale! Why, he makes Gaylord Ravenal sound like a character in George Gissing.

New Yorker, 15 Oct. 1932, 36.

FRED OTTE JR.

Fred Otte Jr. (1884–1956) appears to have been one of Cather's more favored pupils at Central High School in Pittsburgh. He was invited to the McClung's for tea, and Cather tutored him specially so that he might transfer to a better school. The two shared a passion for music and for study. According to John March, Otte eventually became a businessman, but he is remembered best for his participation in his hobby of developing purebred dogs. He wrote many articles about dogs and a popular book, *Simplified Dog Behavior* (1952). He and Cather maintained an occasional correspondence for the rest of her life (March 552).

The Willa Cather I Knew

Willa Cather's name was not in the dictionary when I first saw her. Today, she is listed as Willa Sibert Cather—American novelist. But she was more than that and became one of America's best known highly talented and most respected women.

The first time I met Willa Cather she was an obscure, overworked and underpaid high school teacher. The circumstances were unusual, the surroundings grotesque, the result one of the major experiences of my life— sobering, exacting, maturing, character forming. It was a close friendship lasting more than forty years, to her passing. I had enrolled in what was called "The Academic High School." It was a dingy, decrepit structure, clinging to the top of a grimy cliff overlooking the dirtiest, smokiest railroad yards in what was then the smoggiest, ugliest city in this country. The steel mills made it one of the wealthiest, where often all street and store lights had to be turned on at midday.

At this particular period, the schools and all other public works were ground under the heel of what was commonly known as the Billy Flynn machine, which was said to dip into the money bags and help itself. Apparently the entire school system, including the teachers' pay, was maintained on a starvation diet.

Soiled and stained by the smoke and soot of many years, the floors worn down and the walls defaced, halls and classrooms were cheerless and dun-colored. Looking over the faculty in the assembly hall, they seemed mousey, rather shabbily dressed and collectively funereal. That is, all but one.

In a neat brown suit, wearing a crisp, white shirtwaist with Peter Pan collar and cuffs, this one looked trim, smart and tidy amid her drab surroundings. Her lightly tanned complexion was fresh and clear, with the slight flush of peaches ripened in the sun and wind. Her hands were brown and strong, almost masculine. She sat at ease, looking over the pupils.

This was, I discovered, Willa Cather, the English teacher. Before the end of the first week, one day as the English class ended, I was startled to hear my name. "Otte," (I was pleased that she pronounced it 'Aughty'). I turned to listen. "Will you stay a few minutes, please." What could this possibly mean, I thought, as she straightened some papers on her desk. When the other students had gone, she turned and smiling pleasantly, pointed to a chair.

"Otte, how did you come to enroll in this school? Where do you live? Didn't I see you on the 5th Avenue street car this morning?" After I explained that I lived in the Point Breeze district in the East End, she said she lived on Murray Hill Avenue, a short distance away and rode to and from school every day. I managed to be on the same car almost every day thereafter. It was half an hour's ride to Clyde Street, on the edge of the downtown section. Then we had to walk up a rather steep hill, through a dilapidated tenement district, to reach the high school building.

As we chatted informally about this and that, I noticed Miss Cather walked with a youthful spring to her step; the seams of her hose were perfectly straight and she swung along at a comfortable but steady gait, asking many questions and talking with interesting enthusiasm. And so she taught me the art of easy conversation. When I told her of my gaited saddle horse and that my younger brother owned a cow pony from Cheyenne, she answered with stories of her early days in Nebraska. We were soon on common ground.

I lived near such then-prominent men as H. J. Heinz, George Westinghouse, H. C. Frick and others. Only half a block away, the once fabulous Lillian Russell resided with her husband Alec Moore, who owned the *Pittsburgh Leader*, a well established newspaper, where Willa was on the staff part-time. She seemed greatly amused to hear that by well planned manipulation, we managed to contact these men from time to time when riding. Attracted by the glistening coats and polished leather tack of our mounts, they spoke to us of the spirited performance and good behavior of our horses in jumping natural obstacles used as hurdles, especially in the semi-private wooded tract located behind the Frick home. In this way, we were able to accumulate gaily colored, fancy straw ornaments and some good horse blankets for our own barn, donated from the stables of these kindly neighbors.

I was closely quizzed about these and similar contacts, and required to write countless "themes" about them, for Willa said they might be useful as material for a novel she had in mind to write sometime.

"Otte," Miss Cather said one day as we were walking down the hill after school. "If I were you, I would not return to this school next year. Plan to go to a good school like the one I have heard of in Vevey, Switzerland. The courses are what you want; the experience will be an education in itself. You will save time." The idea fascinated me. It was inspirational. Arrangements were made for Miss Cather to tutor me in English, supplementing my high school work. Lessons were to be at the Judge McClung residence, where Willa then lived. At the suggestion of Miss Isabelle McClung, who was interested in music and had a charming and delightful personality, Willa had moved into the more congenial surroundings of this large and comfortable home. Isabelle later married Jan Hambourg, the celebrated violinist. She passed away at their home overseas while Miss Cather was still active in New York.

My lessons were heard in a small sitting room at the McClung home. As a tutor, Willa was a patient but hard task-master. She insisted upon careful and thoughtful work, however imperfect it might be in quality, for she often reminded me that we learn by doing. She knew how to assign plenty of homework between lessons. I often rose at 4 o'clock in the morning to study before breakfast. I never dared to report unprepared. Willa had been raised with the boys of her family and she understood them. She was the only person I had ever known who made me like study until eventually it became a habit.

Starting with one volume of Shakespeare in the pocket size Temple edition, in the course of time I accumulated about thirty. Meantime, my assignments included the green cover pocket size Temple classics. Her list for study was lengthy and varied. Sometimes it seemed to me that long sentences at hard labor on Devil Island would be preferable. But, recalling just a few, I enjoyed books like "An Iceland Fisherman" by Pierre Loti; Felix Gras' "The Reds of the Midi"; Maupassant's "Odd Number"; "Monday Tales" by Daudet and the Mermaid series of best plays. Willa presented me with that favorite little volume of "A Shropshire Lad" by A. E. Housman. Others, covering different periods of Miss Cather's life, explain her interest in music and the theatre. At her suggestion, I arranged to attend the Sunday dress rehearsals of the old Harry Davis Stock Company in the 5th Avenue theatre in Pittsburgh. It was there I met such well known professionals as Lizzie Hudson Collier, Henriette Crossman, Marian Ballou, the ingenue and Tommy Meighan, then painting scenery, shifting canvas, playing juveniles, but later to become a star of the silent films. There was never any idea that I had any special talent for show business. It was just part of my education. When you studied with Willa Cather, you studied. *The Oxford Book of English Verse* prepared me to appreciate "April Twilights," Willa's little book of verse, which attracted some favorable comment.

Time flew by. S. S. McClure could spot, and recruit unusual talent from the most unusual places. After observing Willa's work in his own way for a while, he decided he wanted and needed her on his staff. McClure was a man of action. Willa was ready. She had been preparing for a long time, although she did not know in what direction the road might open up. Quoting briefly from a note from her, she says:

My Dear Otte: How glad I am to hear from you. Imagine you remembering Dec. 7th again. It was no wish of mine that the new book is to come out on my birthday. That was arranged by the business office because of some technical wrinkle which came up when they sold the rights to The Book of the Month Club.

I always remember our funny seances, when I sat up at the teacher's desk and you sat in front of me at a pupil's desk, in about the dirtiest and bleakest schoolroom that ever was. I am glad that you got something out of it. I liked to teach and I think I might have stuck at it indefinitely if S. S. McClure hadn't seen some stories of mine.

Willa told me of many of her unusual, often difficult assignments from McClure, both in this country and in Europe. Her articles about Mary Baker Eddy stirred up a great controversy, but she impartially reported the facts as she saw them. At one time, she was invited to a testimonial dinner for Mark Twain. It happened that her dinner partner was Charles Major who had written a best-seller titled "When Knighthood was in Flower." He was a small-town lawyer from the midwest with a practice limited to probating wills and filing abstracts of titles, so he had plenty of time for research and thinking up a good plot. The vogue was for historical novels, especially if enough sex appeal had been mixed in to whet the public imagination. Julia Marlowe, a popular actress of the day, was doing the stage version. Never taken very seriously as a literary artist, he was admired for his income-producing astuteness. When the usual small talk of such gatherings had been exhausted, conversation turned to Willa Cather's "The Song of the Lark," in which one of the principal characters is named Fred Ottenberg as a fillip to me—Fred Otte. Charles Major mentioned that he had known me all my life; at one time had held me on his lap while he told me stories; that he had visited our home in Pittsburgh. When Willa said she had been my tutor in English, an unexpected topic of conversation was provided for the rest of the dinner.

After she joined McClure in New York, I saw Miss Cather much less frequently, although at the time I was usually over there once a month, and when possible we managed to meet to talk things over. We both traveled far and wide, but our correspondence continued to the time she was incapacitated and could no longer write freely.

Having seen pictures showing panoramic views of my trips to Cuba, Willa planned to go with me to get the background for a story she had in mind, but the war interfered. Now and then, when in New York, I went to #5 Bank Street to hear and tell the latest news. Here it was, in front of a cozy coal fireplace, with tea and scones, I saw the exciting snapshots of her Mesa Verde expedition. Willa never lost her love for the western country, nor her interest in any personalities or incidents which might have possibilities for future writing. I eagerly read everything she wrote, and just for old time's sake, I imagine, she asked for my opinions.

"Otte," she would say, after I had remembered every one of her birthdays for thirty-five years, "if you ever tell anyone the date of my birth—woe be unto you." Books have been written about Willa Cather's childhood and college days; about her experiences in the later years when she was well known because of her mature accomplishments, but these days in old-time Pittsburgh when comforts were few, work hours long, money too scarce, prospects baffling and uncertain—these were the days they now call "frustrating," but Willa Cather was born with the spark, and nothing, but nothing could extinguish it. It only shown the brighter. It was my good fortune to come under the influence of this truly great but unassuming personality at a time I needed such a contact most. A clever teacher, an exceptional tutor, a strict disciplinarian. Inducement rather than compulsion. Boys like it that way. So do men. It makes you feel important because you get things done.

It has been said that Miss Cather was not an easy person to know. Perhaps this is true. Because of her busy life, she had few intimates. I was just enough younger to occasionally interrupt our serious studies with small-town tales of a rather primitive Indiana, which always seemed to amuse her. But she could always top my stories with one of her Nebraska days.

"Otte," she would say, "the rural mind is entirely different from the urban mind. They see the same thing through quite different lenses."

Incidental to my later interest in rehabilitation work for the handicapped, and my special interest in guide-dogs for the blind, I often think how pleased Miss Cather would be to know that several of her best novels were selected to be recorded by trained readers as "talking books" for the benefit of the blind, as issued by the Library of Congress through many state distributing centers.

From childhood, Willa had always liked animals. She always wanted to know about my dogs. I owned a number of show dogs, including Bedlington Terriers, English Springer Spaniels and German Shepherds. In telling Miss Cather about them, 1 mentioned Norwegian Elkhounds.

"Otte," she said, "you know that dogs are nothing new to me. I have several other friends who have gone to the dogs. In social relations, that is to say, relations with humans, dogs of different breeds seem to have very special and individual effects. I have never known a fancier of Collies who was not very companionable and sympathetic. Perhaps that is because they are all Scotchmen. I think most Scotchmen are sentimental under their grouch. But oh! Beware the Norwegian Elkhound. Social relations with them will contaminate almost any man. One friend of mine who began raising Elkhounds, and taking prizes for them, has become as savage as they are—a biter and snapper of the first order. Beware the Elkhound."

University of Nebraska–Lincoln, manuscript after 1940: 1–7.

PHYLLIS MARTIN HUTCHINSON

Phyllis Hutchinson, another of Willa Cather's students, who later worked at the New York Public Library, was invited to one of Cather's Friday afternoon teas at Bank Street. The teacher who had worn tailored shirtwaists and entertained students at the McClung residence now was dressed in a lovely gown, had her own New York City apartment, and was entertaining well-connected friends, perhaps mixing cocktails (which she had learned to do in Pittsburgh), certainly serving a fine wine.

Reminiscences of Willa Cather as a Teacher

In the spring of 1901 when I was looking forward to being graduated from the eighth grade of an elementary school in Pittsburgh, Miss Willa Sibert Cather was appointed a teacher of English in Pittsburgh Central High School. That fall she and I both started in a new field and I was fortunate enough to be a member of one of her English classes. There were only three high schools in the city at the time — the Academic, the Normal and the Commercial. Central was the academic stronghold and stood on a high hill above the Union Station. The old building was four stories tall, with wooden stairways. Walking was considered good exercise, and as the "D" or beginning classes all reported on the top floor, we had plenty of it. Miss Cather's classroom was also on the fourth floor, as was the auditorium. The latter had moveable benches and was used for entertainments, for chapel once a week, and served also as the indoor basketball field for both boys' and girls' teams. At chapel time, the faculty lined up on the platform and the exercises were led by the principal. As one of the few young teachers, Miss Cather sat in the balcony with the class that reported in her room. Little did anyone dream that there was one person present in that auditorium whose name, someday, would be known all over the world. Willa Cather was then about twenty-six years old, good looking, with gray-blue eyes and dark hair worn pompadour fashion. She had intermittent dimples and beautiful, even white teeth that seemed to flash when she laughed. She affected mannish dress — "rainy-day" skirts were fashionable at the time — and with them she wore severely tailored shirtwaists with stiff cuffs, and collars with four-in-hand ties. This may have been a carryover from her college days when she wore similar clothes, though ruffles and furbelows were certainly in style in the gay 'nineties.

Fifty years ago almost nothing was known of progressive education, or of guidance for students. If one expected to go to college, he went to Central High and was regimented through the same courses, with no electives the first year. We all had ancient history, English, Latin, algebra, botany, and once a week, elocution. Usually there was homework in every subject, and while we complained about it, we really expected nothing else. Schools were co-educational but somehow there seemed to be more girls than boys in each class. "English" in elementary school had been limited to grammar drill, parsing words and diagramming sentences. By the time a pupil reached ninth grade he was supposed to know how to write grammatically, but the world of literature was mostly unknown. I think Miss Cather reveled in opening up the Realms of Gold to us and in stimulating our imaginations with her own enthusiasm. She knew that the only way to learn to write was to write, and she set us to writing themes, one every class day, usually in the first ten or fifteen minutes of the period. We did not know until we came to class what subject she would assign. They were simple subjects like "My first party," "An Italian fruit-stand," "My favorite play," but designed to teach us first to observe carefully, then to describe and narrate clearly. In *The Novel Deméublé* she refers to "that drudge, the theme-writing high school student," and thus described us perfectly.

While Miss Cather had strong likes and dislikes and was generally outspoken, she understood the sensitivity of teen-agers and never held us up to ridicule as some of the other teachers did. I shall always remember and be grateful that she took a *faux pas* of mine in stride and did not give the class a chance to laugh at my expense. Her standard of marking was as low as her standard of what constituted good English was high. Seldom did she grade beyond 85, and that only rarely. Mostly we got 70s and occasionally achieved an 80 on our themes, which were all carefully corrected and returned to us.

We had much required reading, both poetry and prose. She taught us to memorize parts of poems that were in different meters. She had the ability bring out the fine flavor of what we read, and more important, she was able to carry the inspiration of these books over to the duller grind of rhetoric. She stressed the difference between metaphors and similes, and expected us to recognize them as we read. Once she compared a chrysanthemum on a coat lapel to a bunch of coleslaw, an extreme simile to catch our attention and emphasize a vivid description.

A perfectionist, Willa Cather had little patience with the stupid or careless pupil. Personality was all important to her. She made it clear that even a child is not interesting per se, but only if he has an interesting personality. Her own personality could not be ignored. She was greatly admired by some of her students, and just as heartily disliked by others. This condition alone prevented boredom in class. Her classes, however, were never dull. She was too much alive to endure routine and she usually had an interesting story of some celebrity she had known to highlight a point. She spoke repeatedly of Madame Nordica and of Sarah Orne Jewett, whose books she admired tremendously.

She was steeped in the classics, and her knowledge of Latin was always evident in class. Invariably she tried to show us how to derive the meaning of English words from their Latin roots. In *Lancelot and Elaine* Tennyson says: " . . . there is many a youth Now crescent . . ." Miss Cather pointed out that "crescent" is from "cresco," I grow. We were just beginning the study of Latin, so this was a nice tie-in of courses. And the habit she inculcated of tracing meanings through word-roots has remained life-long with some of us. She always made us look up references to mythology, which helped us in our ancient history course. She was the first teacher to give us a list of books for summer reading.

Though young, Willa Cather always seemed very sure of herself. Yet she did not seek the limelight, but always kept inconspicuously in the background. Even if teaching was not her forte, I think she enjoyed it. She tried to impress her own high ideals upon us, and taught us to avoid the tawdry at all costs. "Fine writing" was her *bête noir* and we must despise it as she did. She urged us to seek the right word to express a certain shade of meaning; she made literature come alive; she broadened our horizons and encouraged us to make the most of whatever ability we possessed, and above all, to be ourselves. Those of her pupils who became teachers in turn owe much to her example and inspiration, and for the rest of us her whole-hearted sincerity and the integrity of her character remain a shining memory.

In 1913, I wrote to congratulate her on *O Pioneers!* and frankly mentioned that I liked *April Twilights* better. She answered from Gore, Virginia, a few miles from Winchester where she was born, that the poems had nearly all been written during the two winters she had taught at Pittsburgh Central High School. She said they were rather blue and homesick winters but that some pleasant things had come of them. The loneliness is reflected in the poems, each one a little gem polished to perfection, but with a poignant tinge of sorrow, regret or longing. She closed the letter with a cordial invitation to visit her when I came to New York. Several years later, when I was living in the city, I attended one of her Friday afternoon teas at 5 Bank Street. I was surprised to see, instead of the tailored teacher I remembered, a very charming and delightfully feminine person who was most friendly and gracious as she introduced me to the other guests. The only one I recall was Mr. S. S. McClure who was just back from Europe and full of news of the First World War.

One wonders why in 1920 or thereabouts Willa Sibert Cather dropped her middle name. Presumably she was named for her mother's brother who was killed in the Civil War. At any rate she made good the youthful boast in her poem "The Namesake" which is dedicated to him, that she would be "winner at the game enough for two that bore the name."

Bulletin of the New York Public Library 60, no.6 (1956): 263–66.

JANE SHAW

This final reminiscence, based on information from several of Cather's former high school students, reveals that in the latter part of the twentieth century, Pittsburgh as well as Nebraska was claiming Cather as one of its own celebrities. Jane Shaw (1925–1990), who carried a prominent historical name in Pittsburgh, interviewed Mabel Lovelace, a longtime Pittsburgh resident who had attended a seventy-fifth anniversary tea in the former Samuel McClung residence, the same house in which Cather lived and in which she served tea to her students. For many years, the owners Elizabeth and Robert Mertz cooperated with the Pittsburgh Cather Circle to have tea in Cather's honor.

Seventy-fifth Anniversary Tea Recalls Student Teas

Happy events of seventy-five years ago were recalled when Mabel Lovelace once again had tea at the former McClung home on Murrayhill Avenue.

What's so special about this?

Well, the former McClung residence is where author Willa Cather made her home for five of the ten years she lived, wrote, and taught in Pittsburgh. And Mrs. Lovelace, now in her ninetieth year, was one of her pupils.

Miss Cather, who taught English at Central High School, entertained her students at tea during summer vacation, at Christmas season, during the spring term, and even after they had gone on to college.

"At tea, Willa Cather wanted to find out what we were doing and whether we liked it," Mrs. Lovelace recalled. "She inspired me to be a writer, but I never got to it.

"As a teacher she was tops, but maybe you better not say it that way," she laughed. "She taught composition and would point out what she liked. She also would tell us about things of her own."

Mrs. Lovelace told of Willa Cather's first book of poems, *April Twilights*. "She autographed copies of it and gave it to her students at tea here in this very room."

Mrs. Lovelace remembered many members of that class: her close friends Marjorie Loose and Alline Speer, Frances Kelly, who became head of Carnegie Library School, Margaret Case, later a school teacher at Peabody, Donald Miller, who became principal of Peabody, and Sara Soffel who became the first woman judge in Pittsburgh.

Pittsburgh Post-Gazette, 1 Sept. 1975, 17.

A New York City Journalist

Willa Cather earned her living and practiced her craft primarily in journalism for twenty years. Most of her colleagues, both in the offices where she worked and those she met in her travels, accepted her as a writer and editor of quick mind, firm decision, forceful personality, and well-phrased writing. To further aid her career, Cather displayed stamina, an executive sense, and an ability to meet and talk with talented and important people. The next three reminiscences, however, are not all positive. Each writer has his or her own reputation to think about as well as Cather's. The reflection by Adela Rogers St. Johns, particularly, criticizes Cather as a poor journalist. Anyone who wrote about Mrs. Mary Baker G. Eddy was bound to incite controversy, and St. Johns was a Christian Scientist herself, but she also had her own far-reaching reputation as a journalist, so she had standing to criticize Cather.

FORD MADOX FORD

Ford Madox Ford's (Hueffer) (1873–1939) book of memoirs *Return to Yesterday* appears to be vintage Ford. In other words, he appears to be telling his own version of the truth. Cather indicated in a letter once that Ford could fabricate truths wonderfully.[1] He must surely have been aware that Ida Tarbell and Willa Cather did not work for S. S. McClure at the same time, so one might wonder why he consistently linked them in his book. Perhaps it was because both women were fearless writers and editors. Although knowing Ford's flair for embellishment, readers still get a glimpse of the stimulating world in which Cather worked during her early New York years.

From Return to Yesterday

But by 1906 the domestic note was vanishing even from New York offices. The one that comes most vividly back to me was that of the S. S. McClure Company. That, as I have said, was panelled with polished tulip wood, which gave it a very pretty effect. Pretty is the exact word. It was certainly not august, neither was it opulent, nor yet drawing-room-like as was the case with Lord Northcliffe's private office in Carmelite House. It had already a number of shining, nickelled and black celluloid instruments. But still panelled room opened out into panelled room. There was not a sea of instrument-operating young women in shirt waists or any glass cases. . . .

I passed the greater part of my time in New York in McClure's office not because I wanted to work for the magazine but because I liked the editorial staff. It consisted of Miss Tarbell, Miss Willa Sibert Cather, and Mr. William Aspenwall Bradley, who was then a slim young poet and is now a substantial literary agent in Paris. Miss Isabel McClung, who is now Mrs. Jan Hambourg, was also on the staff, as, I think, assistant to Miss Cather. . . .

I lounged, then, in and out of McClure's office, getting in the way of Miss Cather and Miss Tarbell, being taken about by one or the other of them to tea parties or to lunch at Mouquin's by Mr. Bradley. I bantered S. S. on the Napoleonic nature of his policies and was taken by him to baseball matches, the Tombs and the Night Court on Sixth Avenue. He wanted me to write muck-rake articles for him. One article in particular that he wanted me to write was as to the comparative statistics of crimes of violence in various countries. For this he wanted me not only to get up an enormous body of statistics but to interview thugs in the Tombs and, in the Night Court prison, ladies who had stabbed with hatpins other ladies or their gentlemen friends. I was, of course, to make it hot for the United States. In that respect America was, and is still, I believe, very far ahead of every other civilised country and of several uncivilised ones. According to McClure, crimes of violence were then most frequent in God's Own Country and least so in the Green Isle of his birth. In between came the following countries in their order of precedence: the German Empire, Italy, Spain, France and Great Britain. But Mr. McClure gave to his statistics a human twist. Thus the German Empire came next to the United States in crime because of assassinations of minor officials—postmen, most usually, because they carried objects of value; policemen because they were hated; and firemen because, extinguishing fires, they robbed the public of the chance of profitable insurances. These Mr. McClure included as ordinary crimes of violence, whilst recognising them as being largely political in character. On the other hand in his consideration of Ireland, he omitted assassinations and attempted assassinations of landlords, agents and constabulary because they *were* political.

His proposal was that I should travel in all these countries and, whilst interviewing murderers, collect statistics of all and every sort that could help in denouncing the United States from every angle, material and intellectual. For this he offered me what in those days seemed a princely fortune and he went on making it more and more princely as I successively refused and the hour grew later.

I had of him much the same sort of fear as I had of Lord Northcliffe. I instinctively distrusted mass production whether material or of printed matter; I did not believe I could make the pace of Twenty-third Street any more than of Carmelite House. And, in McClure's case, I could not see that denouncing the United States was any affair of mine. I was in a stage—that has not yet exhausted itself—of being delighted with New York. In and around McClure's office itself I came across what I most wanted. McClure and his young friends who made up his gang were as full of intellectual curiosity as an egg is filled with its contents. It was of intellectual curiosity and a distrust of vested interests that I was most in search. McClure wanted me most, I gathered, to help him attack the American administration. He did not care from what point of view. I could, if I liked, prove that American arts were no good and the American intellect non-existent because of the faultiness of American State education. I could make out elaborate tables to prove anything I liked, as long as it was to the discredit of American authority.

Nothing could have been farther from my inclinations. I was suffering at that time—and I have suffered ever since—from a violent reaction against vested interests in the arts and matters intellectual. In New York I could see no vestiges of the trail of that serpent. Except for the South I knew nothing of America outside New York. But the intellectual and artistic future of Anglo-Saxondom seemed to be in the hands of New York. I could not therefore have attacked what I discerned as the only sign of hope for the race that my skies shewed.

McClure then got it into his head that it would be a good idea to start a muck-rake magazine in England. England surely had political abuses that needed exposing. He suggested that I should start with his capital such a magazine in England. When he came to the country he would edit it as long as he was there. I could edit it for the rest of the time—in conjunction, perhaps, with Percival Gibbon, who knew his mind.

That suggestion, too, I turned down. I could see no need for a muck-rake magazine in England. English political institutions seemed to me—and still so seem—as nearly perfect in their workings as such things can be in this vale. It was only from the aesthetic and intellectual side of English life that I was growing daily more alien. In America the moment I had passed the imitation English cottages on Sandy Hook my heart always seemed to sink a little. I thought that from there to the Golden Gate there was not an old house, nor a mellow one. It was a terrible depressant. But the moment I struck Tilbury Dock and crossed over to Greenwich on my way back to Kent, I knew that a much greater feeling of depression would descend on me. It was the thought of intellectual precedent narrowing down to precedent. From there to John o' Groat's House in the extreme north I should not find one soul who could think without calling on authority.

I had perhaps better illustrate what I mean by a couple of stories.

One Miss Cather told about herself and Miss McClung. Last year I re-related it to both ladies. Miss Cather made no comment, but she never does make any comment. That is perhaps why she is one of the greatest novelists of the present day. Miss McClung said it was very much exaggerated. It is at least very nice.

In Pittsburgh, then, in early days there was a *Shropshire Lad Club*. Beneath the palls of smoke that hang over that terrible valley and in among the slag-heaps that are its most marked features, there existed valiant spirits in large numbers who met for the daily study and reading aloud of Mr. A. E. Housman's volume. (I daresay some of them inhabited one or the other of the rather beautiful hill suburbs of that city. There must have been some such members, since the club was possessed of considerable resources.) But I like to think of them meeting under the presidency of Miss Cather on the sloping side of a conical slag deposit.

In due course, as they would, they decided to do something to make Mr. Housman aware of their admiration. They subscribed therefore for a solid gold laurel wreath and deputed Miss Cather and Miss McClung to carry it to the poet and explain suitably why it was sent.

The ladies got off the boat at Liverpool. They knew Liverpool to be near Chester and Cheshire to be the county next to Shropshire. They visited all the villages whose picturesque names give so much colour to the poems. They called at innumerable parsonages to ask for information as to the poet. The parsons, they said, all seemed to come to their doors carrying napkins and smelling strongly of lunch. Some of them even invited them to share their meals. But none of them had heard of Mr. Housman.

The two ladies then got as far as Shrewsbury—pronounced Shrowsb'ry.

They went to the public library and asked their embarrassing question. The librarian had heard neither of book nor poet. After a considerable pause he said: "Ah, wait!" And consulted his catalogue.

He went away and came back with a copy of the book. It was covered with dust, inscribed: "Presented by the Author," and uncut. But the librarian could tell them no more about the author.

They went to the British Museum and consulted the quite courteous Principal Librarian. Sir E. Maunde Thompson said that he too had never heard of Mr. Housman but would be glad to read the volume of verse that they left with him.

A few days later they had from him a note running:

"Sir E. Maunde Thompson presents his compliments to Miss McCrather and Miss Lung. He has read the work submitted to him by those young ladies and begs to ask: Is there not Milton?

"If the young ladies nevertheless desire to prosecute their search he suggests that they should apply to the publisher of the fascicle. He is Mr. ——."

The young ladies would have done that before but the copies of *The Shropshire Lad* that they had possessed had all been of the American edition. No English bookseller had heard of the work and all refused to book an order for poetry unless the publisher's name could be supplied. They then found their way to Hampstead.

A teeny-tweeny maid opened the door of a boarding-house to the extent of a crack large enough to shew her nose. They were inspected by a landlady from an upper landing. At last they were admitted to a parlour. Its principal ornament was an immense, shiny and very cold-looking grand piano.

They waited a long time. At last there appeared the poet. He exclaimed:

"*Oh!* If I had not thought you were my American cousins I would never have seen you," and disappeared.

They laid the solid gold laurel wreath reverently on the grand piano and departed.

New York: Liveright, 1932. 308–32.

ADELA ROGERS ST. JOHNS

When Adela Rogers St. Johns (1894–1988) wrote her book *Some Are Born Great*, she said clearly that she did so to bring attention to overlooked heroines who had had a hand in creating the story that is America. She acknowledges the importance of written space devoted to people the world would know: "Who would have known . . . even the Blessed Mother herself if somebody hadn't recreated [her] in the time-space continuum. They [great women] *continue*, because of what others have said or written of them" (vi, 5). For the final subject in her chapter on women's contributions in American literature, St. Johns presents Willa Cather as one of these women who should be remembered.

The two women had quite different careers. St. Johns was known as "the country's first woman sports writer," as a Washington correspondent, and as a "Sob Sister," especially for her articles on women in the Depression years. She began her career writing for the Hearst paper in San Francisco and for *Photoplay Magazine* in Los Angeles. Later, she worked on Hollywood scripts and became known as the "Mother Confessor to the Stars."

From Some Are Born Great

Someone is going to ask me about Willa Cather.

Bound to. Just as when I eulogized Tom Mix as the great American cowboy who created the art of the Western, people always asked me about William S. Hart—who was a Shakespearean actor of the third class and afraid of horses.

Willa Cather was a fine—maybe our finest—American woman novelist.

She was a horrid, harsh, repellent woman and a lousy unscrupulous reporter. Truth is the one perfect defense for libel, so I'm going to let that stand no matter what my lawyers or those of my publisher say about it.

I once followed her trail when I hoped to write a life story of that great American woman—*and* writer—Mary Baker Eddy. Probably the greatest all around American woman of all time. Think about her a moment. She is the only woman who ever started a major religion, which Christian Science most certainly is. Her book *Science and Health with Key to the Scriptures* is an all-time top best-seller. The Mother Church in Boston, built by and for her by her millions of followers, now takes in with its Publishing House as much ground as the Vatican. She affected all Christian religions with her insistence that Jesus actually meant what he said when it came to casting out devils and healing the sick. Mrs. Eddy did more for copyright and copyright laws in the years she spent in Washington on this project than anyone else has ever done for us. And when she started her great newspaper, the *Christian Science Monitor*—started it with a brief letter instructing them to begin to publish it at once—she was in her eighty-eighth year. I do not include her as a writer, though no American woman has written a more successful book, because writing was secondary to her propaganda purpose—a good one, of course. And if I find it fascinating because she had to invent practically a new vocabulary for her teaching, she did it to such height that it has now become part of ours.

As I followed Mrs. Eddy's life through New England—she is, by the way, the only woman whose journey through life is put forward in an automobile club road map pamphlet showing each of her homes and the places where important events happened—on the trail I also followed Willa Cather. Out of it, to my amazement, I found Willa Cather had stirred with grim fancy the most vicious and inaccurate of all the attacks on Mrs. Eddy. This contributed to a magazine serial and later a book by Georgine Milmine. Fortunately Mrs. Eddy was the most successful counterpuncher in the feminine history of our country so instead of Miss Cather doing her harm, these attacks were used by Mrs. Eddy to spread her teaching and the truth about herself.

New York: Doubleday, 1974. 128–29.

WITTER BYNNER

According to (Harold) Witter Bynner's (1881–1968) own account, he was a poet whose mother and stepfather traded him a six-month trip abroad after his graduation from Harvard in 1902 in exchange for his working for a publisher for a year when he returned (158). He was on the *McClure's Magazine* staff when Willa Cather arrived in the New York office, although he left *McClure's* for a freelance life of traveling, writing, speaking, and socializing with others interested in the arts, particularly the literary arts (Bynner 165). Frank Luther Mott, a historian of U.S. journalism, gives Bynner credit for improving the "quantity and quality of *McClure's* poetry" (602). Bynner's and Cather's paths continued to cross, even in New Mexico, since both visited Mabel Dodge's ranch.

Another of the persons who frequented the Dodge ranch was Joseph Foster who characterizes Bynner thusly:

> Bynner was a distinguished man—expansive, articulate, urbane. He was very large and self-confident of his peculiarities. He was very darkly handsome and rich enough to have his own way.
>
> Bynner was very famous in academic America—welcome in all the great universities for convocations. He had a surprising cultural drive, a big man with a slight muse. (71)

In a book of memoirs of D. H. Lawrence, Foster said that Lawrence and Bynner "fought constantly . . . Lawrence was outraged by Bynner's academic mummery. 'Leave off fine learning!' he advised Bynner." Bynner, in turn, "really thought Lawrence a beast" (72).

The three books Bynner is reviewing in the following "Triptych" are biographical books all published in 1953: E. K. Brown's *Willa Cather: A Critical Biography*, Edith Lewis's *Willa Cather Living: A Personal Record*, and Elizabeth Sergeant's *Willa Cather: A Memoir*.

A Willa Cather Triptych

Of these three books dealing with Willa Cather, E. K. Brown's, completed after his death by Leon Edel, the first in order of publication and of my reading, is, in my judgment, professorially full and orthodox like the chords of a church organist; the second, by Edith Lewis, Miss Cather's longtime friend and housemate, has the meager simplicity of a one-fingered melody heard from a determined child; but the third, by Elizabeth Shepley Sergeant, a writer better endowed and seasoned than the others, is played on the very air of the years through which these two gifted authors knew each other, sharing and comparing their interests, emotions and aspirations.

It is too bad that the three volumes all appear in 1953, since in large degree they have to repeat one another's objective data. The Lewis account, the shortest of them, was in fact prepared originally as material for Mr. Brown's, the longest; and I wish, since much of her text is quoted in his, that all of it might have been used there, that the two books had been made one from the start either through insertion of more passages from Miss Lewis in fitting order or through general collaboration. Even then, though Miss Lewis calls her record *Willa Cather Living*, the result would have remained, as each of the books is now, biography for libraries rather than for persons, for studious reference rather than for quickening warmth. In Miss Sergeant's record, on the other hand, history and environment come alive around and through a breathing figure, and Miss Cather's works also come freshly alive as they grew in their creator rather than through outer observation and opinion.

All three books narrate, in varying proportions, how their subject at the age of nine left her comfortable Virginian birth-place and its easy-going neighbors behind for Nebraska and its hard-going pioneers; how with this latter material which might have seemed bleak to someone else, she wrought many of her stories and novels, making lyrical nostalgic memories out of the prairies, and heroic figures out of the Scandinavian and other new neighbors whom she had seen face heavy odds and master them; how she went to school and college in Nebraska, contributed to student journals, sought out the most significant persons in Red Cloud, in Lincoln; how she moved to Pittsburgh, first as magazine contributor, then as schoolteacher, and found there wealthy friends who made life easier for her, with Mr. S. S. McClure soon doing likewise in New York through his eager liking for her work and for herself; then her welcoming of Sarah Orne Jewett in Boston as friend and literary influence; presently her trips to Colorado and New Mexico, from which was to come her memorable revival of the Archbishop; her fifteen years at Bank Street in New York with rental of an apartment kept empty overhead to exclude disturbing footsteps and with a return to the world of people on her Friday afternoons; her retreats to New Hampshire and to Grand Manan; her visits to Europe and especially to her beloved France; her love for Turgeniev, Tolstoi, Flaubert, Henry James and grand opera; her family ties and few close friendships; her growing resentment against the mechanization of modern life; and then, apparently because of deaths among her kin and friends and of a world gone wrong, the decline and withdrawal of her spirit.

As I read the Brown and Lewis books, I became more and more depressed and incredulous. This could not be the Willa Cather I had met and seen often in my early youth. Although she had seemed to me then a more calculating and ruthless person than was now being portrayed, she had also seemed a more intelligent and interesting one, whose life could not possibly have become as dry as these two biographers were making it. Brown had not known her; and among his pages especially the phases of her life lay like pressed flowers, with sap long gone and color dim. There were better specimens pressed in the second book; but from Miss Lewis, who had known her well, how could there come only this transcript of a life appearing for the most part dogged, dull, artificial? Where was the gusto, the joy, the warmth, the great joining with the will of spring, which must come again and again to anyone? Had this life been always literary, never wholly human?

And then I began Miss Sergeant's book—and here was the life I wanted to know about, here was "Willa Cather living," here was the person present behind the young woman I had met at the turn of the century. It is right enough for Miss Lewis to note, "She had a poet's attitude toward weather, to her it was one of the rich, contributive constituents of life," or to remark, "She loved people. She had a gift for immediately creating a personal relationship of some kind with anyone she met. . . . Perhaps it was her instant recognition of their common humanity, of the fact that their claim on life was equal to her own." Such statements unbacked are of as minor use to make a vital portrait as are Mr. Brown's documentations. But when Miss Sergeant speaks, it is not statement, it is occurrence. Miss Cather comes to life at the first meeting: "Her boyish, enthusiastic manner was disarming, and as she led me through the jostle of the outer office, I was affected by the resonance of her Western voice and by the informality of her clothes—it was as if she rebelled at urban conformities." And then: "The door closed behind us with a click bringing me face to face with an—adversary? In the sudden hush and aloneness, like animals in a wood, we stared, making the secret circle around one another. Was it the circle of acceptance? A lively sense of clash and curiosity rose between us like smoke from a new fire." And again: "This Willa Cather filled the whole space between door and window to brimming, as a man might do," which is better than Rebecca West's apt describing of the Cather quality as "mountain-pony sturdiness." Miss Sergeant sees and easily describes the surface; she also sees through the surface into the nerves and thoughts of people and can express what she finds. Furthermore she not only makes her reader see with her but ponder on what is seen. Her writing echoes her subject and then echoes it again. Her portrait of Mr. S. S. McClure is both flesh and spirit. To anyone who knew Miss Ida Tarbell's "benign, searching look" the three words are as unforgettable as the three about Miss Cather's "blithe made-in-Nebraska look." And then the latter's "eye-in-every-pore quality that took possession of her when she was bent on her own ends." Again, "she slouched her hat farther over her eyes and sat there like a stone," and, concerning the retreats from New York to Nebraska or New Mexico, or from Nebraska or New Mexico to New York or Grand Manan, "she retreated obliquely." You feel the echoing pulses in Miss Sergeant's descriptions, her narrative; you feel them also in her generalizations such as: "Single women making their way to individual destinies—who in the home circle understands them? If they try to share what they have found in their further reach, who wants it?"

The fact that Miss Sergeant is not afraid to criticize her friend adversely now and then, to see weaknesses as well as strength, rather draws the reader to Miss Cather than estranges him from her. Midway in this third book I found myself wondering why I had remembered resentfully for fifty years Miss Cather's cold harshness in refusing to let us withdraw from publication, in *McClure's* magazine, "The Birthmark" which friends of hers assured us at a tense session with her in Mr. McClure's office might ruin the life, even by suicide as in the story, of another friend of hers and theirs upon whose disfigurement and dilemma it was based. I can hear her now, saying briskly: "My art is more important than my friend." The story was published; and friend, as well as art, survived. Miss Sergeant, though she has made no reference to this episode, has so presented and explained Miss Cather that my pity which had long lasted for the friend has shifted to the author.

It was soon after this point where I paused midway through Miss Sergeant's book, the year in the record being 1920, that its luster began to fail for me, the fault not Miss Sergeant's, but Miss Cather's, for whom, as she herself confessed, the world then broke in two. For her feeling this breakage so deeply, Miss Sergeant suggests reasons other than the world's condition. Perhaps, she says, it was founded on the "poet's response to life, including the typical sense of the lyrical poet that youth and the emotions of youth, because of their great intensity and simplicity, surpass all other emotions. Yet," continues Miss Sergeant, "her ear seems very much less acute in poetry" and might have cited in extreme proof Miss Cather's comparatively youthful but certainly decrepit dedication in "The Song of the Lark."

> On uplands,
> At morning,
> The world was young, the winds were free;
> A garden fair,
> In that blue desert air,
> Its guest invited me to be.

Pursuing her theory that the break in Miss Cather's life came with realization of lost youth, Miss Sergeant quotes from her author a prose dictum on youth's fecundity: "The individual possesses this power for only a little while. He is sent into the world charged with it, but he can't keep it a day beyond his allotted time. He has his hour when he can do, live, become. If he devoted these years to caring for an aged parent—God may punish him but Nature will not forgive him." Not as if God had punished what became in Miss Cather actual filial devotion but as if her" allotted time" of necessary youth had passed, her biographer notes a "spring, now frozen over in talk by fame, or busyness, or just taciturnity!" with the former fervors recurring but rarely. And a particularly pertinent and revealing memory follows: "I never heard the sound of a radio or a musical recording in her apartment and only once the sound of a spoken record. That was the romantic voice of Edward the Eighth, abdicating his throne for love." Miss Sergeant might have wondered if her friend were speaking truly when she said, "Life began for me when I ceased to admire and began to remember." Was it life that began then or a lonely kingdom? Elation only in memory is a single stirrup.

Miss Lewis says in her introduction: "I have written about Willa Cather as I knew her; but with the feeling that it is not in any form of biographical writing, but in art alone, that the deepest truth about human beings is to be found." She means, I judge, that Miss Cather's personality and life cannot be better presented than in the art of the author's writings, that art has reasons reason cannot know; which is partially but not wholly true. She forgets that there is an especial art in biography too and that the art of biography can sometimes by-pass the art of story-telling, that for rounded revelation of "the deepest truth" about himself or herself, one artist sometimes needs the presence of another. The fact that Miss Cather's will forbade publication of her letters indicates that she was shy of rounded revelation, that she may have been afraid of the littlenesses which make greatness and that she chose a mirror rather than welcomed the open sky to reflect the features of an artist's being. Her forbidding that her stories be used in films is a different matter, because such treatment would mean an outsider's tampering with something which, however ineffective, inferior or inconsistent, she herself had done.

Art, says Mr. Brown, "was early and late for Willa Cather the chief expression of her mind." After quoting from one of her earliest stories, which appeared in a Nebraska college journal in 1892, "When the moon came up, he sighed restlessly and tore the buffalo pea flower with his bare toes," and commenting with characteristic lameness, "The phrase is not satisfactory; but like many of the unsatisfactory phrases in *Endymion*, and for the same reason, it is full of promise," he quotes from an article printed the following year in the *State Journal* this "explicit statement of her conception of art": "The further the world advances the more it becomes evident that an author's only safe course is to cling to the skirts of his art, forsaking all others, and keep unto her as long as they two shall live. . . . An artist . . . should be among men but not of them, in the world but not of the world." Crudely expressed in her youth, this was a creed to which she adhered through her years. And yet she could write in 1913 about Isadora Duncan a passage which Mr. Brown quotes from *McClure's* magazine: "I agree with the New York reporter who in summing up Miss Duncan's dancing of *The Rubaiyat* said that on the whole he preferred Omar's lines to Miss Duncan's." Though droll from the New York reporter, this was not droll from Miss Cather, whose serious acceptance of grand opera antics makes the more ironic her dismissal of Miss Duncan's triumph over an ungainly body and a reluctant public, through superb art. To the art in Miss Cather's volumes all three biographers give painstaking and reverent guidance. As to art in detail and in literary style, Miss Sergeant finds that the following passage from *O Pi-oneers!* "evokes" Nebraska's "Divide" "imaginatively and sensuously" and "makes its symbolic image live for us unforgettably, as in a poem":

> . . . The furrows of a single field often lie a mile in length, and the brown earth with such a strong, clean smell, and such a power of growth and fertility in it, yields itself eagerly to the plow; rolls away from the shear, not even dimming the brightness of the metal, with a soft, deep sigh of happiness. . . . The grain is so heavy that it bends toward the blade and cuts like velvet.
>
> There is something frank and joyous and young in the open face of the country. It gives itself ungrudgingly to the moods of the season, holding nothing back. Like the plains of Lombardy, it seems to rise a little to meet the sun. The air and the earth are curiously mated and intermingled, as if the one were the breath of the other. You feel in the atmosphere the same tonic, puissant quality that is in the tilth, the same strength and resoluteness.

Though "as if the one were the breath of the other" is more to my taste than "with a soft, deep sigh of happiness," though I acknowledge Miss Cather's general success in making one feel the atmosphere of her country, and though the people who dwell in it are, I suppose, symbolized by the bodily terms of the writing, this elected passage does not strike me as being indicative of a great artist. It is not Miss Cather's individual style, nor any steady sureness of literary art, which for me makes her work memorable, so much as the cumulative effect of what she is writing about, be it places or persons, and in the long run—despite frequently inept expression—her ability to make that interest count. She seems to me in this respect, though not in what she has called "overfurnishing," to be like Theodore Dreiser. I prefer her naturalness to her "art," though I quickly acclaim both qualities when she gives the sense of a person's whole life in the final four lines of *Lucy Gayheart* or the presence of Nebraska earth and moonlight in a passage like this from the short story, "Two Friends":

> The road, just in front of the sidewalk where I sat and played jacks, would be ankle-deep in dust, and seemed to drink up the moonlight like folds of velvet. It drank up sound too; muffled the wagon-wheels and hoof-beats; lay soft and meek like the last residuum of material things,—the soft bottom resting-place. Nothing in the world, not snow

mountains or blue seas, is so beautiful in moonlight as the soft, dry summer roads in a farming country, roads where the white dust falls back from the slow wagon-wheel.

When I first met Miss Cather, I had a quick sense that, though she was only seven or eight years older than I, her childlike smile was set, as by a jeweler, in an elderly, too authoritative face and that the elder would never let it go into a laugh or, on the other hand, feel it graven with tragic vision of magnificent darkness. I had a prescience that she took herself, not life but herself, too seriously to admit and enjoy the health of humor; and I still think that if she had maintained her childlike response to openness of countryside and people, to human mastery of circumstance and of self against raw odds, and yet at the same time been able to laugh down the world's mischief, as Chaucer or Shakespeare or George Meredith or Mark Twain laughed it down (but after all what woman?), she would not have felt in 1920 that the world had broken in two anymore than it had always broken. No wonder she repined, the smile dead, the laugh unborn. Her own life, in her forties, was what was breaking in two, through inner rather than outer forces, and not so much with the passing of youth as with the discovery that even the finest art man could create would not be the entirety of his being. The world was not behaving for her as she had planned it. War and death and change had always been. The break in her own world was not due to repetition of chronic human tragedy, nor chiefly due to what Miss Sergeant defines as "conflict between the brave ideals of our pioneer ancestors and mounting materialism." It was due, I am convinced, to her middle-aged suspicion that if there had been less art in her life, there might have been more life in her art. About that art she continued to care deeply, rightly, and sometimes bitterly but seldom if ever with the healing humor which, better than any other gift except love or faith, makes one's proportion to the universe tolerable. Bare of humor, and with love hurt for her by time and death, she turned in her latter years to a given faith; but such faith apparently failed to warm her. And in her facing of disappointments, as Miss Sergeant says about the builder's death in *Alexander's Bridge*, "the great chorus of tragedy failed."

New Mexico Quarterly (autumn 1953): 250–58.

A Literary Life

2

In 1911, Willa Cather left *McClure's Magazine* for a six-month vacation, one that grew into fifteen months and beyond. Her journalistic career was over. It had provided her with writing experience, ways to meet people, the luxury of travel, a firm base from which to market her stories and novels, and savings so that she could live without large earnings for an extended time. During that time, while Cather built her reputation as a novelist, she and Edith Lewis, the friend with whom she was sharing an apartment, managed their lives with reasonable comfort. After Cather won the Pulitzer Prize for *One of Ours* in 1923, however, she could consider herself financially secure for the rest of her life.

Cather steadily built her reputation as a novelist, publishing fourteen novels or books of short stories during the next twenty-nine years, a remarkable accomplishment for a writer whose goal was not quantity of work or wealth but excellence in writing. Furthermore, she experimented with each new book, employing different narrative patterns, often different locales, and a wide variety of characters. Each story, as well as its approach, is unique.

Although Cather was able to consider herself a novelist of stature at least since the publication of *My Ántonia* in 1918, she was not reviewed steadily until the later twenties.[1] By then, however, Cather had became a national figure.

Cather's reputation grew, too, after her death, as writers recounted their personal memories of her. The following selections reveal Cather as both a mature woman and novelist, yet they also highlight the unique dynamics of each literary relationship.

An Established Writer

When Willa Cather left *McClure's Magazine*, she was already known as an accomplished writer among her fellow journalists. However, although many people found her vibrant and friendly, she never became a New York City celebrity. She liked praise, but she relied primarily on a few old friends for most of her psychic support. She had steadily moved her narratives away from the style of Henry James and into a more modern stance, but she was not devoted to any movement, not to the avant-garde, nor to the social protest movement, which became increasingly favored by many writers between the wars. Hers was not a presence that entertained or commanded attention; nonetheless, she had a secure role on the literary stage. Elizabeth Sergeant's article sets the Nebraskan Cather solidly in the context of American novelists. Thomas Beer's article places Cather squarely into the busy life of New York's literary world, and the final selections carry Cather's reputation into one of the important literary circles of the time in the United States, that which included D. H. Lawrence.

ELIZABETH SHEPLEY SERGEANT

Elizabeth Shepley Sergeant (1881–1965) was, in 1910, looking for her first editor when she met Willa Cather in S. S. McClure's offices. In her memoir of Cather, Sergeant reflects that afterward, as she stepped onto the elevator that would return her to the ground floor, she felt as if she "had had a cup of champagne" (41). This was the beginning of a long relationship between the two, each a writer, a reader, a lover of France, and a woman of strong opinions. Sergeant's first book, *French*

Willa Cather, about 1912. The necklace was a gift from Sarah Orne Jewett.
Courtesy of the Nebraska State Historical Society, Willa Cather Pioneer
Memorial Collection.

Perspectives, was published in 1914, and her last, published posthumously, was *Robert Frost: The Trial by Existence*. The *New York Times* described her as an "author and friend of several generations of writers." Besides Cather, Sergeant's friends included D. H. Lawrence, Eugene O'Neill, H. L. Mencken, and Robert Frost. Her sister was the wife of E. B. White of *New Yorker* fame.

Sergeant's article is an early, incisive, literary, and biographical piece that presaged the novels, which followed its publication. It reveals a straightforward awareness of Cather's worldview.

Willa Cather

Willa Cather has arrived very quietly at her high place in American letters. Her life, her work and her personality have a simple unity and consistency that are frequently found in Europe but rarely in our own country, though she is the very sort of American whom Londoners would enjoy as "characteristic"—a woman with a western flavor in her speech and bearing that twenty years or so of residence on Manhattan Island have not rendered less invigorating. An editorial interview with her at *McClure's Magazine* in the old days—when her dreams as a writer were still unfulfilled—was like a draught of champagne. One felt life and impatience with life brimming and foaming in her, and went away roused and teased oneself by the sudden swirl and prick of bubbles rising from the depths. She lived then in Washington Square, she still lives near by, and likes to pace the paths below the statue of Garibaldi; if one hails her there on a happy spring afternoon, in her familiar clothes of some fresh brown or green—which challenge a little, as her spirit does, the blandishments of the passing age—her face in its fine maturity shines out with the self-same frankness of her youth, the same warmth and resolute strength of prairie wind and sun. Unless, of course, she has just happened upon some especially offensive gift of the year 1925—such as a paragraph in the gossip column of the press. Then her countenance contracts to closed and negative lines, and her whole person turns aloof and prickly with scorn and rejection.

If all our fiction writers had brought with them to the metropolis this power of rejection we should have had more fine American novels and fewer cheap successes. Willa Cather may not have had a richer creative endowment than many others. But she had more certainty of aim. More insight into the ultimate fruits of easy opportunity and popularity. More character, if one is to speak truly—and if character means certain old-fashioned virtues like faith, grit, determination and unremitting labor. One of the things that a young New Englander recognized most clearly in her long ago was a standard: a standard of living, which made of a modest existence and simple tastes something comely and satisfying; a standard of literary excellence which was based on deep love and knowledge of the "masters." She knew as clearly as a child the proper food of her spirit—Wagnerian opera, for instance, the stories of Merimée and Turgeniev, walks in Central Park, French wine and French cooking, the society of musical artists and old friends from Pittsburgh and the west. She was vigorous and single-minded and thoroughly unaccommodating in temper. The greater part of the people, the ideas, the aims, the social amusements that crossed her path were alien to her, and she made no bones of refusing them as unassimilable and unimportant. She must have been about thirty years old when I first met her, and her objective hung as clear as a new moon above the electric glitter of New York. She would have scorned to create her reputation until she had really earned it. She had accepted as final the hypothesis—or is it the fact—that a complete and loyal devotion to an art means a definite sacrifice of life. "Happiness,"—so she has put it in a story, commenting on Tolstoy's credo—"lies in ceasing to be and to cause being, because the thing revealed to us is dearer than any existence our appetites can ever get for us." A pioneer upbringing may be as fine an armor for art as it is for breaking the glebe, and Willa Cather, by those prairie roots of hers, seems to belong to a more steadfast, as to a more reticent generation than that of her literary contemporaries.

Her eastern existence has always had a western counterpart as essential to her as the soul to the body. Red Cloud, Nebraska, and its hinterland, which in the days of her childhood would have been considered a highly inauspicious place for a writer to grow up in, continues to know and cherish her as its leading citizen. Well it may, since the formative history of the state has been written down more literally as well as more lyrically in her pages than it ever will be in more strictly historical works—or in the stories of a later brood of mid-western novelists, more interested than she in surfaces. Now that her portrait by Bakst hangs in Omaha, now that *My Ántonia* is translated into French and into Czech, and all the books have been translated into the Swedish language, it is natural that young students all over the corn belt should decide to grow to fame by writing up the farm neighbors. Yet how many of these hard-headed young realists will know how to contribute as she has done—with only Virgil as an early guide—to the sum total of happiness on lonely ranches? How many of them shall receive, when they move on to New York, culinary offerings addressed to the "best book writer in the world?" It was related in Hastings last summer that a certain old Bohemian farmer, who had been brought into the hospital, and who wished to recommend himself to his doctor's good graces introduced himself thus modestly: "I am the husband of My Ántonia." The story dovetails very neatly with a paragraph towards the end of this same novel where the boy Jim Burden, studying his lessons in the lamp-light, broods over his professor's explanation of a passage in the Georgics. *Primus ego in patriam meam—deducam Musas. I was the first to bring the Muse into my country.* "This was not a boast but a hope, at once bold and devoutly humble, that he might bring the Muse not to the capital but to his father's fields, sloping down to the river and to the old beech trees with broken tops."

A hope, a wish, they are one and the same when held with intensity. As Mr. Forrester, the husband of the Lost Lady once put it to his guests, it is the secret wish of the heart that turns great dreams—those of railroad builders, those of novelists—into constructive realities. Like most of the boys in Willa Cather's stories, Jim Burden, through whose eyes the story of Ántonia is remembered, is in some sort an incarnation of the author. Reading it, I visualize as observer not a boy but a tomboy: a girl with a charming open face, obstinate blue eyes, and shingled red-brown hair; a girl who drew deep into her lungs the wild, free breath of the land to which she had been transplanted from Virginia, and in the grandiose human outline of its pioneer settlers from old Europe, standing against the broad fields and wide sky, beheld the figures of her destiny. There is something primordial in Willa Cather's voice, her eyes, her gestures, when she speaks of these figures today. It is clear that a few obscure lives—Bohemian, Swedish, French—have contributed as profoundly to the strength of her affections as the richness and glory of the untamed prairie, and its slow transformation into corn and wheat have contributed to her robustness as an artist. In the days when a wild little girl rode her pony twelve miles over the rough red grass of the Divide to fetch the mail—the letters and newspapers of the immigrant neighbors too, with their queer foreign words and strange colored inks—the unwritten history of the country was beginning in her heart, as she has recorded that it began in that of Alexandra, the pioneer woman. And from the hour, many years later, when she was able to renounce her editorship for the career of literature, it seems that her most illumined hours have been spent, not in scrutinizing or absorbing the present, as many writers do, but in looking backward with intensity to her "father's fields," as an Indian remembers the beauties of his legendary world. It is not accidental that *O Pioneers!* and *My*

Ántonia have something of the force of myth or epic. "Mental excitement was apt to send me back with a rush to my own naked land and the figures scattered upon it. They accompanied me through all my new experiences."

Her books, provided one does not take them too literally, or in the order of their writing, are a better guide to Willa Cather's life story than any biographical dictionary. She has told us nothing yet in fiction about Virginia and her early childhood, though she sometimes speaks of them, recalling her revolts from certain polite feudal traditions and stratifications which were borne away on a wild breeze when she reached the Divide. We may think of *O Pioneers!*, her first really achieved long story, as picturing rather closely the conditions which prevailed at the period of her arrival at her grandmother's, when the turf dwellings of the first settlers were being replaced by frame houses, and only great wills could dominate the wilderness, and great visions confront an uncertain future. *My Ántonia* begins also on the Divide at a still more drastic era, which she knew from her elders' stories, some fifteen years earlier than *O Pioneers!* in historical time, and continues into a later day when Red Cloud, (Black Hawk) the pioneer town and the lower road by the creek and the cottonwoods, superseded the Divide in the girl's daily experience. The two novels together, supplemented by the early part of *The Song of the Lark*, weave a sort of tapestry pattern where the most radiant of Willa Cather's early memories, intuitions and impressions of the Nebraska patria on its primeval side stand out like a golden legend.

In *A Lost Lady*, and *One of Ours*, the most recent of the western novels, one feels a greater modification of memory by mature experience, and therefore less of sheer poetry. The former relates a literal human history of the Red Cloud region, in the days when the railroad building aristocracy lived along the Burlington. But while the image of Mrs. Forrester is enshrined by mellow visual impressions of sandy creeks and wide meadows and poplars which the story teller must have salted away these many years in the tears of youth, the romantic and disconcerting "Lady" herself stands before us in the light of a sophisticated knowledge which no young memory has in its stores. As for *One of Ours*, a book that the author ranks, for its stark outlines, above her other works, that brings the Nebraska farmer up to date—at least up to the dull, rich period before the War, when machinery had replaced hand labor, and sharp business methods the hardy faith of the pioneer. This, to her, decadent epoch, Willa Cather knew as a returned and sentimental pilgrim, rather than as a native daughter, and it may be that one reason why she so respects the artistic verities of her novel is that they wounded her so sorely as she set them down. She is enough of a Puritan idealist to take fidelity to disillusion as a sort of penance. The Great War—which one thinks of as the only "world event" which has greatly affected her—enabled her to make up to her "rough-neck" hero for the sterility of the present midwestern farmer's destiny. One of the most endearing things about this vivid and distinguished writer is a suspicion, humbly harbored, that she herself is a rough-neck in disguise who has only happened into fame. I feel in her sympathy for Claude a generous desire to help the others to their great adventure. But here her Muse betrayed her a little. For when Claude's adventure took him to France, it dimmed before our eyes. The prairie farm was the centre where the War affected Willa Cather, and the image of Claude and his mother clinging together "in the pale square of the west window, as the two natures in one person meet and cling in a fated hour," is the one that will survive. For this woman has to touch life at first hand, in order to create it. So much for the western novels as bearing on symbolic biography. *The Song of the Lark*, the theme of which is the artistic evolution of a singer not unlike Olive Fremstadt, and which, in point of chronology falls between *O Pioneers!* and *My Ántonia*, carries over from the western childhood to the period of inevitable artistic and youthful revolt—"artist's youth"—which whirled Willa Cather out into the great world, as it did her heroine, to seek gifts and advantages which Nebraska could not give. She graduated from the university where she had supported herself by newspaper work at the age of nineteen, and having immediately found a job as dramatic reporter on a Pittsburgh paper, plunged eastward to cultivated joys like music, and human relations of which she had heretofore been starved. The best of the very promising short stories which she began to write at this time, such as "The Sculptor's Funeral" and "Paul's Case"—and these best are as fine as anything she has done since—derive their motive force not from the radiation of loving memory, but from the bitterness of revolt from limitations. Originally published in a volume called *The Troll Garden*, long since out of print, they were again made accessible recently in the collection of short stories called *Youth and the Bright Medusa*, most of which were written at a later period. Willa Cather's passion for artists, especially musical artists, has been only second to her passion for pioneers. This book, wholly concerned with art and artists, may be regarded as a sort of commentary on the contacts of the full and ardent Pittsburgh years—the singers and actresses who came through town to get the dollars of the iron kings—continued later in a New York of which music has been one of the basic nourishments. "Coming Aphrodite," that glorious story that heads the volume and recounts the passing love affair of a young painter and a young singer in the Washington

Square of the dear departed days, may be thought of, again in the quasi-autobiographical sense, as making the transition to the city as it looked to a young woman of twenty-eight when, with her own stirring artistic ambition to spur her, she came to join the staff of *McClure's*.

The magazine, under the stimulating direction of S. S. McClure, in the height of the muckraking era offered no real oasis for a writer of novels. Willa Cather was devoted to her "Chief," but she had as much resistance to muckraking and social reform then as she has to the psychology of Freud today, perhaps for the same reason. The spirit of her age, as I have suggested, does not greatly affect her at any time, and she fought the implications of the magazine world, all the six years of her stay in it. If she got some happiness out of a magazine assignment in Boston, that was largely because her sojourn there brought about a significant friendship with Sarah Orne Jewett, whose literary canons of honesty and perfection influenced her crucially at an hour when she needed the support of experience to make her visions actual. She produced, while still an editor, a number of short stories and a short novel called *Alexander's Bridge*. The latter represented in theme and technique more of a concession to popular standards than she ever permitted herself again.

Willa Cather herself says that the moment when she stopped trying to write—that is, to write according to an invented formula—and began to remember was the one when her literary vocation claimed its rights. It was then that the finer novels began to emerge from the matrix of her mind with the west as their most inevitable scene. *O Pioneers!* is not a fabricated thing, but a true recreation of experience, and the act of writing from that day forth became also a recreation: a complete loss of self for three hours a day; "what poker is to my brother." One has only to look at her to know that she has had tremendous fun out of it all. Why should this be so, given the sacrifices and the labor of the craft? That, after all, is the most leading question about her or any other creative writer. On the feeling side it seems that Willa Cather's satisfaction flows from the fact that her books are always transcriptions of friendships for people or places. Though she has distilled the warm and loyal admiration of her nature into the cool stream of art, her relation to her central character or country has remained intense and complete. And there is always a central personage in the books, like a priceless objet d'art on a drawing room table, whose interest and beauty are supreme. Willa Cather's great aim as a story teller has been, as she once explained to a group of English teachers, to get across" to her readers something direct about this beloved object—as a boy would succeed in conveying to a sister just arrived from Europe his feeling about the girl he was engaged to marry. Sometimes she does this through description. Sometimes merely through characteristic speech. In any case character is conveyed. On the intellectual side her fun has largely come in experiments with form. Color of a florid sort is more native to her talent than line, and her progress as an artist, to her own thinking, has come about by making color mean form. She has sought, in Robert Frost's phrase, the purification of her quality, and has accepted as her quality a certain sparseness and austerity in line and contour. Where she has tried for robustness and fullness of life, as in *The Song of the Lark*, she has failed in large measure. Yet she does believe in allowing herself considerable latitude in the general shape of a novel. She conceives that the form it has assumed for her mind's eye at the fiery second of its explosion in her consciousness is the inevitable one. There is always such an explosion for a novel, as for a poem, and the more closely the shape it tears is adhered to, the less it is tinkered with, the better the result. Life for her, so far as her books as yet record it—with the exception of *A Lost Lady*—falls into two great patterns: the pioneer or farm pattern, with its immutable relations, father and daughter, sister and brother, mother and son, grandmother and grandchild, and its dumb, struggling ideals; the artist pattern, with its sparkling superhuman aims and ambitions, and its imperfect and fragile human ties. Through both patterns breaks, now and then, a great wave of overwhelming emotion from below the crust of things; that is her only interest in the "subconscious." Love, to the central character—always a woman up to now, save in the case of Claude, and often seen through the eyes of a subordinate male—is usually incidental to a larger career, usually illicit, usually devastating, or only happy for one poignant and lyrical moment. Remember, for instance, the tragic interlude of Marie and Emil, in *O Pioneers!* The author does not seem to believe in domestic bliss. As for the crust—the visual, tangible, natural world, though so dear to her, she knows to be only valuable to her characters where they touch, smell, look at it. The prairie lives in her books because human beings behold it—and covet it. There Willa Cather is glad to be with the "elders," as she says, rather than with the imagists and the reporterial school.

The most complete expression of her artistic creed is to be found in the admirable preface to a selection of Sarah Orne Jewett's work that she has recently edited: "The artist spends his life loving things that haunt him, in having his mind teased by them, in trying to get them down on paper exactly as they are to him." And to achieve anything noble anything enduring, he must give himself absolutely to his material. The gift of sympathy is his greatest gift, the fine thing which alone can make his work fine. "He fades away into the land and people of his heart, he dies of love only to be born again." Willa Cather's first great prairie death was in *O Pioneers!* But she died a similar death more noble in *My Ántonia*. She has died again in *A Lost Lady* and in the first half of *One of Ours*. There is a river in the Wind River Mountain in Wyoming—one of the happy hunting grounds—that after leaping torrentially down the side of a mountain vanishes, with all its glittering waters into the dark base of the mountain itself. But a mile further down the mountain in a deep, still pool green with marsh grass, another river starts, a gentle smooth-flowing, level stream. These two are one and the same. So Willa Cather conceives the artist's life as it should be; so, when one visits her in her book-lined rooms in Bank Street, one feels that it is. About the rooms are evidences of the more torrential course: paintings of Italy and the southwest; autographed photographs of famous singers and writers of European fame; lithographs of Czechoslovakia. Courbet's Georges Sand is over the mantel, and Keats—a Boston literary heirloom—is in the background. The author's skin is warm and ruddy, her eyes are sailor blue, her bluff, almost boyish addresses modified by a little catch at the beginning of a sentence that might be shyness or just eager zest of life restrained by thought—as the river is caught in the weight of the mountain. And if she talks, as she may of her friend Ántonia, with her fourteen children, who doesn't want to die because she would have to stop cooking, I feel again what it has meant to my friend to grow up in a land that was "not a country at all but the material out of which countries are made." A country "with motion in it." A country where she learned so young the happiness it is "to be dissolved into something complete and great."

New Republic, 17 June 1925, 91–94.

THOMAS BEER

Thomas Beer (1889–1940) was a well-known journalist, novelist, social critic, and, according to Burton Rascoe, "the author of one of the most distinguished socio-critical studies in modern literature, *Stephen Crane*" (62). Beer's biography stimulated a great deal of interest in Crane, who was never a self-promoter, an inconvenience for Beer, Cather once commented. Beer himself seems to have been a name-dropper. In the following reminiscence, Beer sets Cather into the New York City writing and cultural landscape, mentioning in the same article people as diverse as Lotta Faust (1880–1910—a talented and popular actress in musical comedies),

Laura Benét (1884–1979 — sister of William Rose and Stephen Vincent Benét), Edith
Wharton (1862–1937), and Theodore Roosevelt (1858–1919).

Miss Cather

She strolled to the other side of the very clever Cameron Mackenzie's desk
in the office of *McClure's Magazine* and interrupted my adolescent diplo-
macies just as they reached concert pitch and I felt reasonably safe in asking
five dollars for use on a Saturday afternoon of my seventeenth year. I gave
the young woman a glare of justifiable hatred. Lotta Faust was dancing in
some show at two o'clock and somebody had to be my momentary banker,
else the world would crack. Miss Cather idled, rapping a piece of paper on
Mackenzie's inkwell, and whatever she had officially to tell him went on
for several epochs. When she finally strolled off, the editor said, grubbing
five dollars from his waistcoat: "She writes better than Edith Wharton," and
pronounced her name, which struck me as infinitely absurd. Lotta Faust was
dancing somewhere that afternoon. But, having seen Lotta Faust dance, the
rosy young woman's name survived in my sticky mind and I charged her
first volume of tales to my father's account at a bookstore with a willingness
to investigate. For Mackenzie, when nobody else had mentioned the novel's
existence, threw a copy of *Sister Carrie* at my head, and ten years later sent
me an odd affair called *The Rivet in Grandfather's Neck*. He died too soon to
establish himself in his proper calling, that of aid to collectors of rare first
editions.

My unimportant figure now retires. It was presented merely as a symbol
of the Americans as facing a distinguished artist. Miss Cather was always being recommended by the intelligent to dullards in a hurry to see Lotta Faust,
or to write an article on Lucas Malet. Her stealthy advance in estimation is
now the first convention of any essay on her work. The other conventions
are equally established, and a pattern for appreciating or deprecating Miss
Cather can be simply copied. The points are already patented. She is, or is
not, at her best in sketches of middle western life. She does, or does not,
produce types rather than characters. She is, or is not, the leading female
writer of the United States. (Imagine Miss Cather, Mrs. Wharton, Miss Ferber, Miss Suckow, Mrs. Gerould, Mrs. Scott, Mrs. Benet, Miss Hurst and
Mrs. Miller wrestling on velvet mat for such a cracked opal!) She is, or isn't,
the final exponent of objective realism. And so forth and so forth to the lim-
its of endurance. Coasting around this weary thicket, one comes to a core
of solid achievement which nobody, outside the patrician group of young
critics bred in Mott Street and finished in Paris, seems ready to flout.

The decade of Muck, the calamitous ten years from 1900 to 1910, represent the flimsiest period in modern literary history, as far as the United States have a literary history. Theodore Roosevelt, spiritually, reigned and under his favor the adoration of journalism came to an amazing height. Everything from the Standard Oil Company to the sexual nature of mankind was being tabulated and reformed; novels were either subtly debauched romances, demonstrating that a pure woman clad in a sheer nightgown, alone with a drunken rake in an empty house, could repel him with one freezing stare, or soggy imitations of Arnold Bennett and H. G. Wells. Miss Cather, appearing sparsely as an author of brief tales, had nothing to put in competition with the Englishmen or with such native powers as Upton Sinclair, Robert Chambers and twenty-seven humorists now half forgotten. She was not didactic, loud or funny. She was, in certain stories, deliberately fighting against the grain of popular taste.

In the '90's the western scene had suffered doses of severely realistic representation from Hamlin Garland, Stephen Crane and, in his earlier manner, from Owen Wister. But under the good Theodore, the necessities of flattering the west were sufficiently clear to editors, and it was innumerably declared that a hardy westerner was worth three easterners — the formula was useful to Mr. Sinclair Lewis as late as 1917 — and that the life of small towns was full of human charm. Miss Cather instinctively answered the current values with "A Wagner Matinee" and "The Sculptor's Funeral," saying in the two stories by inference nearly everything that has since been beaten into the public and critical ears with immense insistencies of drums. It may be supposed that a series of sharp attacks on these anecdotes of isolation and intellectual poverty on the prairies would have brought a premature fame on the writer, but nothing of the sort happened, and Miss Cather was left with one or two handsome compliments from reviewers, and the rather irritating solace, if she was given to reading fiction between 1910 and 1916, of seeing three admirable passages from her prose imitated with sharp promptness. It may be said, therefore, that she became an influence in American letters from her first publication.

She herself was not immune to influences — who is? — and the excessively curious will find a phrase of "The Beldonald Holbein" and a simile from "The Pace of Youth" transmuted in this early work. A paragraph has been modeled, here and there, after Sarah Orne Jewett. The didactic method of Mrs. Wharton showed a little later, but sparely, in her first novel. There was a tendency toward hard work with a hammer in the psychologic frames of characters, and this, one imagines, was a nervous consciousness that the system of inferences, on which so much of her narrative based, might not be understood. Having made all these admissions against the work, there remains an astonishing balance in favor of Miss Cather. She had already demonstrated an art within an art; the people of the stories moved in a defined landscape, illustrated and indicated in a series of deft, swift strokes of the highest pictorial quality. And this continuous illustration leaves an inevitable satisfaction, even when the stories collapse, as two did. You have seen lads squirming like eels into sudden sight when the belated engine nears the wintry station; a woman's hysteria has made embarrassed men mere splinters in the gloom of a vulgar parlor, a cab has slithered on the icy glaze of a street. Forlorn turkeys in a dooryard have become momentary symbols of an intolerable isolation. All this was done unobtrusively; the pictures interspaced the narrative and did not present so many arrangements, pauses for a little "background." Where she failed, she failed by selecting the wrong material, rather than by lack of mastering her form. Add to this that she was already infinitely clever in her simplicity of exposition. The weary woman of "A Wagner Matinee" is left at a precise point; sympathy for the "steel pathos" of deprivation has been evoked, and the case rested.

Taken as a whole, Miss Cather's printed world is an exhibit of the finest literary tact. The dangerous episode tempts her constantly and she yields to the temptation, then carries us with decency through scenes that might, in careless handling, become explosions of inferior emotionalism. Such a business as the old railroad builder's confession to the lad in *A Lost Lady* or the recitative of the defeated singer in "The Diamond Mine" would easily fall into sweet sorrow. Beyond the question of legitimate emphasis, lies a subtler danger inherent in playing, as she often plays, with contrasts in sentiment. The narrator of *My Ántonia* is a successful man of affairs, married to a perfect lady whose terrors are allowed to remain half formed in the reading mind so that her husband's hymn to Ántonia takes on the wistful modulations of regret and frustration without a direct evocation of one's pity. Miss Cather exposes human mischance and leaves the witness to his own emotions. This is all that time has preserved of the tragic idea. The characters are shown in their own value, and you may weep or yawn as you please. So it is only when Miss Cather has forsaken the grave impersonality of effect that she has opened herself to scoffing. At her best she has achieved the suspense and grace which Henry James gave to the last chapter of *Washington Square* and to long passages of *The Awkward Age*; at her weakest she has been so immeasurably superior to averages that one's hat comes off. She is the least sentimental student of sentiment now active in American letters.

Anybody can play the satirist and anybody can indulge in irony, especially by using the applauded devices which pass as irony in American criticism—i.e., A conceives an intense adoration of B who drives trotting horses or paints pictures and then discovers that his or her idol takes morphine or has a taste for low women. (This small gibe is directed not at Mr. Sherwood Anderson but humbly offered for the consideration of literary auctioneers who call a good thing by the wrong name.) Miss Cather has had the courage to stroll on eggshells, and her heels have been light for so much of the parade that her self-control rouses envy, at least among those of us whose shoes are caked with yolks. Recite again the platitude, now ninety years old: "Every writer begins as a sentimentalist," and then speculate on the distance that Miss Cather's will has carried her from the crude core of the matter.

With the tact mingles a pleasant disdain of the easily managed "strong scene." The passional murder in *O Pioneers!* is seen retrospectively, a simple document of an event. The Lost Lady's hysterical screams to her lover pass into the black mouth of a telephone. The bridal night in *One of Ours* ends with the sound of the compartment's door closing serenely as the young idealist's wife locks herself away from the contamination of mere marriage. A dramatization of "Paul's Case" would ruin the swift anecdote. It is true that this indirection has, once or twice, defeated itself. Very well, but we have never been bored by an obvious dialogue between a cheap clerk and his conscience or by a woman facing a recreant client of her body. For all the outcry against "externalism" just now current and tedious, the two foremost practitioners of the novel in English have manipulated their introspective characters away from the conceded scene as adroitly as has Miss Cather. But, pending the establishment of a school of criticism in England and America, which won't express its passion for the obvious on seven days of the week with an augmented yell for plain narrative of the inessential in Sunday editions, it is useless to defend the economy of artists. To the intelligences whose concept of the art of fiction demands that they see Stephen Dedalus at his mother's deathbed refusing to pray or to know what passed between Jurgen and Anaitis when the candles were blown out, Miss Cather's refusal of interior legend is naturally offensive. The reduction of the novel to a primer of psychiatry is going on rapidly enough, the last manifestation being a complete chapter devoted to the emotions of a virgin while washing her dead father's shirt. There is an end of all things save banality. . . .

The woman who protested the flattery of the West in 1906 became presently a pioneer in the representation of its people, the humane representation, which Miss Suckow and Mr. Wescott continue. Miss Cather long since made the choice at her disposal. She shed the urbanity which glitters in "Scandal," shrugged away the chance to play the analyst of art, as art, and forswore the attitudes available to a clever girl familiar in the long library where Mrs. Fields and Sarah Jewett poured tea for all that was most suave and most gracious in fading Boston. She walked backward into a territory where nobody knew the difference between Cezanne and Seurat, and again evaded the obvious profit of repeating that the west was ignorant of these toys. With the vision of that resolute stroll my capacity as a critic ceases. . . . There is a species of indoctrination which prevents any act of appraisal. Every year of my childhood there was a cloudy bustle of packing and farewells, and a horror of fear that the long tickets had been forgotten. Water trembled in fascinating blots on bright nickel of basins in the sleeping car. One woke in a thick silence to the chink of hammers testing halted wheels and heard voices drawling that there'd been the hell of a wreck down by Saint Jo or that there was a new traffic manager on the C. B. and Q. It seems to have been always summer when the train passed by flickering grain in which men's blue shirts were remote scars of color and at the journey's end there were dusky rooms that faced a street in which cottonwoods delicately whirled their bi-colored leaves. There was a park and a lost lady walked in it with adoring lads at heel behind her yellow parasol until her husband shot the tall man who stopped off once too often on his way to Chicago. There was a deep voice that told how General Dodge shoved the Union Pacific through the desert and you could see the general himself roaming with his cigar along the sloping street that led up sandy bluffs to a plateau whence the entire universe was comfortably apparent with the Missouri shimmering importantly past the sweep of Omaha; and once there was a ride through illimitable wheat with Swedish songs wailing from field to field. For these reasons I am a very bad judge of Miss Cather's novels. It seems to me that they contain occasional errors, flakes of heavy writing—so do those of George Moore, Thomas Hardy and Joseph Conrad. A perfect writer would be an abominable creature and one to be stoned to death by cooks. But there is too much else in Miss Cather, and to that excellence of content I am too susceptible. But I doubt that the excellence is available to people who know nothing of the region on which such an integrity and a justice so fine in its intention have been expended.

As to the gentlewoman poised under the heavy plush curtains of literary renown, there follows no paragraph of personal depiction. She walks a good deal in Washington Square where ashcans are prevalent. This book would be unseemly entombed with dead kittens and broken bottles. Miss Cather once asked me what an intelligent person was. Perhaps he is one who does not commit the vulgar treachery of public familiarity with his betters.

The Borzoi, 1925, 23–30.

DOROTHY BRETT

The next two reminiscences are included not because they reflect the views of highly placed or well-known critics but for what they reveal about the relationship between Cather and D. H. Lawrence, "the most gifted writer of his generation," Cather said (Woodress 354).

Dorothy Brett (1883–1977), a shy, deaf artist daughter of an English viscount, became a close friend of Lawrence and a believer in his dream of a utopia in Taos, New Mexico. She tells, in an oblique manner, of being invited to have tea with Cather in New York City with Lawrence and Frieda, Lawrence's wife. Frieda later comments, "We had been warned that we might not like her. . . . Everybody said she was blunt and abrupt, but we got along famously" (Nehls 414). Lawrence also mentions Cather matter-of-factly in a letter to Thomas Seltzer: "Will you please send to Willa Cather, 5. Bank St, Washington Square, New York a copy of *Kangaroo* and a copy of *The Captain's Doll*" (Lacy 131).

From Lawrence and Brett: A Friendship

We [Frieda, D. H., and Brett] go to a concert, to hear Madame G—— sing. The place is dark. During an interlude, you get up to go. You are going to see Willa Cather. You lean down and in a loud whisper you say that Madame G—— comes onto the stage as if she were wheeling her stomach in a wheelbarrow in front of her. The people around laugh, but some of them give a scandalized "Shhh!"

It is very late. Frieda and I have been home from the concert for hours. You have not returned. I am beginning to get scared, think you have been run over. At last you come.

"Why are you so late?"

"Oh, you couldn't find the street?"

And you say that you liked Willa Cather and have had a nice time, and that she has invited us all to tea the following day.

We are sitting in Willa Cather's room. Miss Lewis has been showing me some pictures. They are very kind and hospitable. The tea is very good. And you are teasing Willa Cather about art. She is serious, probing you about your ideas; you are evading, mischievously.

"I hate literature and literary people," you say. "People shouldn't fuss so much about art. I hate books and art and the whole business. "

The more amazed, the more indignant Willa Cather becomes, the more you storm against art. What fun you are when you begin knocking art about!

Philadelphia: Lippincott, 1933. 39–40.

JOSEPH FOSTER

Joseph Foster (1898–   ) reveals that Cather did, at least occasionally, mix with the Bohemian set that gathered around Lawrence in the West, particularly at Mabel Dodge Luhan's ranch, although Elizabeth Sergeant is careful to point out that Cather loved and visited the Southwest "before . . . D. H. Lawrence and other celebrities brought Taos into the news" (Sergeant 141–42). Foster's recollection of Cather is interesting in the way in which he includes her without focusing specifically on her. Cather was not one of Lawrence's loyal followers, although she thought he was an outstanding writer, nor was she one of Mabel Dodge Luhan's protégés; nevertheless, Cather was clearly a part of the New Mexico literary scene.

From D. H. Lawrence in Taos

Trinidad, Lawrence's friend—a beautiful, lithe, naked boy—was dancing, dancing, the older Indians chanting encouragingly. The Indians were the truth of life. Their joyousness was real. They sang and sang their reality.

Ai yo Ai yo.

A new Round Dance was forming, everybody was crowding in. The Indian voices rose higher and higher. The whites loved this moment, dancing shoulder to shoulder with the Indians. Yes, they loved being Indian for a short while.

The people were shouting around us now. The voices of the Indian chorus rose and fell. The soft-footed Indian girls had refilled the huge punch bowl again and again with pink champagne.

Margaret pointed out a middle-aged woman in starched white, spinsterish, wide-eyed, disdainful, at the edge of the circle. "That's Willa Cather. She's a botanist enthusiast. She's writing a novel about Santa Fe—the Archbishop or something—"

Albuquerque: U of New Mexico P, 1972. 180.

A Novelist

The next group of selections is not reviews, although each of the authors was a well-known reviewer. The first selection is a personal reminiscence by a friend who knew Cather well from the time Cather went to Lincoln. Dorothy Canfield Fisher, too, moved east from Nebraska, and over the years became an established writer and critic. Her viewpoint reflects a deeply integrated personal and professional understanding of Cather's work. Fanny Butcher, primarily a Midwestern critic, began her critical career reviewing *Alexander's Bridge*, a review for which she received a personal note from the book's author, beginning a lasting critic-friend relationship. Finally, Henry Seidel Canby's article, given his national influence in reading taste, sets Cather into the mainstream of established American novelists of her time.

DOROTHY CANFIELD FISHER

When Cather matriculated at the University of Nebraska–Lincoln, Dorothy Canfield Fisher's father, James Hulme Canfield, was chancellor of the university, and his bright young daughter Dorothy (1879–1958) was in the eighth grade. She and Cather became good friends, and when Canfield accepted the presidency of Ohio State University in 1896, Fisher, then in her last year as an undergraduate, visited Cather in Pittsburgh, an experience relived in the first article. Fisher later admitted that she probably romanticized this experience; nevertheless, the story reveals the sort of relationship one young woman may have with another who is slightly older; the latter delighted to show off her beginning success, and the former appropriately impressed and excited, not only about her friend's achievement but also about her own beginnings as an adult. The Heinrich Heine poem that Cather translated on the

"How I Found My Rabbit Traps," Willa Cather on her 1913 trip to Virginia. Courtesy of the Nebraska State Historical Society, Willa Cather Pioneer Memorial Collection.

evening Fisher is describing was published the next December in the *Home Monthly*, the magazine Cather was editing:

> The star now stops above Joseph's roof,
>   And they enter the cottage lowly;
> The oxen bellowed, the infant cried,
>   While sang the three kings holy.

The second article, a retrospective piece about Cather and her novels, again reveals much about its author. Although Cather and Fisher experienced some rifts in their friendship over the years, the article shows no personal animosity but is a professional and personal appreciation of Cather's work by a woman who was an arbiter of literary opinion. Fisher was a member of the review board for the Book-of-the-Month Club and a well-known writer herself, writing more than forty books for children and adults, primarily fiction, but many in essay form.

Novelist Recalls Christmas in Blue-and-Gold Pittsburgh

Willa Cather came to enter the University of Nebraska, from her small hometown of Red Cloud (one of the loveliest of place names, I always thought), when I was in the eighth grade of a public school in Lincoln. No great gap in actual years, as you can see. In fact, Willa was a class-mate of my brother, only five years older than I. But the gap was enough, at our then respective ages, to set Willa well above me in the hierarchy of the years. A brilliant freshman in college had the prestige of a grown-up, compared to a little girl still in grade school.

Later on, of course, as we both grew on into the twenties and thirties, this difference in years dwindled to nothing at all, as such differences do to adults, so far as any barrier to our close comradeship went. But my lifelong admiring affection for Willa was, at first, strongly tinctured with the respectful deference due from a younger person to a successful member of the older generation.

The year (1894) when Willa was graduated from the University of Nebraska, my father, who had been chancellor of that institution, became president of Ohio State University. The Canfields moved to Columbus, and—great good luck I thought it—Willa Cather, looking for an earning-your-living job like other new college graduates, got a job as headline writer on a Pittsburgh newspaper. Or did she begin by editing a little local magazine? I can't be sure. Pittsburgh is not nearly so far from Columbus as is Nebraska. And, more important to me, the incessant journeying to and from Arlington (the Canfields' permanent home) could by a little determined shaping be bent around to include a stopover in Pittsburgh.

So it happened that the first Ohio Christmas was not an Ohio one at all for me, but was spent in Pittsburgh with Willa. By that time she had more prestige than ever over me, because she was earning her own living, was getting (as I remember it) the magnificent salary of $100 a month.

This kind of success and independence for a young woman was not in the least taken for granted in the '90s, or now. It cast a glamor over Willa which enhanced the admiration we had all felt for her during her college years, because of her gift for writing. I was immensely grateful for Willa's invitation to me, not in college yet, only in the last year of preparatory school. My occasional brief stopovers in Pittsburgh were golden days for me. When people talk about Pittsburgh as a dirty, dark, noisy, grimy city, I can't imagine what they are talking about. Over it hangs, for me, a shining cloud of young memories.

Especially that first Christmas, when everything was new and exciting to Willa's youthful inexperience of big city life. She had made wonderful friends, she thought. So did I. Especially (this was natural to anyone who read so voraciously as Willa) among librarians. It did not take long, I suppose, for the trained eye of a librarian to see that the eager young reader from Nebraska was no ordinary person. By Christmas time she was on delightfully friendly terms with the Andersons, among the very nicest people in the whole American library world.

Since I am asked to make this a reminiscence of youth, perhaps I should in honesty add that my own enjoyment of Willa's presenting me to her new, cultivated city friends was slightly damped by their laughing at me. My mother had allowed me to celebrate this visit—the first one I had ever made away from home—by having my first grown-up skirt, really long, like a lady's. I wore that dress proudly to the Anderson's. Their house was set on a steeply inclined street. As we climbed up towards it, I had a dim recollection that the proper thing for ladies to do with long skirts was to clutch it at the back and hold it up, to keep the hem from the dirt. So I did. Mrs. Anderson chanced to be watching us approach and was tickled to a laughter she could not suppress when she saw that I was holding my skirts up at the back, although of course the steep pitch of the street made the hem swing far about the sidewalk we were mounting.

She and Mr. Anderson were still smiling when Willa and I went in. Mrs. Anderson's first words to me, after her pleasant welcome, were: "That's your very first long skirt, isn't it?"

With idiotic astonishment that she could read minds, I exclaimed blankly, "Why, how did you know?"

This was too much. Both Andersons burst into laughter. Not wounding. Like that of a friendly, humorous aunt and uncle. All the same, my new dignity had been denied.

Nothing of the sort happened at another librarian's house where we went later. (Was Mr. Seibel a librarian already, I wonder, or did he become one afterwards? I can't be sure.) Here we had a deep draught of the most concentrated essence of Christmas I've ever had—yes, because it was so new to me, even more than the gay, boisterous later Christmases when my own children were little.

Mr. Seibel was, I suppose, of German tradition, and so was his sweet, motherly wife. Their celebration of Christmas was trimmed with every bright, homely, traditional German touch, most of them new to me.

As I look back on that evening I see the Seibels' house swathed in Christmas greens, fragrant wreaths, garlands, and ropes of evergreen.

There was talk too, wonderful, cosmopolitan talk. The Seibels were very cultivated people, knowing French as well as German.

That evening, I remember, Mr. Seibel standing before that enormous tree, looked up at it and quoted to us a Heine Christmas poem:

Der Stern blieb stehn über Josephs Haus,
Da sind sie hineingegangen:
Das Öchelein brüllte, das Kindlein schrie
Die Heil'gen Drei Könige sangen.

It sounded wonderfully fine as he rolled it out in his rich German. Willa was enchanted by it, got the book out from the shelves back of us, copied off all the poem, and before I had gone on from Pittsburgh to Vermont, had made an admirable rhymed translation of it, the first translation I had ever seen made.

And that poem was accepted by a magazine, a real magazine that paid checks, and was published in their next Christmas issue.

I still have that—one of Willa's first literary successes, very thrilling to her and to me. I never look at it without seeing the Pittsburgh of those days, so different from anybody else in Pittsburgh. It shines in my memory as bright-colored and enlivening as any elaborately illuminated mediaeval manuscript.

"*Der Stern blieb stehen*," the Anderson's friendly laughter, the adored Hasenfeffer, the genial Seibels, the young Willa at the beginning of her career, everything possible to her—it all shines gently and glitters softly in my backward-reaching thoughts, like a great Christmas tree.

Chicago Tribune Magazine of Books, 21 Dec. 1947, 9.

Willa Cather, Daughter of the Frontier

Scientists seem to think there is no better entertainment than to set up a hypothesis in the intellectual bowling alley and see how much of it is standing after the evidence is in. Why leave all the fun to them? I offer you a hypothesis about Willa Cather's work: that the one real subject of all her books is the effect a new country—our new country—has on people transplanted to it from the old traditions of a stable, complex civilization.

Such a hypothesis, if true, would show her as the only American author who has concentrated on the only unique quality of our national life, on the one element which is present, more or less, in every American life and unknown and unguessable to Europeans or European colonials. For Americans (whether originally from Norway, Scotland, Poland or Bohemia) are the only people who have given to the shift from the old to the new life the stern dignity of the irrevocable.

English and French colonists seem to take the attitude of those married people who can't bear to give up thinking of themselves as somebody's children rather than as grown-ups: for whom not their own, but their parents' house is home. Psychologists tell us that the definite break with the past and the assuming of adult responsibility involved in marriage is too much for many people who for no matter how many years after their weddings continue to long for mother's pies and father's protection.

Americans have no choice but to accept the definite break with the past. They are like people who have married against their parents' wishes, and know they must make the best of their bargain. Every American finds himself shut out from the home of his father and married to a new country, with no arrangement made for divorce if he does not like his bride.

Is there one of Miss Cather's novels which is not centered around the situation of a human being whose inherited traits come from centuries of European or English forebears, but who is set down in a new country to live a new life which is not European or English, whatever else it may be? Isn't Miss Cather's chief interest what happens to him in this country, as opposed to what might have happened to him if his family had stayed on the other side of the Atlantic?

This hypothesis cannot be fully examined without looking to see what Miss Cather herself has made out of being an American. For it is not only in her books but in her own experience that she has wrestled with the grave problems and perplexities of transplantation. In her own person she lived through the typical American experience of going from a stable old society to live in a new world. She was born in Virginia of a family who had been farmers for generations, and lived where she was born till she was eight years old. That means she was born and lived for what is traditionally the period of life which most influences personality in a state which had the tradition of continuity and stability as far as they could exist in this country, and in a class which more than any other is always stubbornly devoted to the old way of doing things.

By the time she was a child of eight, Nebraska was being settled by one of the greatest floodtides of rural immigration in the history of the United States. In one decade half a million people pulled their roots from the soil—Danish, German, Norwegian, Bohemian, Virginian—where they had been for centuries, and transplanted themselves to a new country where, strangers not only to the land but to one another, they had the full responsibility of creating whatever communal life was to be.

Along with the half million, out to a ranch near Red Cloud went the Cathers. Their sensitive, intelligent, gifted little girl, marked to the marrow of her bones by her experience of life lived according to an old, stable, orderly and unquestioned tradition, found herself in what from this distance looks rather like social chaos and anarchy. But the sight of chaos is, everybody knows, the most potent stimulus the creative impulse can encounter; and anarchy taking away the props supplied to the weak in settled societies gives infinitely more elbow room for the strong.

Our little Virginia girl was not only sensitive and gifted, she was endowed with wonderful vitality and with what I feel to be a *prime* virtue, perhaps the prime virtue—the will and the ability to enjoy life. And what vital young creature could fail to respond to the stirring drama of hope enacted in those first years of the new settlements? Nothing being yet done, everything was still possible. The pioneers had left behind them stability and tradition, but they had also left social barriers and class inhibitions. They might live in sod houses and have few and plain possessions, but horses—old Aryan symbol of the ruling class—were cheap and, symbolically again, there were no fences.

The women of the little girl's family probably were sometimes homesick; most pioneer women were. But the child with a pony of her own to ride in a world without fences probably enjoyed life very much indeed; most frontier children did. No matter how widely she rode, in all that unfenced prairie, the only people for her to see were transplants; and for the first few years most of them half drunk with the exquisite and unforgettable elixir of frontier hopefulness.

The tragic souring of that wine coincided with her growing up. By the time she was twelve the tide had begun to turn. Successive droughts had brought terrible crop failures to those farmers from rainy climates, pitifully unprepared for a hot, dry land. In one decade the population of Nebraska increased more rapidly than that of any other state west of the Mississippi; but in the decade following, so violent was the revulsion of feeling, the increase was not only less than in any other state of the entire Union, but an actual numerical decrease took place in half of the counties.

This dismal period, full of disappointment and bitterness as dramatic as the preceding hope, began when Willa Cather was about twelve. Till she was twenty—twenty-one—out of college, out of the state, she lived in the midst of one of the greatest disillusions the American pioneer movement has ever known. She had lived through years of hope so blinding that the defects of frontier life could not be seen; she had lived through years of reaction so bleak and black that its fine qualities were invisible. Is it surprising that her writing centers around the theme of the varying ways in which new life in a new country affects those transplanted to it?

Now she was not merely a wonderfully sensitive instrument for recording accurately and storing away all these impressions. She was also a vigorous individual in her own right, who wanted what she wanted with the invincible energy of health. Nebraska might, as people sometimes then gloomily prophesied it would, crumble into deserted desolation; she was twenty-one years old, as intelligent as they come, fearless, determined, eager. From deep roots the sap of life poured up into her young heart. She intended to live, not to brood over a communal heartbreak she could not help. She put out a strong hand and began to take what she wanted. Why not? What she wanted was hers by right. She took it away from no man.

She had already taken something of what she wanted from her student days. When she came up from Red Cloud to the State University, Lincoln was a new little prairie city, the university a rough approximation to an institution of learning. But they offered the brilliant young freshman something different from what she had had.

Sharp-set, fortunate owner of one of the finest appetites mortal ever had for the best in art and life, the girl from Red Cloud fell ravenously on the new opportunities. She amazed and sometimes abashed some of her professors by caring much more fiercely about their subjects than they did. Especially French. There seemed to be a natural affinity between her mind and French forms of art. During her undergraduate years she made it a loving duty to read every French literary masterpiece she could lay her hands on. Judge how disconcerting she was to the head of the French department! When she graduated it was the general conviction of those who knew her that she was the most brilliant student the university had ever had, and was destined for more striking success than any other member of her class.

Then, full of love and hate for the frontier, she moved eastward, to a job on a Pittsburgh newspaper. Being eminently natural and vigorous, she went right on wanting what she wanted and what she had not had; that is, what farm, ranch, and small town life and state university education had not been able to give her; she wanted the best music, the best plays, personal contact with artists and actors and other interesting creative-minded people out of the common run; she wanted knowledge of the niceties of fine food and good wine and good service and of the work of the great painters and the great writers of the world, of where to go and what to see in Europe—but, above all, she wanted then, and always, to write.

I don't live where I hear much of what is said in literary chat, but I understand a legend is going the rounds which presents Willa Cather as a pale victim sacrificed to art. It is true that her art has always been first and foremost in her life, center and core and meaning of her existence, but she has sacrificed herself to it as much as a person who enjoys good eating sacrifices himself in eating good meals. Of course, he can't do other things at the same time, but what of it when he is already doing what he likes best? As well sympathize with Tilden for the fancy dress parties and bridge playing he has missed because of his tennis, as well sympathize with a fish for being in water instead of gasping in the dust, as sympathize with Willa Cather for what she hasn't done while she has been writing.

In no time (as such things go—say in ten years) she had her diploma from the University of the World, again with very high standing. She had worked on that Pittsburgh newspaper. She had changed from that to teaching in a public high school (which she did extremely well). She had read ever so many more first-rate books. She had heard much good music. She knew interesting people, as many as she liked. She knew Europe. She moved from Pittsburgh to New York to edit a magazine and met more stimulating people. Presently, having had the best out of various kinds of life, she was what she set out to be—an accomplished woman of the world and an accomplished writer.

Then, feeling her power ripe within her, she set herself at the business of writing. What did she write about? Why, about what but the different ways in which life in a new country affects different personalities exposed to it. About human lives in which the qualities coming from heredity must be adapted to an environment slowly evolved. Isn't that the thread of unity tying all the beautiful and various Cather works into one whole?

You will hear people say, commenting on what they call the disconnectedness of her work, "The unity of Balzac's work comes from the fact that he is mostly concerned with showing how people react to the presence or absence of money in their lives. Hardy concentrates on the reaction of human beings to the brute element of chance which so often wrecks their lives. Thackeray's main interest is in the action of worldly and social ambitions on naturally noble and disinterested impulses. But what common element is there in Willa Cather's work? Show me one thing in common between *A Lost Lady* and *Shadows on the Rock*."

There is, of course, everything in common; they are two treatments of the same theme. Any one wishing to depict marriage as an institution would naturally show cases where it succeeded and others where it failed. Miss Cather shows that the institution of America also varies in its results. Cecile finds that she can be and is happily married to her new country, bringing a grand dowry of fine traditions with her. But America fairly breaks *A Lost Lady* on the wheel. What is Mrs. Forrester but Mme. Récamier in Red Cloud? As Miss Cather presents her her tragedy is not universal, like the clash of Richard Mahoney's temperament against human existence in general. It is a tragedy not of life but of frontier life, which needs so sorely other qualities than charm in its women that it has not the tradition of delight in charm that would have made Mrs. Forrester a joyous and joy-giving woman in an eighteenth century French salon.

But my space limit is more than passed. Why don't you go on testing this hypothesis on the Cather novels? It will not by any means cover everything. What hypothesis does? But I think that you'll see at once that *My Ántonia*, like Cécile, is one who makes a rich and fruitful success out of her union with the new world; and that Claude is one of those—who would have done infinitely better if the family had never left the old countries. Claude's going to war is only an escape from a hated marriage (both with his country and with his flesh-and-blood wife who is perhaps its symbol). What the war really gives him is a glimpse, that makes his heart ache, of a country where he could have developed innate qualities of taste and skill and discrimination and power which his America would have none of. And the Archbishop—but I was going to leave the rest of this to you.

Still, space or no space, I must not close without pointing out that if this hypothesis is true, it explains, among other things, the otherwise inexplicable lack of general enthusiasm abroad about her splendid books. Her name is well known, but she is not as much read as many authors of half her worth. Intelligent and fair-minded English critics have said, "Yes, I recognize that hers is fine work. But somehow it doesn't interest me." Such comment has always reduced us to the sort of speechless indignation felt by lovers of A. E. Housman's poetry for people who "can't see so much as all that in those little verses."

Our hypotheses would suggest, you see, a perfectly simple explanation for this British obtuseness—namely, that Miss Cather's work is all about an experience which no one but an American can have had; that, like Dante, she is the first to write in the true folk language of her country, which naturally is not understood by outsiders; that she is deeply and mystically our own.

Omaha World-Herald Magazine, 4 June 1933, 7. First published in the New York Herold Tribune Magazine, 28 May, 1933, sec. XI.

HENRY SEIDEL CANBY

As a co-founder, editor, and chairman of the board of the *Saturday Review of Literature* until his retirement in 1958, Henry Seidel Canby (1878–1961) knew the literary world well. In his position as chairman of the board of judges for the Book-of-the-Month Club from 1926–1958, he also knew the reading public. In addition, he was familiar in the academic world for he was a professor at Yale and often published educational books concerning writing and literary history. Cather found him a sympathetic reviewer. After his review of *Sapphira and the Slave Girl* appeared, Cather wrote to him that she appreciated his clear representation of what she was trying to accomplish in the novel. In his article, he recalls conversations in which he and Cather talked about writing. Like most good writers, he had an eye for a telling incident, such as the one which graces the end of this article, a touching momentary reunion of Cather and S. S. McClure near the close of their lives.

Willa Cather (1876–1947): A Reminiscence

Among the novelists who reached their height of achievement in the twenties was Willa Cather, whose death on April 24 ends a great career in American literature. She had already, before the twenties, shown what Americans could do with the rich experience of pioneer life. A personable woman, of finely cut features, with a delicate flush which deepened when ideas warmed her imagination, she was definitely an intellectual aristocrat. She had a way of summoning you to a tea or a conference which proved not the less stimulating because commanded. Actually, as one soon found out, she was guarding her working hours and working energy. She had a fierce devotion to her art which was not vanity, but came from a clearer view than that of most of her contemporaries of the difficulty of achieving even a relative perfection. You can read about it, written of others but applicable to herself, in a book of her essays called *Not Under Forty*.

Willa Cather's mind had the precision of a scholar's, the penetration of a critic's, and the warm intellectuality of a creative artist's. She had led an active editorial life on the staff of the old *McClure's*, which had put the vitality of new European minds and the audacity of the American muckrakers into a cheap and readable magazine just when the genteel periodicals were going stale. It could be tough; it was sensational; respectable editors regarded it as a portent of vulgarity—which only shows that the vulgarity of one generation may prove to be the respectable realism of another. She had done her job in the literary, not the muckraking department, and had wholeheartedly retired into the art of fiction.

As we sat talking, she would ask me the news of that old editorial world; what had happened as a result of this or that, or where were the old fighters now and what were they doing. I could only reply that I lived in an ivory tower in those days and did not know the answers. But this was an introduction to our real talk. Miss Cather was one of the few writers I have known who passionately desired to talk of the craft of good writing with only the most indirect reference to her own work. In this she had what I should call a Gallic mind. The subject matter of her most important books was taken from what was most vital in American pioneer experience, yet the tradition of her craftsmanship was certainly French. The name of Flaubert was often on her lips. She had the not uncommon passion for perfection—but what she liked to analyze as we talked was what constituted perfection for a given situation or a theme. This is French rather than English or American, and when pursued in writing by an Englishman or an American often leads to artificiality. Not so with her. She wished to know how the great ones achieved, not to imitate them. Her idea was that the consummate artist in fiction gave himself entirely to the situation he chose for his story, following its *nuances*, not shaping it to preconceived effects. That was what she wanted to talk about; what she did herself in *O Pioneers!* and *Death Comes for the Archbishop*.

Not long ago I sat with Miss Cather at a meeting of the National Institute of Arts and Letters, at which she was to be given the gold medal in fiction, their highest honor. She had been ill, her face was drawn, her pace a little unsteady. That day a special award for lifetime service was given to Samuel McClure, then well into his eighties. When he was helped to the platform, the color came back to her cheeks, and, with the warm impulsiveness one finds always in her best heroines, she ran forward and kissed and embraced him. I do not suppose that Willa Cather was the greatest American novelist of the 1910's and '20's, bigness was not her *métier*—that she left to the Upton Sinclairs, who had less art. Certainly she was the most skilful, and one of the best.

Saturday Review of Literature, 10 May 1947, 22.

FANNY BUTCHER (BOKUM)

Fanny Butcher (1888–1987) wrote features, social and travel articles, music and literature reviews, and criticism for the *Chicago Tribune* from 1913 to 1963. After Butcher reviewed *Alexander's Bridge*, she and Cather became correspondents. She continued to review each new Cather novel, and at the time of Cather's death, she wrote a substantial reflection of Cather's writing career, much of which is reflected in the following selection. Butcher, a Midwesterner herself, was in a position to know the literature and art of the Midwest and Cather's relationship to that specific culture.

Willa Cather

Of all the people it has been my happy fortune to know, there was never any other who, I felt, was so wholly fulfilled within herself as Willa Cather. By fulfilled within herself, I do not mean selfish or egotistical or careless about everyone else. I mean that somehow she had found what so eludes most of us, exactly what she wanted of life, and had managed to achieve it. What she wanted wasn't fame. It wasn't fortune. It wasn't adulation. Material possessions meant to her only what they could do to make her life unencumbered, freer to devote herself to doing what she wanted most in the world to do—and that was to write. It has always been said that creative writing, the true vocation to it, is a compulsion that cannot be denied, and as essential to the spirit as breathing to the body. In a lifetime of association with writers, I never knew anyone who seemed to be more wrapped around by her work, to be almost encircled in it like Laocoön in the coils of the sea serpents. Once she said to me that nothing mattered to her but writing books, and living the kind of life that makes it possible to write them. I never forgot those words, for they were her credo. Despite everything during the thirty-six years that I knew her, between the publication of her first novel, *Alexander's Bridge*, and almost her last hours, despite distractions, even of illness, she seamed to me to have managed to live that sort of life in so far as it was possible to do so.

Our long friendship started—when *Alexander's Bridge* was published. The author's name on the title page was Willa Sibert Cather, unknown as a novelist. I was not only an unknown, but a completely inexperienced reviewer. She had previously published a volume of poems, *April Twilights*, had been an editor on *McClure's Magazine*, and was known, as editors are, only to the writers with whom they deal or to the owners of the magazines or newspapers for which they work. Except in rare cases like those of Edward Bok, George Horace Lorimer, Bob Davis, Frank Munsey, or S. S. McClure, in the forgotten past, few even constant readers of a periodical ever know the editor's name.

Alexander's Bridge was one of five or six assorted books I carried under my arm when I walked out of Floyd Dell's office at the *Chicago Evening Post* feeling like Balkis, the Queen of Sheba, loaded down with the treasure of Arabia, for when I went in I was tremulous with fear that I would walk out with only chagrin at having dared in my such salad days to ask for a book to review. I haven't the faintest recollection of what the other books were, except that I am sure they were not either poetry or drama because I remember Floyd's saying to me, "I suppose you want to review poems or plays like all the other young hopefuls," and my, unequivocal reply, "I want to review books."

Because I wasn't important enough to have a review signed, only the initials F. B. appeared at the bottom of my review of *Alexander's Bridge*. A long time after it appeared, Floyd sent me a letter he had received from its author, addressed to the Literary Editor, *Chicago Evening Post*. It came from 1180 Murray Hill Avenue, Pittsburgh, Pennsylvania, and was signed Willa Sibert Cather, the signature she used until (as I remember) the publication of *My Mortal Enemy*, when she discarded the Sibert.

In Willa Cather's will there is a prohibition against any of her letters being published, a legal ban that in her case seemed to me a major deprivation, for the many letters Willa Cather wrote me contain the most illuminating comments on her work, her ideals, and especially that marvelous sense of joy that comes from having a creative goal. I can understand why anyone might not want to share with the world the intimate details of one's life that often creep into letters written in a moment of emotion or petulance, but if Willa Cather's other letters resembled those she wrote to me, they could do nothing but add to her stature as a great writer and as a rare human being, both of which she was.

If what she wrote to the "Literary Editor, *Chicago Evening Post*" cannot be quoted verbatim, its gist can be shared. The letter was written some time after the review appeared because, she said, she had just returned from an absence of some months. The fact that she wrote at all was unusual, because few authors write to reviewers in gratitude for a reviewer's perception, though few are reticent about resenting an unfavorable review. They usually attribute adverse criticism to some personal grudge on the reviewer's part.

For a half-century I have reviewed books, and I am often asked about my tenets of reviewing. Not necessarily in the order of their importance, they are, first: the audience by whom the review will be read of necessity gives the review its form and, in a sense, its content. A review meant for a scholarly quarterly has no place in a newspaper with a million readers. A scholarly review must be contemplative and philosophical about both the subject matter and its treatment, and it may rightly be minutely argumentative. But that kind of review in a newspaper is simply not read by men on the eight-fifteen or women looking, through the paper over a cup of coffee, after the children have been packed off to school. And if a review isn't read, it defeats its own main purpose, which is, in any kind of media, destined for no matter what audience, to entangle and stimulate the reader's interest and to help the reader decide whether the book is one he wants to spend his time reading. It is as simple as that. An insidious virus often attacks some reviewers—the "see what a great boy am I" bug. They try so hard to tell the world how good they are with a scalpel that can neatly cut out the book's heart, how clever *they* are at tossing words around, that when the reader has finished the review he has neither desire nor the intention ever to look at the book. I deeply believe that book reviewing should never be used for the personal aggrandizement of the reviewer, only to help increase and widen the inestimable pleasure of reading.

Newspaper reviewers of any of the arts are essentially, I have always believed, reporters, and they should be judges of what the author has accomplished, or failed to accomplish, and make an honest attempt at understanding the author's intent. A novelist, for instance, may never have intended to write a contemporary *War and Peace*, a poet a *John Brown's Body* of today, or a historian a modern *Decline and Fall of the Roman Empire*. For a reviewer to castigate a light tale of human foibles for instance because it does not try to settle all the racial, economic, and social problems of the day is, it seems to me, bad reviewing. There was a period in my memory as a reviewer when, if a book did not have reforms of social injustices as its hard core, the most popular reviewers automatically treated it as a smudge on a windowpane to be wiped away with a couple of good swipes.

At the moment of this writing, there seems to me to be a real smudge on the windowpanes of most fiction, the smudge of intentional pornography. It may be just a part of our period of self-cleaning ovens and self-adjusting air conditioners. But whatever titillation there was earlier in seeing four-letter words in print (and don't forget that "love" and "duty" are four-letter words, too) or in reading clinical descriptions of intimate wigglings and screams of ecstasy, wears off when one encounters them on every other page. A kind of "ho-hum, so what" feeling sets in, even with readers who deplored the suppressions, evasions, and innuendoes of the Victorians. Take the word of an old lady who has watched literary booms and busts over a lifetime: the present sex kick in fiction will wear itself out by overindulgence, just as the era of three- or four-generation family chronicles, the era of historical novels, the era of social-injustice stories, the era of what were called omnibuses—enormously long, books sometimes printed in two, even three, volumes—wore themselves out.

But for a reviewer to say a book is "good" or "bad" because it is as sexy as a pomegranate is seedy is to miss the point. If the author intended to write about a sex relationship and does it with skill and literary grace, he has, it seems to me, done his task honorably. It is not literarily "good," but dishonest if he uses sex like freshly ground pepper on the morning oatmeal.

Nothing could be farther from any kind of literary dishonesty than the writing of Willa Cather. She was never diverted from what she knew was right in her work, by any of the temptations that literary success often brings: money, fame, or the pressure to write another book like its best-selling predecessor. Like all great artists she experimented—saw and added new dimensions to her work. But she did it with such skill and subtlety that few readers realize how experimental all of her writing was. For instance, *Death Comes for the Archbishop*, which became a classic, was so great a departure from the usual fictional treatment of the relationship between a man, his God, and a land he loved that some top reviewers denounced it as not a novel at all, or said, as the *New York Morning World* did, that judged as a novel it was a very poor performance. When we talked about that book, Willa told me she had always wanted to try something in the style of legend, with a sort of New Testament feeling. "I think I succeeded fairly well, but a story with no woman in it but the Virgin Mary has very definite limitations. It is a very special kind of thing and you like it or you don't." I remember saying in print that I liked it (as did and still do hundreds of thousands of readers). But in my review I used the word "folklore" instead of "legend," and Willa Cather, who was almost uncanny in sensing subtleties in words, pointed out the difference to me, that folklore is inarticulated, detached, but legend a sort of interpretation of life by faith—words I never forgot. She went on to say that it was the order and discipline in their background that gave the missionaries she wrote about in *Death Comes for the Archbishop* proportion and measure and accent like a work of art. And then she told me that some time—preferably in the country—I should reread the book the way I had read Swiss Family Robinson when I was little, not as a piece of writing but as someone living with the characters as one of them, in the milieu of those early missionaries, one in which miracles seemed to them a part of the day's work. Another time she told me that *The Archbishop*, like *Robinson Crusoe*, was a kind of writing colored by a kind of country, like a folk song.

When I was in Santa Fe I saw the setting for *Death Comes for the Archbishop*. I sat inside the tiny chapel where the Archbishop celebrated the mass. It is hardly large enough for six people. I shut my eyes and became again a part of the historical Archbishop Lamy's time and thought, as I had felt I was when I first read the book.

Whenever Willa Cather went to her family home in Red Cloud, Nebraska, she of necessity changed trains in Chicago, and even if she didn't stay over a few days with her childhood friend, Irene Weisz, we always had at least a few hours together. Incidentally, Mrs. Weisz has given the Newberry Library of Chicago all of the letters from Willa Cather that she received during that lifetime friendship. I read them, of course, with interest, but with disappointment, for in them Willa never wrote about her work as she invariably did to me, as if it were a living entity to her. Sometimes she would write to me how it was progressing, how it had been received. Often she wrote with gratitude for what her work had done for her, helped her through a crisis of physical or family stress, or simply given her a glorious summer or year. Once when we talked about *The Archbishop*, she said, "It's an altogether new kind for me, and how I loved doing it. It was as if you had, after playing only modern composers, taken the time and used the control to practice Bach awhile without any comparison."

Happily, she shared her creative thoughts with me. We had a rare and wonderful friendship, and although it was between a writer and a reviewer, she knew that I would never be influenced in what I wrote about her work by my affection for her as a person; and I knew that as a friend she would understand and respect my honesty with myself as a reviewer.

Once, I remember, she worried about my thinking she might have written a lauding preface to Thomas Mann's *Joseph* series only because her publisher, who was Mann's also, had asked her to help sell the book. We both had found Mann's *The Magic Mountain* dull, and she reminded me of that, but she said his Biblical trilogy seemed to her a great work. She told me she had read it twice for pleasure before she even thought of writing about it. Then after the third reading she decided she wanted to write the introduction, for she so seldom found a new book that carried her into a new world, and this carried her back into the oldest world of all.

She could have piled up fortunes if she had allowed her books to be made into movies, but after seeing what happened to her *A Lost Lady*, she was adamant against any more of them being put on film. After her death, Edith Lewis, her devoted friend and her literary trustee, wrote me that *A Lost Lady* was produced as a silent film and later as a sound film, that Willa always regretted having let it be made into a movie, and that the decision to do so was made hurriedly over the telephone.

The first I heard of *A Lost Lady* was in a letter from 5 Bank Street in Greenwich Village, where Willa Cather lived for years, until the building was razed. In that letter she told me that it seemed that everyone who professed to like one's writing did all in his or her power to prevent the writer from having one untroubled day in which to write again, but that, in spite of everything, she had done a new story of forty thousand words, and both Alfred and Blanche Knopf, her publishers, liked it better than anything she had done before. It was *A Lost Lady*.

A very short book of Willa Cather's, *My Mortal Enemy*, seemed to me to tell more in a little over a hundred pages about marriage and the man-woman relationship of love than tomes could have told. It filled me with wonder that any writer could make a book so profound out of so slight a story of a vivid and beautiful woman who loved a man against all of her traditions, married him, and watched love disintegrate until he became in her mind her mortal enemy. That is what I said in the *Chicago Tribune* Willa's reaction to my sincere praise of the overpowering task she had set herself, and her brilliant success in achieving her goal, was characteristic of her. She was not elated over its being a review that would lure readers, she said, but it was worth writing a book to have someone get the point of it absolutely, and what she had written about was, as I had said, just that fundamental, both the attraction and the antagonism between two strongly individual people who love deeply, truly, the irresistible attraction of being one, and the fierce resentment at no longer being two unentangled individuals.

Out of *The Archbishop* inevitably came her novel about Quebec, *Shadows on the Rock*. If Willa Cather was converted to Catholicism as was often said, I did not know it, but the long months she spent in research about Archbishop Lamy took her also to Quebec, and there she found something that impelled her to write *Shadows on the Rock*. To me it was a magical book, the sheer writing in it an experience that nourished the roots of a reader's mental being. No title ever more aptly fitted a novel than *Shadows on the Rock*, about the fortress rock of Quebec in the eighteenth century when a little band of French planted their culture in the unwelcoming crevices, a rock against whose impregnability the human beings were only shifting shadows.

After the book appeared, she wrote me that she was up on the Canadian island of Grand Manan in the Bay of Fundy and glad of everything, which meant that she had had a happy hard-writing summer, when her mother died suddenly in Pasadena, that since then life had been a tough pull, and that my review of *Shadows on the Rock* had given her a hand up when she needed it. It had made her feel that she had been able to transfer to me the unreasonable and unaccountable glow that trying to relive the little details of life in primitive Quebec had given her, which was like a child's feeling about Christmas, she said, with no reason to it, just something that brings happiness.

Most of the reviewers in New York criticized her for what she didn't write—a book including the larger dramatic incidents of history. Talking about *Shadows* later, she said, "Doesn't one have a perfect right to love a small Georgian pitcher better than the Empire State building, and can one choose what one loves anyway, or how one should love it? As I wrote you, I did this book to keep me going and I'm well satisfied if a few old friends, like yourself, get a little happiness out of it." A good many people must have got a little happiness out of it because it was chosen by two book clubs and around a hundred thousand copies were sold in bookshops.

One place in Quebec made such a deep impression on her that she told me she could think of no other where she could die wrapped so securely in peace. It was a home for the indigent aged, the dedicated work of an order of nuns that had been in existence almost from the time Quebec was founded. She urged me to go to see it, to tell her whether I, too, felt the supreme peace she had felt when she visited it. You can look down on it from a room on the unpopular side of the Hotel Frontenac, she wrote me, so I should be sure not to reserve a room on the St. Lawrence side.

My husband and I made a sentimental journey to Quebec, and did as she said, eschewed the pleasure of having breakfast watching the exciting water life of the great river and seeing (as we once did on another trip) a whale spouting. When we sought out the convent, we found that only one person could speak to us, not that no one else could speak English, or that my meager French couldn't have served, but because it was the home of an order in which a vow of silence had been taken by every sister. The mother superior, with whom alone we could talk, welcomed us almost tenderly when she found that Willa Cather had sent us. She showed us where the old people were cared for, in the partitioned alcoves that I had seen in old French hospitals that were part of some vast medieval chapel. If there was an omnipresent sense of peace it was smothered for me in my pity for the broken bodies that limped or crawled in their clinging to a life whose tomorrows were menacing, not because they were numbered, but because they were doomed to pain.

After the French fashion, the building was built around an inner court. Never have I seen grass so brilliantly, exultantly green. When I told the mother superior how startlingly beautiful it was, so vividly alive against the gray walls she said, "The courtyard has been ever since the walls were made, the last resting place of the nuns of the order when they joined their God." I left wondering why sadness, not the comfort of serenity, had so gripped me, while to Willa that spot had spoken almost joyously.

Willa Cather had such a sense of gratitude to *Shadows on the Rock*, for helping her through crises of two years—the death of her father, her mother's unexpected illness, and her own lack of health—that she wouldn't sell the book as a serial, although she was offered a large sum for serial rights. "It simply isn't a serial," she told me, "and to have it read piecemeal would be unfair to it. So, although I need the money, I just couldn't do it, Fanny. You understand, I know." Of course I understood, and somehow, because she chose thus both to respect her art and to prove her gratitude to it, I understood a little better the whole creative urge and gratification. I never knew Willa Cather to speak of the actual writing of a book as anything but complete satisfaction. Most writers, understandably, complain of the very real agonies of creation, the inevitable loneliness, the grind of galley slavery. To Willa writing was the breath of life, the corpuscles in her blood, the great love.

Although *Shadows on the Rock* was a title that perfectly and subtly fitted the book, the perfect fit was evident only after it had been read, and in the book business a title has often made the difference between a winner in the literary horse race and the forgotten nag. To name only a few of Willa Cather's—*Youth and the Bright Medusa, Sapphira and the Slave Girl, Death Comes for the Archbishop* (a title with "death" in it is always risky), *The Professor's House*—almost all are classic examples of titles that puzzled rather than allured. But Willa was adamant about them, and she always had her way until it came to a novel about a Nebraska boy who went to war. His name was Claude, and she called the book *Claude.* Her publishers and the members of the sales conference all told her it wouldn't do. She said it was the book's title and she wouldn't change it. They argued with her, they pleaded. Name titles do not necessarily discourage sales, nor have they from the eighteenth century days of Richardson's *Clarissa Harlowe. David Copperfield* brought in a pretty penny for Mr. Dickens, as did *Anthony*

Adverse for Hervey Allen. But a given and a surname identified a character as an individual, and a given name alone in a title unconsciously makes the reader think of a type rather than of a person. Of course there have been successful first-name titles, but the success has come after the book proved irresistible; *Lolita* a good example. *Lolita* did not pique the reader's curiosity at all the day it appeared. Its career was a chain reaction, certainly not triggered by the title.

The argument over *Claude* went on for some time between Willa Cather and her publishers, both growing more and more stubborn. Finally, she said she was going to Nebraska; on the way she would see me in Chicago, and let me settle the dispute. I was then a bookseller as well as a reviewer, so I had a double-barreled gun with which to do the settling. I told her without hesitation that *Claude* wouldn't do. She had a list of titles she had considered. Not one of them seemed to me to give that little nudge to curiosity which a good selling title does. (Nobody, for instance, who picked up a book called *Gone With the Wind* could resist flipping the pages out of sheer curiosity about what was blown away.)

Of the many titles she had thought of, I felt the best was *One of Ours*, for the book was about a young midwesterner who became one of our fighting men. I persuaded her to relinquish *Claude*, which she did reluctantly, and happily *One of Ours* received that year's Pulitzer award.

One of Ours is, it has always seemed to me, the least good of Willa Cather's novels, especially in its war scenes, for she had had no firsthand contact with either battle or life behind the lines, as did such novelists as Ernest Hemingway and John Dos Passos. You will probably cite Stephen Crane's *The Red Badge of Courage*, an unrivaled classic of war, written by a young man who never was touched by war, except emotionally and philosophically, but Stephen Crane's book is an introspective, reflective picture of war, not reflected and refracted, as was *One of Ours*.

The title *My Ántonia* had the same selling handicap, in its way, as did *Claude*. Many readers think it her first novel, but three—*O Pioneers!*, *The Song of the Lark*, and *Alexander's Bridge*—preceded its publication in 1918. *My Ántonia* always had a special place in Willa Cather's heart. She certainly hadn't much affection for her *Alexander's Bridge*, as is evident by what she wrote on a picture she sent me. It is a photograph of the young, sensitive Willa, who had a haunting beauty. It is dated February 16, 1920, and came to me with this inscription: "For Fanny Butcher who wrote the first discriminating review of my first novel. In this case my interest in the reviewer has outlived my interest in the novel, for I don't think much of that book now."

My Ántonia is now accepted and studied as an American classic but, surprisingly, when it came out it was not well received by either the critics or the public. In 1918, the year it was published, the world was more concerned about war than about a gentle servant girl in Nebraska. The book was not advertised widely and was treated by the publisher as just another novel. Willa once told me that Grant Overton and I were the only reviewers in the country who liked it. I certainly did, and I was astonished that every reviewer didn't recognize that in its quietness it was as true a record of the pioneer days and spirit as the most flamboyant covered-wagon chronicle. Of course, part of its lack of success was that the nation was war-oriented. The public wanted to read either books directly or indirectly concerned with the conflict or the future of the world and mankind, or else what is known in the book trade as "escape literature," anodynes like adventure tales, Zane Grey westerns, detective and mystery stories. The best sellers of 1918–1919 were Arthur Guy Empey's *Over the Top*, a vivid record of trench fighting; *Dere Mable*, by Ed Streeter, a funny book of letters written to his sweetheart by a more ardent than literate doughboy (it is said to have sold over 600,000 copies), and the translation from the Spanish of Blasco-Ibáñez' spectacular spy story, *The Four Horsemen of the Apocalypse*. (The four horsemen were conquest, slaughter, famine, and death, in case you don't remember.)

My Ántonia had not the jaunty content to allure readers who wanted to forget the war and it had no contact with what they wanted to escape from. Its allure was in the art of beautiful writing, its hold on the reader a gentle touch of a tender hand. Willa felt that her publishers had not done their utmost to make it a success, and she was willing to go to another publisher for her next book. News of her dissatisfaction with her publisher seeped out, and other publishers hovered. Why she chose Alfred Knopf, then one of the youngest publishers in the book business, instead of one of the oldline firms is a comment on her ideals.

Willa Cather always had a deep love for music. Her novel *The Song of the Lark* reflects it, as does *Lucy Gayheart*. Although that book is actually a love idyll, technically it seems to me as plainly influenced by Miss Cather's interest in music as anything she wrote. Before *Lucy Gayheart* was published, Miss Cather stopped off in Chicago, on her way West, to see me and she said to me something I never forgot. I quoted it in my review of the book: "I see no reason why one cannot write a novel as a composer writes a symphony." You can feel Willa Cather's use of the technique of music also in *The Professor's House* and in *My Mortal Enemy*, which is a tense contrapuntal exercise. Her passionate interest in music took her to every concert available. In that winter of her discontent she found nourishment for her spirit in music, and gave herself, she told me, two or three afternoons of serenity at concerts each week.

In the predominantly feminine audience, she often noticed a handsome, Spanish-looking young man who was plainly listening, as she listened to music, with his whole being. "When I found that he was a book publisher," she said to me, "I decided then and there that any young man who would neglect his business to listen to music in the afternoon was the publisher I wanted." This attunement happily lasted for both until Willa Cather exchanged her seat in an earthly concert hall for whatever music of the spheres is available. I remember going to see Willa soon after Christmas one year, and her showing me the new machine on which a dozen records could be played from one stacking of the discs and saying, "Alfred gave me this for Christmas. It was music, you know, that made him my publisher."

There was always something apart from the world about Willa Cather. It was none of the cynic's contempt for mankind, but more the philosopher's wide observation of man and his motives, his dreams and his failures, and then choosing what, given all of the potentials, she wanted her own life to be. What she wanted was simply to write books. She did not want, as many writers do, to have written them, to bask in their sun socially and economically.

She never married. I never asked nor was told why not. She must have been lovely when she was young, with her blue eyes seriously but eagerly looking at a world that could hold all the joys of life—for that is the way she looks in early photographs. She refused all social invitations except from a few old and cherished friends. She lived comfortably but not lavishly and had, so far as I could see, no extravagances and no intense prejudices, except against anyone or anything bent on interfering with her work. She wasted no working time, as many of us do, on causes, though she wrote about them so subtly that a reader scarcely realized it. The "race question" was not in her day the inescapable problem it either intentionally or involuntarily has become in all of our lives, but there is in her last novel, *Sapphira and the Slave Girl* (published in 1940)—a tale of pre-Civil War days—a deep understanding of what slavery meant, what made it unbearable not only to the enslaved but to the innately freedom-loving white person.

I have often wondered how Willa Cather would have adjusted herself in today's world to what often seems the complete breakdown of real and honest communication and understanding between governments, generations, races, families, even between eternal nature itself and man. Marcel Proust, born only a few years before Willa Cather, shut himself up in a cork-lined room to insulate himself from the world, to write his monumental *Remembrance of Things Past*. Willa was no eccentric like Proust, but she was so completely dedicated to her work she avoided all distractions, even the allure of a room with a view.

Once when I told her about visiting the studio in Meudon, where Rodin had created some of the greatest of all modern sculpture, she said that she had spent almost a year nearby with her friends, the Jan Hambourgs (Mrs. Hambourg was the dear friend of her Pittsburgh days, Mr. Hambourg, the violin virtuoso and composer). When she arrived, she said, they offered her a choice of two rooms in which to work: one a large, sunny one whose window looked out on a garden of almost lyric beauty, the other, a room found in almost all French houses, with a view of a blank whitewashed wall. "Of course you know which one I chose," she said, "I was determined to let nothing, especially that lovely garden, keep me even for a few moments of joy from my work." Sometimes illnesses interfered with her work—once she told me she hadn't been able to write for over a year—but she never doubted what she wanted in life, and that clear-eyed, unquestioning certainty gave her a peace, a serenity of mind and heart that emanated from her like the beams of the little candle Portia cited in *The Merchant of Venice*, which shone like "a good deed in a naughty world."

In *Many Lives—One Love*. New York: HarperCollins, 1972. 354–68.

The Legend Grows

Just as Willa Cather's journalist colleagues found that they had anecdotes to tell about her, so writers and artists began to recall anecdotes that revealed their awareness of her growing reputation as a novelist and artist. The following pieces are all short but telling vignettes of Cather. In them, we witness Cather as she appeared to others while she was dedicating her energies increasingly to her fiction.

FRANK SWINNERTON

Cather's royalty checks grew after the publication of *One of Ours* (1922). So, in 1923, after completing *A Lost Lady*, she spent seven months abroad where she visited the Jan Hambourgs, nursed a sore right shoulder, and sat for the Leon Bakst portrait, which hangs in the Omaha Public Library. On the return trip to New York, she met Frank Arthur Swinnerton (1884–1982), an English journalist, editor, literary critic, and novelist known for portraying complex ideas or feelings in a vivid and clear style. He and Cather seemed to have much to discuss.

From Swinnerton: An Autobiography

Having first helped to plant three magnificent young sycamore trees in our garden, I left England in November, 1923, by the *Berengaria*, then one of the three largest ships afloat; and I had hardly stepped aboard that immense movable hotel before I was accosted by a young American business man of most engaging character. He was a delightful fellow; and as soon as he had introduced himself he began ingenuously to boast, not of his own

Willa Cather's 1920 passport photo. Courtesy of the Nebraska State Historical Society, Willa Cather Pioneer Memorial Collection.

prowess, but of his country and its glories. As we tramped the decks of the *Berengaria* together the song he sang was of the indescribable superiority of the United States to any other land in the world. England he despised; it was small, dirty, effete, and contemptible. It could be put away in a corner of the United States and never noticed except as a regrettable slum that needed to be cleaned up by some honest-to-God pioneers. America, young, free, gigantic, had everything of the best and vastest within its confines. The biggest buildings, the greatest hospitals, the finest industries, magazines, men, women, and bosses, the most magnificent mountains, prairies, flowers, waterfalls, lakes, and mammals, were to be seen there amid the finest civilization known to man. And so on. As he talked we passed two other American passengers, who must have been speaking of the *Majestic*, for one of them said: "Of course, she's a bigger ship than this"; and I remarked to the young man, who had also heard the speech: "I suppose that's a boat on one of the American lakes?" For a moment he was taken aback. Then he seized my shoulder. "*You're* all right!" he cried, giving it an enthusiastic shake. It was unnecessary, after this, to boast. Hitherto he had been talking to an Englishman. From that moment I was a human being, which, though something lower, was more tolerable.

At Cherbourg, according to the deck-steward, whose duty it is to know everybody's business, another writer was coming aboard the *Berengaria*—a "Miss Cayther." I said—rather nimbly, I thought: "Miss *Willa* Cayther?" He did not know, but, perhaps thinking that writers like to get together, which is but a half-truth, offered to point her out the next day. I demurred. That night, however, a lady joined the table for four at which I had been sitting with two English business men, and took the seat next to mine. She was not a tall lady, but was of middle height, fresh coloured, rather broad-cheeked, and decidedly self-possessed, and when I saw a scribble on the label of her wine-bottle I jumped to the conclusion that this must be Miss Cather and demanded to know if it was so. She demurely said: "Yes. Why?" from which I inferred that as I had been told about her she had probably been told about me; and having boldly named myself I began to talk at once upon that assumption. There was no constraint about Miss Cather, who, when she found that I had a ready tongue, used her own with similar readiness. We talked unstintedly for the rest of the voyage.

What we could not discuss in five days we left for the future, when there will always be plenty of material; but in five days one can cover a good deal of ground and we did our best. The two business men—both agreeable, simple souls—said almost nothing at all, except, towards the end of the voyage and in the exhilaration of anticipated farewell, that they had enjoyed themselves very much; and it was Miss Cather and I, helped in chief by Miss Cather's luminous intelligence, complete freedom from egotism, intense interest in life and living, music, Europe, and men and women, who were indefatigable. She talked excellently, without show of wit but with beautiful candour. Her mind is strong and clear, her humour, though undeclared, shows in every acceptance of meaning; she is full of wisdom. And, finally, she is one of those happy persons whom the minor exasperating incidents of existence cannot ruffle. It is a rare gift.

This happiness of temper triumphed over the most amusing unintentional persecution on the part of our young boaster, who was always on the wrong foot with her, was always crowding her, and who, like a boisterous great affectionate dog, gambolled up at all hours of the day, full of *naïf* communication, even as she walked thoughtfully on deck in the very early morning. Her patience was deplorably fine. However, in the end the young man came to me, comically and pathetically wounded, because after nearly a week of long-suffering, endured perhaps also (I fear) at meal-times, she at last had turned upon him an hour before breakfast with the heart-rending cry: "Am I *never* to be permitted to cerebrate?"

I liked her, and like her, very much indeed. But then I like, without exception, all the American woman novelists I have ever met. Either I have met only the really interesting among them or as human beings they are superior in what I shall call essential quality (say, in character) to all but half-a-dozen of the English women writers whom I have met or known. They talk without trying to impress. They are neither self-important nor in a bad sense self-conscious. They are not always, it appears, thinking of themselves as Writers or as Women (or as Women-Writers). And they are entertaining. Different as they are in themselves and in their work, Ellen Glasgow, Willa Cather, Fannie Hurst, Edna Ferber ("Noo Fannie Hoist, noo Edna Foiber," as I heard a book-selling boy call at a New York terminus), Anne Parrish, and Alice Duer Miller, to take six whose names immediately occur to me, are all real people who would strike the mind and imagination if they had never written a line.

New York: Doubleday, 1936. 316–19.

MARY WATKINS CUSHING

As Olive Fremstad's secretary in the broadest sense of the term, Mary Cushing (189?–1974) was, in her own word, Fremstad's "buffer" against the world. It was in this capacity that she met Cather, who became Cushing's "ally" in helping Fremstad to relax during her busy season. Cushing's lively memoirs of Fremstad's quirks often call to mind Cather's own characteristics of intense attention to her muse, and, at the same time, they show Cather's relationship to another artist from the point of view of someone whose central concerns were not the making of art but the serving of one who did.

From The Rainbow Bridge

Miss Willa Cather, the writer—not then so famous as she later became—was my most steadfast ally. She too felt that Fremstad ought to see more of her fellow men, and often took her to matinees or invited her to wonderful little French meals at her apartment on Bank Street. Madame, while unresisting, would still protest, "But I get nothing from people!"

"An artist learns from everyone she meets, from everything she sees!" Miss Cather would remind her.

"What I learn, I find here!" Olive Fremstad insisted, in a cello voice, her eyebrows climbing, both hands pressed to her heart.

This melodramatic gesture might have seemed absurd in another, but she was in deadly earnest and was, to her own knowledge, absolutely right. A smile would have been an impertinence.

We had met Miss Cather during the latter part of the previous season; actually, I am told, on that very day when Fremstad sang at such short notice the role of Giulietta in *Hoffmann*. Madame had blithely gone for a drive in the country and left me to cope with an expected interviewer from *McClure's Magazine*. This proved to be Willa Cather, at that time one of the magazine's editors, who was preparing a special article about three American singers: Homer, Farrar, and Fremstad. The first two had been duly disposed of; Miss Cather was saving until last, she frankly said, the one who interested her most. This was no reflection upon the other artists, but Cather had then in the works a new novel, *The Song of the Lark*, based in some measure on what she had imaginatively reconstructed of Olive Fremstad's early life. She now wished to prop up the fiction with fact and fill in occasional blanks by personal observation.

In this she was somewhat thwarted that first afternoon. How deadly to be confronted by a humble young acolyte instead of by the priestess herself! I was much embarrassed, and expected to see her turn on a peevish heel and slam the door in my face. But this was not Willa Cather's way. She sat down quite happily with me and asked me all the questions which she thought it would be fair for me to answer. She laid the groundwork for her article, and had a fleeting glimpse of her heroine—rather tired and windblown—as a consolation prize at the end. Later, upon a more leisurely occasion, she was able to have her interview, unhampered by the need for gathering statistics.

This was the beginning of a rewarding friendship which lasted well into the years when Miss Cather's own work began to make demands for which she had to conserve her energies. She was a gay companion and always a sympathetic student of the artist's nature. Madame was delighted with the article when it appeared during her final Metropolitan season, and told the author that her penetration and insight were uncanny. But she was less enthusiastic about *The Song of the Lark*, which was published a little later. "My poor Willa," she once said in my hearing, "it wasn't really much like that. But after all, what can you know about me? Nothing!"

Miss Cather took this in good part, neither complaining nor explaining. She knew what she knew, and she had got what she wanted. The book was quite a conspicuous success, and actually, her Thea Kronberg had never been publicly labeled Olive Fremstad. So she and Madame remained on the best of terms. Later that season the singer, followed by me with the collected floral offerings from a performance of the night before, went to see Miss Cather in the hospital where she lay ingloriously stricken by an infection from a hatpin, having lost an important section of scalp. The sufferer was invited to visit Little Walhalla that spring to recuperate. Much to my surprise she accepted, and actually stayed there with us for a week.

During that visit I came to know her better and admire her even more, for we had a week of typical storm and stress. The cook left; the plumbing ceased to function; and Madame's mood was joyless and grim. Miss Cather lent me a cheerful hand in the successive emergencies, mopped up my tears, and exhorted Madame to a higher heart. Presently, through her efforts, the sun came out and the clouds rolled away, and when she departed—doubtless with secret relief—she left at least one staunch disciple behind.

New York: Putnam, 1954. 242–44.

ELIZABETH YATES

Elizabeth Yates (1905–2001) grew up on a farm south of Buffalo, New York, then moved to New York City after her high school graduation, where she began writing articles, book reviews, and short stories. After living in England from 1929 to 1939, she and her husband settled in the New Hampshire countryside where she continued to write and to teach at writers' conferences. Although she was a writer of books of adult fiction and biography, including one about Dorothy Canfield Fisher's life, she is best known for her award-winning works for younger readers. The sensitive tone and graceful mingling of the fact and art that mark her children's books are evident in this article.

The article also highlights an important aspect of Cather's mature writing years: she relied heavily on her excursions to retreats in the northeast, usually in late summer or early fall, for uninterrupted and tranquil writing or recuperation times. There was Jaffrey, New Hampshire; Grand Manan, New Brunswick, where she had her own cottage built; and Asticou in Maine, which she found during World War II when limited sea service kept her in the United States. Yates's article is occasioned and enlivened by the reminiscences of Eleanor Shattuck Austermann, the daughter, then the wife, of the owners of the Shattuck Inn at Jaffrey. A letter from Katherine Savage of Asticou presents a picture of Cather similar to that in Yates's article:[1]

> Mr. Savage knew Willa Cather rather well — a formal acquaintance really, but naturally more significant than many summer guests of the Inn.
>
> I doubt if Miss Cather attended *regularly* any church here, but if and when she did I suspect she would have much preferred the simple "small" church at Seal Harbor — St. Jude's. Saint Mary's in the summer is highly social — that phase of the scene here was far from *any* interest to Willa Cather — a quiet very private person — and Miss Lewis, her devoted companion, did much to insure her privacy at all times.
>
> If you are familiar with the record of her "surface" associations with the three Northeast resorts she visited you perhaps are under the impression that she made the same impressions at all three — quite the contrary. At Grand Manan she may have been considered "a character" but not at Asticou. We found her a perfectly delightful, gentle, scholarly — yes a modest guest. Her wishes were few as far as material needs were concerned, and every effort was made to respect her privacy. I suspect that is why she returned and lived in the same room (simple indeed) each summer. Her common type early hotel writing desk is still in the same place it was when she drafted one of her last books — in fact, in my own old cottage where I live. It happened a Library of Congress musicologist was a guest of my family and was more than thrilled to use her old writing table, this past August.

Required Reading

It was 1925 and a group of Wellesley juniors were discussing the books in their English course. One of them picked up a copy of *My Ántonia* and began reading from it.

"But that's by Willa Cather!" Eleanor Shattuck exclaimed.

"Of course, it is. Three of her books are on the list. She's required reading."

"Miss Cather is required reading?" Eleanor Shattuck spoke the words as if they came strangely together.

The girl who was reading from *My Ántonia* put the book down, carefully keeping a finger in the place. "Do you know her?" she asked, her tone as filled with awe as her friend's had been with surprise.

"Why, yes, I know her. She's a guest at the Inn. She comes every year." Then Eleanor Shattuck put back her head and laughed. "I don't know what Miss Cather will think about this—" She picked up the list of books the English juniors had been given. "Required reading!" she exclaimed. "Wait till I tell her."

Eleanor Shattuck knew Willa Cather as a frequent guest at the inn her parents ran in Jaffrey, New Hampshire. She knew that she was a writer, too, but somehow that had never seemed so important as the fact that she was a quiet, friendly person who came yearly to the Shattuck Inn and one whose visits were welcomed.

As the years passed and Eleanor Shattuck married George Austermann and together they managed the Inn, Willa Cather's visits continued. Two months or longer every year over a period of twenty years, she came with Edith Lewis to Jaffrey. During that time, Eleanor Austermann grew to know her well and to cherish her as a friend; that she was a celebrity was of small importance. But because of what Miss Cather was, she required a measure of protection, which the Austermanns gave to the full. She was never asked to sign the register during all those years; her need for quiet was answered, and her need for solitude respected.

Some time before, at the beginning of Willa Cather's career, Sarah Orne Jewett had written her a letter which was to become memorable, for its effect not only on Miss Cather but on the many who would read it in the various biographies and books on writing in which it would later be published. Miss Jewett spoke of Willa Cather's responsibility to herself as a writer so that her own work might mature as it should. "You must find your own quiet center of life and write from that," Miss Jewett wrote. "To write and work on this level we must live on it—we must at least recognize it and defer to it at every step. . . . To work in silence and with all one's heart, that is the writer's lot; he is the only artist who must be solitary, and yet needs the widest outlook upon the world."[1]

Willa Cather found her quiet center within, and during the years she found many quiet places in which to work, but much of her finest work was done at Jaffrey. Carrying her typewriter and her canvas chair to her working studio in the pines, she lost herself, as she loved to say, for three hours every day. Coming back to the Inn, she would enter by the rear door and go quietly up the stairs to the two little rooms on the third floor which she always requested and which were always kept for her. She liked their sloping ceilings, the way the rain sounded on the roof, and the near feel of the sun; but best of all she liked the view from the windows across the green tops of pine trees and the pastures overgrown with blueberry bushes and juniper to Monadnock. Blue-green in the daytime to black at night, the light on the mountain was constantly changing, but the mountain itself was always serene and dominant.

Coming downstairs to her meals, she would greet friends and visitors cordially, and in the evenings she would often join a group of people talking in the lounge or by the fire. She preferred to be with the people she sought out—many of them elderly women who could not walk abroad as she did—rather than with those who sought her.

Alice Edwards, who was a frequent visitor at the Inn, recalls how her husband, Neilson, would talk with Miss Cather about his hunting trips and the animals he saw on them. "I never knew anyone to listen so intently," Mrs. Edwards said. "She just drew things out of people—things she could use in her books."

As we were speaking, Mrs. Edwards' gaze rested on the mountain. "How Willa loved Monadnock! Once she told me that though she had been in the Alps and the Rockies she always came back to Monadnock. It satisfied her, was the way she put it. She was indeed a most wonderful person and friend. But if she did not like anyone, that was different. I remember saying to her once about a young woman who was staying at the Inn, 'Isn't she pretty?' And Willa replied, 'With that little small mean mouth?'"

"Of all the places Willa Cather knew and enjoyed during her life—and places, different kinds of country, were rather a dominant note in her scale of enjoyment—Jaffrey became the one she found best to work in," writes her long-time friend, Edith Lewis. "The fresh, pine-scented woods and pastures, with their multitudinous wild flowers, the gentle skies, the little enclosed fields, had in them nothing of the disturbing, exalting, impelling memories and associations of the past—her own past. Each day there was like an empty canvas, a clean sheet of paper to be filled. She lived with a simple sense of physical well-being, of weather, and of country solitude."[2]

"What was Miss Cather like?" I asked Eleanor Austermann, reaching across an area of surmise to one who held a certain knowledge.

"She was a shy person, deeply kind and by nature considerate," the answer came slowly, as Mrs. Austermann remembered her way back through the years. "She was always sincere and never did she say what she did not mean. She saved herself for her work, and she was a demon for work—all morning she spent in her outdoor studio, and it was every morning, too, except when weather kept her indoors, and then her work went on in her room. Often, in the afternoons, she would take long walks through the country or up Monadnock's slopes. She had a vast correspondence, and much of her free time went in keeping up with it. She wrote notes to people for little things—a small favor shown her, a call made, a time of illness. I shall never forget the letter she wrote to me when our little boy died. There's small comfort anywhere at a time of loss, but the fact that Miss Cather wrote to me from her heart and that she attended his burial in the Jaffrey churchyard on a gray rainy day meant a great deal. She knew, better than many people, that there are things in life one has to live through, but she knew the support that friendship could give."

I would not be shown that letter, and I doubted if anyone but the Austermanns had ever seen it. To Willa Cather, correspondence was as intimate as it was sacred. What went from one heart to another was not for alien eyes to see. After her own death she knew that she could not escape the searching of biographers and critics, but in her will she protected her letters and what they might reveal of her relations with her friends by saying that none were ever to be made public.

"She had her friends in the town and in nearby Peterborough," Mrs. Austermann continued, "and she often went out to tea with them. There were times when some special friend of hers from New York, or elsewhere in her world would come to the Inn for a rest or a recovery from an illness, but as a rule she and Miss Lewis kept to themselves."

"There was a feeling that she withdrew from people, wasn't there."

"Yes, but what seemed to many to be withdrawal was to Willa Cather self-preservation. She was a dedicated person, my husband has always said. People are so much more prone to misunderstand attitudes than to try to understand them; by her reserve and her desire for times of aloneness, Miss Cather was only doing what it was imperative for her to do—save herself for her work."

I thought of Edith Lewis' words about Willa Cather, "The one thing needful for her, as for most artists, was solitude—solitude not only to work in, but to feel and think in."

Perhaps people could not see it, but one wonders if those who criticized Willa Cather then for her devotion to her work and her disciplined retirement from society would think differently now. Every individual works within certain limitations—physique, environment, intellect, culture. A distinction between an artist and an ordinary person may be that the artist knows his limitations and must work within them. As Willa Cather once said, "An artist's limitations are quite as important as his powers; they are a definite asset, not a deficiency . . . and go to form his flavor, his personality . . ."[3]

She did not return to Jaffrey after the hurricane of 1938. Among the hundreds of pines leveled by the wind were those that had formed her outdoor studio, but she never lost touch with the Austermanns, and in letters through the years she often embraced the friendly comfort of the Inn she had come to love so well and the mountain that rose behind it. On an April night in 1947, a few hours after her death, the Austermanns received a telephone call from New York. Willa Cather had asked that she be buried in Jaffrey. Would they see to the arrangements?

Four days later, after a large impressive funeral in New York, Willa Cather's body was laid to rest in the hilltop cemetery in Jaffrey. Only a simple burial service was held at the grave; only a few people attended. Stalwart as ever and serene, Monadnock Mountain looked down on the small scene in the southwest corner of the ancient burying ground. The pale green of new leaves on the trees softened the April light; the cries of returning birds quickened the air.

A plain but solid marker watches over the grave to which many people come every year to read the eloquent words cut in the granite, to remember, and in reverence to rejoice that such a one once lived and continues to live on.

WILLA CATHER
December 7, 1876–April 24, 1947
THE TRUTH AND CHARITY OF HER GREAT SPIRIT
WILL LIVE ON IN THE WORK
WHICH IS HER ENDURING GIFT TO HER
COUNTRY AND ALL ITS PEOPLE
" . . . that is happiness, to be dissolved
into something complete and great."
From *My Ántonia*

"Sanity, magnanimity, love of beauty, enthusiasm for living—these are the outstanding qualities of Willa Cather's work at its best," says Edward Wagenknecht in his *Cavalcade of the American Novel*. The people of Jaffrey, and the Austermanns in particular, know something of what made it possible for that work to come to its perfect fullness.

"Yes, she saved herself for her work," Eleanor Austermann repeated quietly, as if in that way she could best sum up her knowledge of Willa Cather.

NOTES

1. *Letters of Sarah Orne Jewett.* Houghton-Mifflin Co., 1911.
2. *Willa Cather Living,* by Edith Lewis, Knopf, 1953.
3. *Not Under Forty,* by Willa Cather, Knopf, 1936.

New Hampshire Profiles, Dec. 1955, 17–19.

PAUL HORGAN (GEORGE VINCENT O'SHAUGHNESSY)

Paul Horgan (1903–1995) wrote about many subjects in many genres, but he is best known for his histories of the Rio Grande and of Bishop Jean Baptiste Lamy, both of which won Pulitzer Prizes for history. Horgan's interest in the Bishop was piqued by anecdotes told by a family Horgan visited summers in Santa Fe, where he went to escape the heat in Albuquerque. Horgan's hostess had known Lamy as a visitor to her parents' home when she was a child and willingly answered questions for Horgan. Gradually, Horgan came to study documents relating to the Bishop in Catholic archives and libraries. His accidental intrusion upon Cather writing in Santa Fe occurred many years, however, before his own book, *Lamy of Santa Fe: His Life and Times,* appeared in 1975.

From "In Search of the Archbishop"

I cannot now recall any of the anecdotes which my charming and animated little hostess used to tell of Archbishop Lamy. She had seen him in her girlhood. It was taken for granted that he was often a guest in her father's house. He was the most famous man of Santa Fe, and to know him was cause for pride. The power and the charm of his memory came to me through the recollection of the lady who evoked him. Abrupt, impatient, and merciful in the face of my ignorance, she gave him to me. Who built the college? Archbishop Lamy. The convent and its chapel? The archbishop. The hospital? He. The cathedral? Who else? Loved trees and gardens so much that he gave away cuttings and seeds and saplings, and even on occasion went to plant young trees with his own hands for particular friends? Himself. Used to stop and talk to people every day walking in the plaza? Made many trips across the plains in wagons and even once had to fight Indians at a river crossing? Left when he died a feeling of deep sorrow not only among the people of his Church but in everyone else, too—those who knew what he had done for such a vast land, those in whose doorways he used to appear as a friend. She had seen him. I had not. Yet so I came to feel his quality and his effect, and ever afterward, when I went to the cathedral at Santa Fe, or walked along the long wall of the Bishop's Garden, or heard the angelus clapping its rings of sound over the city, he was somewhere behind my thought, my eye, my ear; and one day he would move me to vest him, however poorly, in my word.

But in this preoccupation I was anticipated by others. Without knowing it at the time, I one day intruded inadvertently upon the literary tradition of Archbishop Lamy. It was during the summer several years after my first view of Santa Fe. La Fonda, the modern hotel on the site of the first inn at the end of the Santa Fe Trail, has a number of balconies and porches which catch shadow and seclusion in the manner of the pueblo style with its little setbacks and terraces. One morning quite idly I went through a heavy panelled door leading to one such porch and knew at once that I must go away.

In the deepest corner of the porch were two steamer chairs, and upon them reclined two ladies whose concentration I disturbed. They were busy with papers and pencils. I have an impression of many accessories—notebooks, opened volumes, steamer rugs against the vagrant breezes which feel cool to someone out of the sun in Santa Fe, perhaps a thermos jar containing hot bouillon, possibly a fly whisk, and what else? If I invent it, it is because I have forgotten, and if I have forgotten it is because the nearer of the two ladies turned upon me a light blue regard of such annoyance and distaste at my intrusion that I was gone too quickly to take more than a sweeping impression of where I had been. But I was there long enough to recognize that it was Miss Willa Cather whom I had interrupted at work with her secretary, and I was already so devoted to her work that my chagrin rose equal to my respect. Decades later, and myself the victim of countless interruptions of my own working situations, I know acutely what it may have cost Miss Cather to recover through deep breaths in the mind that wonderful, removed, beautifully lost sense of utmost communion with one's subject which every artist must develop for himself every time he works, and which I had shattered for her.

What was she working on that morning? I did not know, and I cannot now say, but a year later her novel about Juan Bautista Lamy was published. She called it *Death Comes for the Archbishop*. When I saw her that day—it was the only time I ever saw her and I always regretted that I never had the opportunity to tell her how sorry I was for my transgression—she was working only a hundred yards from his cathedral, whose humble beauties she was the first to recognize. I remember the eagerness and excitement with which I awaited my first edition copy of her Lamy novel in the following year, 1927.

Catholic Historical Review 46 (January 1961): 412–13.

TRUMAN CAPOTE

Truman Capote (1924–1984) published his first novel *Other Voices, Other Rooms* about six years after the incident he relates in the following anecdote. He wrote many articles and stories that combined his reportorial skills with his ability to render the fine line between reality and dream. The best known of these efforts is his "nonfiction novel" *In Cold Blood* (1966), based on a grotesque series of murders in Kansas. In his memoir, *Music for Chameleons*, Capote admits both that he considers his "journalism as an art form" and that he has placed himself "center stage" in this book that tells stories about the people he has known. He includes Cather in a section devoted to outstanding conversationalists, mentioning her with others such as Marianne Moore, Isak Dinesen—"a *conversational* seductress"—and Diana Vreeland—"Abbess of High Fashion"—a thought-provoking mélange.

From Music for Chameleons

When I was eighteen I met the person whose conversation has impressed me the most, perhaps because the person in question is the one who has most impressed me. It happened as follows:

In New York, on East Seventy-ninth Street, there is a very pleasant shelter known as the New York Society Library, and during 1942 I spent many afternoons there researching a book I intended writing but never did. Occasionally, I saw a woman there whose appearance rather mesmerized me—her eyes especially: blue, the pale brilliant cloudless blue of prairie skies. But even without this singular feature, her face was interesting—firm-jawed, handsome, a bit androgynous. Pepper-salt hair parted in the middle. Sixty-five, thereabouts. A lesbian? Well, yes.

One January day I emerged from the library into the twilight to find a heavy snowfall in progress. The lady with the blue eyes, wearing a nicely cut black coat with a sable collar, was waiting at the curb. A gloved, taxi-summoning hand was poised in the air, but there were no taxis. She looked at me and smiled and said: "Do you think a cup of hot chocolate would help? There's a Longchamps around the corner."

She ordered hot chocolate; I asked for a "very" dry martini. Half seriously, she said, "Are you old enough?"

"I've been drinking since I was fourteen. Smoking, too."

"You don't look more than fourteen now."

"I'll be nineteen next September." Then I told her a few things: that I was from New Orleans, that I'd published several short stories, that I wanted to be a writer and was working on a novel. And she wanted to know what American writers I liked. "Hawthorne, Henry James, Emily Dickinson . . ." "No, living." Ah, well, hmm, let's see: how difficult, the rivalry factor being what it is, for one contemporary author, or would-be author, to confess admiration for another. At last I said, "Not Hemingway—a really dishonest man, the closet everything. Not Thomas Wolfe—all that purple upchuck, of course, he isn't living. Faulkner, sometimes: *Light in August.* Fitzgerald, sometimes: *Diamond as Big as the Ritz, Tender Is the Night.* I really like Willa Cather. Have you read *My Mortal Enemy*?"

With no particular expression, she said, "Actually, I wrote it."

I had seen photographs of Willa Cather—long-ago ones, made perhaps in the early twenties. Softer, homelier, less elegant than my companion. Yet I knew instantly that she *was* Willa Cather, and it was one of the *frissons* of my life. I began to babble about her books like a schoolboy—my favorites: *A Lost Lady, The Professor's House, My Ántonia.* It wasn't that I had anything in common with her as a writer, I would never have chosen for myself her sort of subject matter, or tried to emulate her style. It was just that I considered her a great artist. As good as Flaubert.

We became friends; she read my work and was always a fair and helpful judge. She was full of surprises. For one thing, she and her lifelong friend, Miss Lewis, lived in a spacious, charmingly furnished Park Avenue apartment—somehow, the notion of Miss Cather living in an apartment on Park Avenue seemed incongruous with her Nebraska upbringing, with the simple, rather elegiac nature of her novels. Secondly, her principal interest was not literature, but music. She went to concerts constantly, and almost all her closest friends were musical personalities, particularly Yehudi Menuhin and his sister Hepzibah.

Like all authentic conversationalists, she was an excellent listener, and when it was her turn to talk, she was never garrulous, but crisply pointed. Once she told me I was overly sensitive to criticism. The truth was that she was more sensitive to critical slights than I; any disparaging reference to her work caused a decline in spirits. When I pointed this out to her, she said: "Yes, but aren't we always seeking out our own vices in others and reprimanding them for such possessions? I'm alive. I have clay feet. Very definitely."

New York: Random House, 1980. 253–56.

A Mature Professional

In her daily life, Willa Cather encountered many different kinds of people, often professionals in their own sharply defined worlds. Many of them found even a short relationship with Cather rewarding. In a short review of the posthumous *The Old Beauty and Others*, Lorna R. F. Birtwell remarks of Cather, "Her reticence became proverbial. And yet what a warm and hearty human being she became among just people." Although asked more than once to teach at Bread Loaf, Cather taught there only one summer. Birtwell's article provides a vignette of Cather in that rare role as teacher. Marion King was one of the many librarians whom Cather came to know over her lifetime. Mary Ellen Chase was a professor at Smith; thus, her article reveals what someone responsible for teaching literature thought about Cather. Alfred Knopf, of course, was her longtime publisher, major business associate, and personal friend.

LORNA R. F. BIRTWELL

In the summer of 1922, after a busy year of traveling and a couple bouts of serious illness, Cather taught at Bread Loaf. Her old friend Dorothy Canfield Fisher was instrumental in arranging this. After *One of Ours* was published and Cather had won the Pulitzer, she probably did not need the money as much as she did at the time she agreed to teach at Bread Loaf. She had already begun to protect herself from spending time and energy with the public, saving herself for the intense creativity she showed over the next few years. She wrote *A Lost Lady*, *The Professor's House*, *My Mortal Enemy*, and *Death Comes for the Archbishop* all within the following four

Willa Cather on her sixty-third birthday. Courtesy of the Nebraska State Historical Society, Willa Cather Pioneer Memorial Collection.

years. It would appear from Birtwell's article, written for the magazine of the Young Women's Christian Association of the U.S.A., that Cather could have been in great demand as a workshop teacher had she chosen to accept such invitations.

Remembering Willa Cather

A little fire snapped briskly in the fireplace, for even summer mornings can be chilly in the mountains. At one side, leaning on the mantel with a manuscript in his hand, stood a tall young man. At the other, seated in a low wicker chair, was a sturdy handsome woman speaking apparently into the fireplace. Behind her a group of youngish people leaned forward intently. Outside the windows was the soft rolling sweep of the Green Mountains. This was the creative writing class of Professor Whicher of Amherst, held in the living room of his cottage at the Breadloaf School of English, and the critic was "Cather" (to rhyme with gather), so named by Professor Whicher's little son, Jackie, who had taken her on as a rather special friend and whose shrill pipe demanding "Cather" might be heard at every meal across the Inn's dining room tables. Cather was with us for a few weeks, as several other celebrities had been, to give a series of talks on writing. Her informal criticisms in the creative writing class were undertaken purely out of her generous interest in a group of young aspirants whom she was kind enough to take with a seriousness almost equal to their own.

After Professor Whicher had finished reading an anonymous manuscript, Cather would comment. She had stipulated the back-to-the-class position to avoid embarrassment to herself or the student whose work was under discussion. As it was, I can quite remember the coral ears of a promising stripling when the trite verbiage of his story was remarked. He had written about a bride in the kitchen of her new home, but never, never was the reader allowed to suppose that it was a mere kitchen in which the young woman, whom he had already described as "a delicate flower," was functioning. It was her "holy of holies," her "inner sanctum"; it was "the scene of ancient household rites." Miss Cather's kindly, chuckling criticism of this amateurishness led to a discussion, far from amateurish, on live diction, dialogue, and the effective use of dialect.

Another yearning bit about a musical virtuoso caused Cather to observe how very dangerous it was for a young writer to get a violin into the story. She cited her own case. Those who have read of the old Bohemian immigrant, Shimerda, in *My Ántonia*, will remember his suicide in the harsh prairie winter. In a youthful collegiate story about the same character, she had made of him a former first violinist in the opera at Prague. Between that lush story and the tragic, beaten old man of *My Ántonia* who did, indeed, love the cities and the dances and the songs, there was a lifetime of artistic evolution.

Cather's lectures were held at four o'clock in the little auditorium of the Inn so that the whole school could attend. They were made with effort, hewn out of her artistic sincerity, out of her desire to give us as truly as possible the heart of the matter. They were not glib; they were not funny, except as laughter bubbled up spontaneously from time to time.

It was at a time when America was just starting on its literary renascence, on a beginning of its own cultural evaluation. (Robert Frost was to continue the next summer the same deep-going criticism of poetry that Miss Cather was giving us on the novel.) There was a great turning over of the material of fiction, of the element of plot—Miss Cather had been accused of being weak in the manipulation of plot—of the difference between the synthetic, "formula-made," popular product and the novel with an inner life and growth of its own. She told us how Sara Orne Jewett [*sic*], whose exquisite stories of Maine are now too seldom taken down from the shelf of classics, first directed her away from the purely artificial, if polished sort of thing toward stories of her own pioneer country as *O Pioneers!, The Song of the Lark* and *My Ántonia*.

The first two books had been given scant attention, by most critics, but Mencken had proclaimed *My Ántonia* the most beautiful book ever written in America and Heywood Broun was making almost daily mention of it in his column. And other critics were catching fire.

One of Ours, a novel of the first World War, was due to come out that fall. It did not jibe, however, with the bitter mood of the young writers who had experienced the war and was given little praise by the critics.

Miss Cather was then already working on *A Lost Lady*. With her exacting craftsmanship, her books were spaced two and three years apart. A little volume of poems, *April Twilights*, was being reprinted too. At this time, 1922, Miss Cather had before her twenty-five more years of artistic achievement, and, as I think of it, it seems to me that she had reached a Great Divide.

With *Death Comes for the Archbishop*, a serene mountain peak of literary distinction, the toilsome but glorious ascent had been made; the slope of ripened reputation lay before. Yet despite all its sureness and conscious mastery this period lacked, I feel, some of the vitality of those years of struggle, of which she makes Mrs. Ferguesson say in "The Best Years" (from *The Old Beauty and Others*), "Our best years are when we're working hardest and going right ahead, when we can hardly see our way out."

From that time on Miss Cather's novels dealt with evocations from the historical past, although a book of short stories, *Obscure Destinies*, among which is "Neighbor Rosicky," considered by the author to be her best piece of work, and a novelette, *My Mortal Enemy*, still give us scenes and persons from her own life span. But I have thought, or rather wondered, if, when Miss Cather named her novel of the early French settlement in Quebec, *Shadows on the Rock*, she was not tacitly admitting that such evocations must be "shadowy." In this book the shadows are exquisite, indeed, and out of the night of the past, the universal human things shine like stars in the cold northern sky.

Dorothy Canfield Fisher has said of Miss Cather's work that it always has within it the theme of pioneer America. If this be accepted to mean pioneer, not only of new land but of cultural frontiers, it would seem to be true. No one has a deeper sense of the richness of the European heritage than Willa Cather. This is, in a way, her theme in "Neighbor Rosicky," in which the narrow, provincial prejudice against the 'foreigner' is overcome in little Polly, young Rudolf's wife, by her love for her father-in-law, a love which stretches her cultural horizon.

Miss Cather's own special love, a compensatory one perhaps, is the ordered beauty and decorum of French tradition. Unlike Sinclair Lewis, Dreiser, Anderson, she did not reject Main Street with angry vehemence: but she had her own revolt. She loved, one feels, the ugly, comfortable opulence of old New York and has evoked it memorably: the soft lilac sky of spring above Diana when she stood atop the old Madison Square Garden at Twenty-third Street; the glow of rose-shaded lamps through the falling snow when the old Astor sprawled in brownstone where the Empire State now stands; the Opera House on a night of Wagner. The men, too, she sang, the titans who built the railroads out into her pioneer country, the banker, the powerful, industrious, self-assured, feeling their weight and worth as new Americans, sensing little, if at all, of the industrial battleground they were preparing.

The novel which I still regard, in spite of imperfections, as the most vibrant with life and genius is *The Song of the Lark*. It was re-issued a few years ago with a new preface by Miss Cather. The book's heroine is Thea Kronborg, a Swedish American opera singer; it portrays the consecrated struggle of every great artist to get away from the cheap and tawdry, the bribes of shallow success, into the depth of his own genius. In *The Song of the Lark*, it seems to me, all the themes of Miss Cather's work fuse into a glowing whole, sometimes almost molten in its passion, sufficient to project into the air a lifetime of creativeness. The young student Thea, poor and beaten down by her work as accompanist in the studio of a "fashionable" musician, is sent by one who values her to recuperate on a ranch near the ruins of the cliff-dwelling Indians. Among these ruins, her mind and body steeped in sun, she comes to certain understandings, "ethics of the dust," from the fragments of pottery that the Ancient People had left behind them:

This care expended upon vessels that could not hold food or water any the better for the additional labor put upon them made her heart go out to these ancient potters. . . . Food, fire, and water, and something else—even here in this crack of the world so far back in the night of the past! Down here at the beginning that painful thing was stirring, the seed of sorrow and of so much delight. . . . When Thea took her bath at the bottom of the canyon in the sunny pool behind the screen of cottonwoods, she sometimes felt as if the water must have sovereign properties from having been the object of so much service and devotion. . . . One morning something flashed through her mind that made her draw herself up and stand still until the water had quite dried upon her flushed skin. The stream and the broken pottery: what was any art but an effort to make a sheath, a mold, in which to imprison the shining elusive element that is life itself—life hurrying past us and running away, too strong to stop, too sweet to lose? The Indian women had held it in their jars. In the sculpture she had seen in the art museum, it had been caught in a flash of arrested motion. In singing one made a vessel of one's nose and throat, caught the stream in a scale of natural intervals. . . . Suddenly an eagle, tawny and of great size, sailed over the cleft across the arch of sky. He dropped for a moment into the gulf between the walls, then wheeled and mounted until his plumage was so steeped in light that he looked like a golden bird. . . . Thea stood rigid on the stone shelf, straining her eyes after the strong tawny flight. O eagle of eagles! Endeavor, achievement, desire, glorious striving of human art! From a cleft in the heart of the world she saluted it. . . . It had come all the way; when men lived in caves, it was there. A vanished race; but along the trails, in the stream, under the spreading cactus, there still glittered in the sun the bits of their frail clay vessels, fragments of their desire.

The summer weeks at Breadloaf ended; the visitors had gone. And the students most ungratefully put on a review burlesquing their mentors. Once more Edwin Markham tossed his white beard to the hills and made them reverberate with the sonorities of his poetry; Richard Burton twiddled the broad black ribbon of his eyeglasses; Louis Untermeyer spoke drolleries; Katherine Lee Bates trundled across the stage followed by her airedale, Tansy—Tansy brought down the house. We had loved them all, but we had fun.

Only one figure was lacking. No one could be found who could, or would, take off "Cather." It just didn't seem to be among the possibilities. Perhaps no one could throw back her head and laugh so richly.

To be inimitable! It is the hallmark of the great artist. The verdict arrived at by the Breadloaf Summer School at play will, one is sure, be the serious judgment of American letters as it takes Willa Cather into its lasting heritage.

Women's Press (Nov. 1948): 8–12.

MARION KING

For over four decades, Marion King (1902–1998) was a librarian at the New York Society Library, New York's oldest library. The library lay on the path Willa Cather often walked for exercise, and since King also liked to walk, their paths often crossed. Cather and King struck up a respectful relationship, as King did with numerous patrons.

From Books and People: Five Decades of New York's Oldest Library

For some time I had been seeing a new person in the neighborhood, a rather short, stocky lady in an apple-green coat and matching green pork-pie felt hat, which she alternated with a similar habit in red. One day, passing at close range, I recognized a famous face and began to hope that she would discover the library.

Of course she soon did, with opening words as characteristic as they were unforgettable. "I'd like to subscribe here if I may," she said. "My name is Cather. I'm by way of being a writer."

She had a husky, rather boyish voice that came in little gusts. Her hair was brown, but her fresh pink and white skin and large blue eyes gave an effect of blondness. She was sturdy and wholesome looking.

She had given up her apartment in Bank Street and was living at the Hotel Grosvenor, missing her own books she told us. We had heard a good deal about her seclusion and reserve, and we treated her with an incurious matter-of-factness that won her confidence. She began to come in often, to look over rows of books and sometimes sigh. "It's easy enough to see what you *don't* want to read."

After a while I would venture a suggestion. She liked *Miss Mole* and came back for E. H. Young's other books but found them disappointing. Once I gave her *Miss Hinch*, an excellent short tale by Henry Sydnor Harrison, and when I asked her if she liked it, she said with a smile, "I did indeed. I bought that story for *McClure's*." I offered her only the straightforward, the veracious, and the sound. I never tried her with my oblique fancies, The *Innocent Voyage, The Flying Yorkshireman, His Monkey Wife.*

Soon, when we met as she took her morning exercise, she would turn back and walk to the library door with me. My memory of Miss Cather is filled with a succession of those five-minute chats—about this and that, books of course, green vegetables once, which she wanted only in their season, and expertly cooked, not "covered with cold water and slowly introduced to heat," incompetent Congressmen, about whom she was quite vehement, the Christmas boxes she loved to make up for her Nebraska farm friends. She asked me to guess what one gift they liked above everything else. It was large white linen handkerchiefs.

Some time later, when she wanted an apartment again and found one on upper Park Avenue, she told of sitting alone in it for hours—I almost feel she said all day and night—to test its quiet, before signing the lease. Legend has it that in Bank Street she rented the apartment above hers, just to keep it empty—oh, enviable luxury!

When she was writing *Shadows on the Rock,* she came often to consult old herbals, old maps, and histories of Paris, before finally going there. She told me that book had seemed a disappointment to her friends, who sent her many scolding letters. They had wanted something else, not that. But she would always be grateful to it for carrying her over a hard stretch of life. Her mother was in her last illness, and Miss Cather traveled with the manuscript many times across the country to see her.

I think the book, lovely as it was, was the first signal of diminishment. The power if not the beauty began slowly to run out with the sands of her vitality. To me "Old Mrs. Harris" in *Obscure Destinies* was the last splendid thrust of her pen. When I met her the morning after it was published and told her how wonderful I thought it was, "I rather liked that myself," she said.

Miss Roseboro', who had been her devoted friend from the old *McClure's* days, described her once as having a heart like a great anthracite furnace. When V. R. was very ill at the last, Miss Cather asked me to find out quietly and let her know if there was any need of money, but there wasn't. I heard from someone else—not her!—that she had paid off many of the mortgages on those Nebraska farms.

She was a sunlit peak of that decade, and she stayed with us until the end of her life, two decades later.

New York: Macmillan, 1954. 208–10.

MARY ELLEN CHASE

In a presentation to the American Association of University Women, Mary Ellen Chase (1887–1973), a professor at Smith College and a well-known short story writer and lecturer, called Willa Cather "the greatest American novelist." In an interview given to the *Monkato Daily Free Press* in 1929, Chase asserted that "there are two measures of literature, one the universality of the theme, the other the excellence of the workmanship." Chase said she valued books that give the reader "lines that sing in the mind for hours after reading them." This was the test of great "workmanship." Chase quotes one of those lines for many of Cather's readers: "The precious, the incommunicable past."

From "Five Literary Portraits"

Willa Cather. At fifty Willa Cather was a handsome woman, perhaps even beautiful. Of only average height and without doubt overweight, she had certain arresting features which one never forgot. Her complexion was clear and smooth, not like Dresden china, that tiresome comparison, but rather like the outside of any well-washed plate just off a white colour, perhaps like cream. Her face was startling in its absence of lines. Her mouth was generous and good-humoured. Her eyes were her most memorable feature, long rather than round eyes and of a clear blue, neither dark nor light.

She always looked directly at one with a flattering expression of deepest interest, which, I am sure, was a mannerism rather than any sign of genuine concern. In spite of the efforts of biographers who like to stress her outgoing nature, she was not a person who craved for or who sought many human relations. The people she most cared for were not those whom she met, but, instead, those whom she created: Mr. Shimerda and Old Rosicky, Ántonia and Father Latour. She had great physical energy and vitality. When I knew her on Grand Manan Island in the autumn of 1929, she spent hours each day in clearing away undergrowth near her home there with an axe. Her hands were broad and strong, and she made excellent use of them. She used them in talking, too, spreading out her thumbs and fingers as far as they could go, raising her wide-open palms backward toward her shoulders in moments of interest or excitement.

At just that time she was about to go to Quebec to garner material for
Shadows on the Rock.

"That's just what the book is going to be," she told me. "Shadows. They
mean far more to me than mere substance. It won't have a trace of what is
called *movement* or *suspense.* It will just have people and a lot of *things.*"

She was at her best when she talked about writing, that of others more
than of her own. Among novelists she admired Flaubert; Balzac, though
she thought he "over-furnished" his books; Hawthorne; Sarah Orne Jewett,
whom she had known well. I remember most vividly her ideas of design and
pattern as opposed to situation and plot.

"I can't write plots," she said once. "Sometimes I wish I could, but we
have to do with what we have. I don't see life in terms of action. Persons like
me who see it in terms of thought and imagery would best keep away from
suspense. It's design they want, not conflict."

All who admire *My Ántonia* know precisely what she meant. That lovely
book is held together only by design: its pattern, the recurring red grass of
the Nebraska prairies. This red, waving grass comes again and again into
her simple, spare pages. The little boy, Jim Burden, sees it upon his arrival
from Virginia, and to him it is the vast new country moving on and on. The
servant girls on their picnic see it, bent by the strong wind. It blows over
Mr. Shimerda's grave at the crossroads. To Jim Burden upon his return after
many years to see Ántonia and her sons, it is the symbol of "the precious,
the incommunicable past" which he and Ántonia share.

Shadows on the Rock is given whatever form it possesses by those "things":
the wooden beaver which the little boy, Jacques, brings for Cecile's crèche;
her silver cup which he envies because it has her very own name upon it; the
old French candlesticks, which lend dignity to dinner in the Auclairs' simple
house; the parsley, *le persil,* which is never allowed to freeze; the glass fruit
of Count Frontenac; the daisies "drifted like snow in the tall meadow grass"
of the Ile d'Orleans; the five sea-battered French ships, beating up the St.
Lawrence from home.

Like Charles Lamb, Willa Cather "knew the genius of places," that inde-
finable spiritual atmosphere which certain places possess for those who understand them. For her: Avignon; East Jaffrey in the shadow of Monadnock,
where she is buried; Santa Fe; Red Cloud; Grand Manan.

She deplored letters from strangers about her books and avoided answering them as much as she could. Certain of her chroniclers deny this. They
say she answered thousands with vast pleasure. Perhaps she did; but she said
once to me:

"The happiest moment of my whole life was when a suitcase full of unanswered mail fell down the Grand Canyon!"

Massachusetts Review 3, no. 3 (1962): 511–13.

ALFRED A. KNOPF

Alfred A. Knopf (1892–1984) enjoyed a personal and professional friendship with Willa Cather from the time he was a twenty-seven-year-old ambitious young publisher interested in excellent writing and artistic typography until her death in 1947. When Cather decided to leave Houghton Mifflin and its editor, Ferris Greenslet, who was also a friend and remained so, she chose well. But whereas Greenslet was her publisher when she was a younger and newer writer, Knopf seemed a publisher more appropriate for the increasingly ambitious Cather. In his autobiography, Greenslet recalls his meeting Cather: "a fresh-faced, broad-browed, plain-speaking young woman, standing her ground with a singular solidity—Willa Sibert Cather!" (116). Knopf, however, like Cather, was a connoisseur of fine music, fine food, fine fabrics, and gracious living. A description of him from a *New Yorker* "Profile" sounds much like that of a male Cather: "A man of commanding presence, compelling mustache, and resolute practical mien, he is plainly contemptuous of tumbrils." His tastes, too, echo Cather's: "his liking for the better by-gone days when he enjoyed, among other things . . . spacious, well-staffed houses and uncrowded streets; and of books published because they contained good writing and/or valuable information." Knopf and his wife, Blanche, became close social friends with Cather. In a *New Yorker* column entitled "Flair is the Word," Lillian Hellman reported that Knopf said of Cather: "she was a regular dinner party on the phone." The comment belies partially the stories of Cather hating the telephone and being brusque with people. It appears that for those special few, like the Knopfs, Cather could be highly captivating socially and still insist on her own terms professionally.

Publishing Willa Cather

Here you may ask if we didn't steal Willa Cather from Houghton Mifflin. We did not. She simply walked unannounced into our two-room offices on West Forty-second Street one day, introduced herself, and was astonished that I knew her work and had read her most recent novel, *My Ántonia*. She brought me *Youth and the Bright Medusa*. She didn't ask for an advance then—or ever.

As Willa Cather was so different in so many respects from any author I know or know about today, I will speak of her at some length. She was a lady of a very special kind—now all but extinct. Loyalty was one of her great qualities; if she was on your side it was almost impossible for you to do anything that she regarded as wrong. And if she was not on your side you simply couldn't do anything of which she approved. She left a most unusual will, but I know it expressed what she strongly believed. It forbids motion pictures or dramatizations to be made of any of her books. She used to say to me that if she had wanted to write a play or a motion picture she would have written a play or a motion-picture script. But she didn't—she wrote a novel or a short story or a novelette. The will also forbids the publication of any of her letters. She had, to be sure, once allowed a motion picture to be made of one of her best-known novels, *A Lost Lady*. But the experience was so disillusioning that she determined never to risk its repetition. One day Benjamin H. Stern, our close friend and long-time lawyer, who also represented her for many years, told me in his office that he had an offer from Hollywood for her that ran into six figures. Ben's office was on the thirty-fifth floor of the French Building, and I immediately told him that I would as soon jump out the window as mention this offer to Miss Cather. I added that I thought, if he wished to retain her good will, that he should not mention it to her either. He didn't.

She also refused to permit any cheap editions of her books to be published. Here again, she once made an exception and allowed *Death Comes for the Archbishop* to be included in the Modern Library. But as soon as this contract expired she would not permit us to renew it. One day Ferris Greenslet, himself a man of letters, who directed the editorial work at Houghton Mifflin and had published her first four novels, came to my office to tell me that he had a proposition which would enable us—and Miss Cather—as he put it, to clip coupons from bonds for years to come. His plan was to include some of her books in the celebrated Riverside Press series of school and college editions of classics. She refused this offer out of hand, telling me that she did not want boys and girls to grow up to hate her because they had been forced to read her books when they were students.

Like many intelligent authors, she had a shrewd idea of the relative value of her own work, and when she brought me the manuscript of *Death Comes for the Archbishop* she said that our son would one day be paying royalties on it to her niece, and asked for special terms. But she was not greedy: she wanted an increase of one percent in the royalty, and refused to accept this on any later book.

She was opposed to book clubs, and for many, many years refused to permit us to offer them anything of hers. She said she felt most strongly that only people who really *wanted* to read her books should be asked to buy them. How she came to make an exception in the case of *Shadows on the Rock* is a small story in itself. The steady refusal of so important and popular a novelist to permit any of her work to be offered to members of the Book-of-the-Month Club was, naturally, a matter of some concern to the Club's management. Harry Scherman, with shrewdness that was not uncharacteristic, had one of his judges write a very long letter to Miss Cather explaining the workings of the Club and the advantages which it brought to authors. The judge selected to write this letter was Dorothy Canfield. She and Miss Cather had been friends since they had been undergraduates together at the University of Nebraska, where Dorothy's father was Chancellor. Miss Cather in her usual way brought the letter to me and asked my advice saying that while she hadn't changed her mind about book clubs she hesitated to offend Henry Seidel Canby, the chairman, and the other judges.

At that time the retail book trade was conducting a vehement, though ineffective, campaign against book clubs. I decided to telegraph each of our salesmen to ask the most important bookseller he visited that day whether or not we should let the Book-of-the-Month Club have *Shadows on the Rock*. I naturally assumed that these booksellers would live up to their public protestations and support Miss Cather's position. I couldn't have been more mistaken. With one exception, they all said that they would like to see the book taken by the Club because this would increase their sale of it. The buyer in a department store—a very small and unimportant outlet—voted in favor of what he thought was the position of the entire retail book trade. It was this refusal to sacrifice immediate sales for a longer objective that made the victory of the book clubs inevitable in this battle. Thus I remember visiting a favorite midwestern shop whose owner was always denouncing book clubs and finding right in the middle of his store—indeed in front of his own desk—a big display of the latest Literary Guild selection.

In the fall of 1921 Paul R. Reynolds, the dean of New York literary agents, wrote me that a publisher had told him that in his opinion there was no reason why Cather's work shouldn't be as well known as that of Edith Wharton, and that he would like a chance to make it as well known as Edith Wharton's. Reynolds asked if Miss Cather would not like to meet this man. I sent her Reynolds' letter, and she returned it without comment, simply writing in the margin: "I wonder who?" Nothing came of this proposal.

But I would not like to give you the impression that she was not interested in what happened to her books after we published them—and, indeed, before. She concerned herself about their typography, their bindings, their wrappers, and the copy that appeared on the wrappers. She followed our advertising closely—only once in all the years we worked with her did she complain that there was not enough of it. She watched our copy and objected when she found it, as she sometimes did, "dull and uninteresting." Then as likely as not she would sketch out and send us the sort of advertisement that she felt did her work justice. In the case of *Death Comes for the Archbishop*, she supplied the text for the wrapper and we printed exactly what she gave us. She said, wisely, that a jacket should tell readers what they want to know—something about how and why the book was written, for that, she said, is what strangers usually write authors letters about.

With it all she was extremely modest and always showed the greatest pleasure when Blanche and I wrote or wired her enthusiastically after we had read a new manuscript. She told me that *Shadows on the Rock* was the only book she had ever felt nervous about, and that it was a great comfort to her that Blanche and I and other people in the office had confidence in it.

In August 1931, when *Shadows on the Rock* had sold over 65,000 copies, I wrote her: "I am glad that you feel as you do about the New York reviews. I am pretty sure that it has taken the better part of four years for most of these people to become convinced of the greatness of the *Archbishop*. I suppose when your next novel comes out they will be writing what a grand book *Shadows on the Rock* was."

She had written me that the New York reviews had not disturbed her and recalled that when the *Archbishop* had come out the reviews, with few exceptions, were very nasty. Indeed, she said that the worst reviews she ever got were for *My Ántonia*—that in the whole country there were only three enthusiastic ones—that only *A Lost Lady* and *Youth and the Bright Medusa* had had good reviews. In fairness I must add that *Shadows on the Rock* did get some very good notices, especially those written by Governor Wilbur L. Cross of Connecticut (formerly a very distinguished professor at Yale), by Fanny Butcher in *The Chicago Tribune* (she was ever faithful to Cather's work), and by the reviewers in *The San Francisco Chronicle* and *The Atlantic*. And in 1934 when she was traveling in Europe I wrote her that "*Lucy Gayheart* pursues the even tenor of her way—without benefit, as usual, of the reviews." And a little later when the sale had nearly reached 50,000 copies: "I hope you don't read many of the American reviews—vicious is the only word to be applied to most of them. I almost wish we had sent out no copies of the book for review at all."

So I think another generalization holds: reviews alone don't sell books.

Bulletin of the New York Public Library 68, no.9 (1964): 560–63.

Friendships

3

In her book *You Just Don't Understand*, Deborah Tannen observes that "When people talk about the details of daily lives, it is gossip; when they write about them, it is literature: short stories and novels." By her own admission, Cather was always interested in news about the people she knew. For her, those details led to a greater understanding of the characters she put into her novels and into the ways in which she framed the novels. She was, as George Seibel said, "always wondering." Learning more details about Cather's life from those people who knew her gives critics one more tool in building a foundation upon which to stand to gain greater insight into the house of her fiction.

The reminiscences in this section are primarily by those who considered Cather as friend, mentor, or spiritual companion, although there is also one by a Bohemian "neighbor" and one by a member of the Cather family.

In the Neighborhood

Carrie Miner Sherwood and her sister Irene Miner Weisz were constant correspondents and provided regular stops on her travels all Cather's life. Weisz lived in Chicago, so Cather could stop over on any train ride east or west, and Sherwood married a local banker and lived in Red Cloud until her death. Sherwood was not only an old friend but also an intimate connection for Cather with Red Cloud and the people and country around it. She, her sister, and copies of the local newspaper, which Sherwood had sent to her in New York, kept Cather apprised of the conditions of the country and of the marriages, births, deaths, needs, and dreams of the people she had known during her years in Red Cloud.

Newspapers were important to Cather's start in becoming a writer and an independent person, and they have been important in keeping her reputation before the public, especially, but not exclusively, the Midwestern public. The recognition of her talent began early. When Cather was twelve, the following notice appeared in the *Webster County Argus*:

Children's day at the Baptist church last Sunday was celebrated with every evidence of enjoyment. The church was elegantly decorated with flowers arranged in all kinds of shapes by the young ladies and children. In the evening a very large congregation assembled and were pleasantly entertained for an hour by the songs, readings, recitations, etc. of as beautiful a band of little ones as can be found anywhere. The recitation by Miss Willa Cathers [sic] was particularly noticiable on account of its delivery, which showed the little Miss to be the possessor of extraordinary self control and talent.

The work of Red Cloud citizens in providing support for Cather studies is invaluable. Groups devoted to authors often provide the base of devoted archival work that sustains literary and critical studies. The Willa Cather Pioneer Memorial, centered in Red Cloud, fostered by such people as Carrie Miner Sherwood and Mildred R. Bennett, has been doing that service for Cather. In addition, the WCPM has preserved many of the sites that served as prototypes for the settings in Cather's novels.

The following three newspaper articles appeared when local residents were building interest in archival material in the area and when it became crucial to have a record of memories of Cather's last living girlhood friend in Red Cloud—and one of her closest friends for over fifty years—Mrs. Sherwood.

The final piece in this group of reminiscences is a personal letter relating a visit Cather made to Frank Sadilek, a Bohemian "neighbor," to gather material or details, in this case, names for people in her stories.

DEAN TERRILL

For many years, Dean Terrill (1925–) was a full-time roving reporter for the *Lincoln Journal*. His beat was Southeast and Central Nebraska, so Red Cloud was part of his regular territory, and he wrote numerous stories about Cather. "It was nice to have a celebrity in the area," he said. "Cather was and still is good copy. I don't think the market is saturated yet."[1] Carrie Miner Sherwood must have been "good copy," too, for many people interviewed her for radio, press, and video.

Willa, Carrie Shared Human Story

Call her a Willa Cather character and right away you're in trouble with Mrs. Carrie Miner Sherwood.

Proud as she is of her companionship with the late Nebraska author, the saucy 92-year-old insists there is only one real portrait in all Cather writings. That was of her own mother, Mrs. James L. Miner, re-created as the Mrs. Harling of *My Ántonia*.

That book, among the writer's first but the one she considered her best, was dedicated to Mrs. Sherwood and a younger sister, now of Chicago. A half dozen autographed copies still sit on her shelves, part of the complete works reminding her of a lifetime friendship.

"There's no question but what some incidents of my life appear," she explained with sharpness belying her age. "But there must be a sameness of character to achieve universal appeal. That's what Willie saw in any of us."

Carrie Miner in riding outfit. Courtesy of the Nebraska State Historical Society, Willa Cather Pioneer Memorial Collection.

"Willie" is Mrs. Sherwood's pronunciation and the spelling used by the author Willa herself in their decades of correspondence. The nickname, along with original book sketches and pictures hanging from the walls, hints at the women's closeness.

"She was a dual personality, even as a child seeming older than her real age," the bright little lady continued. "For example, I was four years older, so my two younger sisters were her playmates, while I was her companion."

The Miners and Cathers, both Webster County pioneer families, lived a block apart in Red Cloud. But obviously it was more than a childhood acquaintance which drew Miss Cather back for frequent visits until her death in 1947.

A reason for their deep friendship is hinted at in the inscription penned on the cover of *The Song of the Lark* as early as 1916. "To Carrie Miner Sherwood, my fellow student of human stories," it reads — and this brings more tears to the aging widow than any other memento.

Mrs. Sherwood visited the writer twice in New York after she became famous and is certain she never lost her nostalgia for Nebraska.

"She came back at least half a dozen times planning to retire here in town, but just never got it done," she continued.

The Red Cloud woman was an important source of information for her neighbor, Mrs. Mildred Bennett, in writing the book, *The World of Willa Cather*. She is also vice president of the Willa Cather Pioneer Memorial.

Her father and husband founded the bank now known as People's Webster County Bank. She is still a director, and sons Miner and Phil are president and chairman of the board.

Was Miss Cather's success a surprise to her old schoolmate?

Not really, she remarked, except she had anticipated Willie might do best working with plays. This was her first love as a youngster — and Mrs. Sherwood even recalled the author's part in a benefit play for victims of the 1888 blizzard.

Determined never to exploit her friendship with the renowned writer, the elderly woman acknowledged that this sometimes conflicts with her desire to publicize Miss Cather. But on one point she has been stubbornly insistent — no pictures.

She never had a photo taken with her friend, she remarked, and will not let their relationship weaken her now in this regard.

"Any photograph of me now," she rationalized, "wouldn't show the same person who knew Willie."

Lincoln Evening Journal, 1 Feb. 1962, 12.

TOM ALLAN

Tom Allan (1918–   )is another Nebraska roving reporter: "the best and most re-warding job on earth," he said, when interviewed after he had been at the Omaha World-Herald for fifty years. Like his counterpart in Lincoln, Dean Terrill, Allan interviewed Carrie Miner Sherwood. Terrill called her "saucy" at ninety-five; Allan calls her "peppery" at one hundred. If the character Frances Harling had been real, one feels, she would have approved of her future. One of Allan's favorite observa-tions about Cather's reputation in Red Cloud is "Half the town is maddern' hell because she didn't put them into her books, and the other half is maddern' hell because she told the truth about them."[1]

Allan's anecdote about the rubber plant in the background of the Bakst portrait of Cather gives us insight into the nature of the feisty woman who remained best friends with Cather from the time they were girls together in Red Cloud throughout Cather's life, and in interviews, beyond Cather's death.

Memories of Cather Abound for Centenarian

The characters of the novels of Willa Cather, Nebraska's world-renowned author, are ageless. So it was Monday for one of the best loved of them all, Frances Harling of *My Ántonia*.

In real and "worthwhile adventure" life she is Mrs. Carrie Miner Sher-wood, a tiny, lovable lady, who at 100 years of age still exudes the peppery enthusiasm she did as friend and adviser to the author from Miss Cather's childhood until her death in 1947.

The greatest treasure of all for Cather scholars is the memory of this woman, the only one outside of Miss Cather's parents to dare call the author Willie.

The Cather family had moved from Virginia to the Red Cloud area in 1883, and in turn moved from a farmstead into town the following year. Willa was nine when her father brought her into the general store of Carrie's father, J. L. Miner. Carrie, then fourteen, was working in the store.

"I can see her today as well as I do you," Carrie recalled. "Her father had sat her on a base shelf, and my father was fitting her with shoes. We were friends from that day on, and I mean really friends. I don't know why we got along so well. In all the years we never had a bit of misunderstanding. She used to tell me so many wonderful stories of the South and Virginia when I was a little girl."

Carrie revealed that Willie had a passion for music, particularly violin music.

"She took piano lessons from a Professor Schindelmeisser," she said. "But writing was her forte. You know, I think Willie inherited a great deal of her story telling from her Grandmother Boak. Her grandmother toured the country time and time again."

Carrie stopped wide-mouthed. The music lesson mention had brought to mind her efforts to obtain the piano Willie used from a North Loup woman who had purchased it at the sale of the Cather estate.

"I'm still going to keep on fussing about it until that woman sells it to us for the museum," Carrie fumed.

"It's rather strange how much she cared for music. She used to go clear across the country to hear Yehudi Menuhin play his violin. They became close friends.

"It's hard to tell what I liked best about Willie. She was always good-natured and very free with information. She occasionally asked my advice, and we discussed her characters in the books she was writing quite often. We'd sit on the swing on the big porch for hours without stopping. We talked mostly about people. She loved people. But she also had a way of brushing people off—not verbally, emotionally I guess."

She paused and bid me go to her bedroom to look at the photo of Willie above her bed. It's the one most used in Cather portraits.

"That's my favorite," Carrie said. "She had a good face and was always a very nice looking woman."

Then, chuckling, she led me to another photo. It is the picture of the portrait painted of her by Bakst which hangs in the Omaha Public Library.

"She asked me once how I liked the picture," Carrie said. "I told her I liked the rubber plant in the background. She replied, 'All right; you keep the rubber plant, and I'll get another picture.' Of course, she didn't."

Omaha World-Herald, 31 Dec. 1969, 25.

MARJORIE SMITH

Marjorie Smith (1901–   ) prepared for her teaching career at Kansas State University at Manhattan, then taught in an ungraded rural school in Kansas for ten years before she moved to Nebraska, where she taught English to high school students at Superior, then at Guide Rock. She also enjoyed writing freelance articles for the *Hastings Tribune* and the *Lincoln Journal*. She especially liked to interview local people who were a little different from others, "not run-of-the-mill." At Guide Rock, whenever she taught a work by Willa Cather, she would invite Janet Sherwood Crary, a sixth grade teacher, to talk to the class about Mrs. Crary's grandmother Carrie Miner Sherwood. On the occasion of Mrs. Sherwood's hundredth birthday, Smith interviewed her, and three years later, after Mrs. Miner's death, Smith interviewed Crary.[1]

In Neighborhood, It Was Willie Cather

"Grandmother will be 100 years old on December 19. She is my finest source of information on early Nebraska history," said Mrs. Janet Sherwood Crary, a teacher in the Guide Rock elementary school. "It's always Willie, never Willa, when grandmother refers to her girlhood friend, Willa Cather. But let Grandmother tell you."

Carrie Miner Sherwood looks from her living room windows upon the very same neighborhood where she, her sisters, and the Cather children spent hours sharing books, food, and talk.

"It was always talk," Mrs. Sherwood said, "with Willie asking the questions and I answering, since I was four years older.

"Our family had this whole block eighty-eight years ago when Red Cloud was young. And like many small towns the population was twice what it is today. It's about 1,500 now."

Mrs. Sherwood looked across the street to the house where she grew up, and where Ántonia of *My Ántonia* was the hired girl.

"We had an orchard, a big barn, horses, and cows. Willie was deeply interested in everything outdoors; we all were. I think if Willie hadn't been a writer she probably would have been a botanist. She was always investigating.

"Yes, perhaps I was the inspiration for Frances Harling in *My Ántonia*. Everybody thinks so. And my sister Mary is Julia, the musical one in the book. Willie had to have background characters for her stories, and we, as childhood friends, fell naturally into place. The only actual portrait Willa ever made was of my mother in *My Ántonia*.

"I left school at fifteen. I didn't like the professor, and in that I had parental backing. He was not a scholarly man. One day when I could take no more of his attempts at discipline I walked out. I have always been a rebel, I guess. I remember the morning very well, even though it was more than eighty-four years ago. I had my ruler in my hand, and it clicked out my rejection of formal education as I raked it along the banisters as I descended the stairs.

"Father put me right to work in the office of the general store. This was the first big department store in the Republican Valley.

"It was at the Red Cloud store where I first saw Willie. I was on my way home from school and stopped in to walk home with father. Mr. Cather was buying Willie a pair of shoes. They had driven in from the country.

"In 1884, the Cathers moved into Red Cloud and were our neighbors;

there was no house between theirs and ours. During vacations Willie spent more time at our place than she did at home.

"We were steeped in story telling. Just living life in Red Cloud at that time was romance itself, but we didn't know it then, not even Willie. The coming of the railroad and the unusual people who came here—most of them from the East and quite a few from Boston—made the culture here unique.

"We were just as fond of Grandmother Boak, Willie's maternal grandmother, as the Cathers were. She was a little southern lady who had lived through the war. She held us spellbound with first-hand accounts of the Civil War. As I remember it, she had sons in both armies.

"We loved to have her tell and retell about the time the soldiers took possession of their home near Shenandoah, Virginia. And how, at night, she would go with supplies for the boys to the Confederate camp, and the following night take supplies to the Union camp.

"My father's motto was live and let live. We traveled, and became acquainted with many kinds of people. I think the keynote of my relationship with Willa Cather, the core of our friendship, was people. We both loved people.

"My favorite book is *My Ántonia*, naturally. It is the one that gives me, you might say, an emotional reaction. However, the first part of *The Song of the Lark*, in the chapter, "Friends of Childhood," I think, is the loveliest thing she ever did.

Ántonia, or Anna Sadilek, came to live in our home when she was fifteen. The Sadileks came to Nebraska with the hope of owning land, and after Mr. Sadilek's death, the mother's driving ambition made slaves of them all.

"Annie became self-reliant very early. She had a peculiar combination of independence and dependence which I think Willie brought out in the book. She worked in several homes in Red Cloud, at one time in the Silas Garber home. The former Governor and Mrs. Garber were just as fond of her as we were.

People came here from all over the world to talk about Willa Cather. Yet plenty of people who live very near here have never heard of her. Mrs. Mildred Bennett's book, *The World of Willa Cather*, has brought new interest to this part of the country."

In later years Willa returned to Red Cloud now and then to rest. Even here people were constantly seeking her for pictures and interviews.

"One morning," Mrs. Sherwood recalled, "a large car drove up in front of our house, and two men carrying camera equipment came to the door. They wanted to see Willa, and when I told them they couldn't, they were angry. After I was rid of them, and I'd tried to do it quietly in order not to disturb Willie, I found her standing at the top of the stairs, laughing. She had heard everything.

"Reminiscing is very pleasant," Mrs. Sherwood observed with a smile, "but a friendship that began in childhood and remained close throughout a lifetime is filled with memories so poignant that it is difficult to speak of them. I share them as I near my Centennial birthday only because I want the young people, particularly Nebraskans, to become acquainted with the writing of Willa Cather."

Lincoln Sunday Journal and Star Nebraskaland Focus, 21 Dec. 1969, 5.

ELSA SKOCPOL

Unfortunately for students of American literary history who study the quotidian, there are few sources in print that reflect memories of Willa Cather by everyday folk, people who were often quite important to her in building the world of her novels. Elsa Camilla (Stastny) Skocpol's (1896–1987) grandfather in the following letter, whom Cather visited, was Frank J. Sadilek (1851–1933), a man who eventually performed over a thousand funeral orations. A native Bohemian, he seems to have been a popular choice of speaker because he had memories of many years, people, and languages and because "He serves when called regardless of nationality, financial standing or position of the deceased in life, or of his family. He has no set oration, but dwells on the life of the deceased." The writer of the letter is a daughter of the second daughter mentioned in the letter—Dr. Olga Stastny. The family's history is one that would interest Cather. Family members whose ancestors were immigrants in Nebraska now have positions in leading world universities.[1]

Willa Cather in Wilbur

In the Spring of 1917 someone in Lincoln told Willa Cather that the best place to ask anyone for Czech names was the little town of Wilber, in Saline County. So, one Sunday she took the morning train to Wilber and walked up Main Street to a drug store. When she asked the druggist who would be the best person to ask about Czech names, he told her, "That would be Mr. Frank Sadilek. I think he knows every Czech family in Saline County, and has spoken at hundreds of funerals of Czech descent. Just walk three blocks up this street, cross the walk through the court house yard, then cross the street to the west and knock at the door of the second door to the left."

She was welcomed by my grandmother who was happiest when she could cook for company. Grandfather was sitting by the window in the sunshine. He was delighted to acquaint her with the Czech names of his countryman, and told her how it happened that he was called as a eulogist in the early days in Saline County because there were no Czech ministers available. In later years, when his people had learned to speak our language, many of them asked him (continued to ask) that he speak a few words in their native language. He then made friends with many ministers who conducted the regular ceremonies, not only in Saline County, but in other places in Nebraska and northern Kansas. Even after he walked with crutches because of the removal of one leg to his knee, my husband drove him to funerals of many friends who still asked for his eulogy.

After grandmother had served a hearty meal, they settled down to the discussion of typical Czech names. Grandmother had told Willa that they had eight children. When Willa had asked Grandpa, "What did you name your eight children?" he answered that the four girls were named Ántonia, Olga, Sylvia and Irma. The boys were named Charles, Frank, Walter and Victor. Willa pondered awhile and then said, "I think I would like the name Ántonia best for my young heroine." Her father's name was Anton.

All this was told to me the next day when I visited my grandparents. Grandmother had given Willa some crochet lace and some of her good kolace, and Willa had returned to Lincoln on the train which had returned from Beatrice (usually at 3 o'clock in the afternoon).

During the Fall of 1918 my grandparents were delighted to receive an autographed copy of Willa's book, *My Ántonia*, and it was loaned to good friends and neighbors, and we never found it in the bookcase when we were disposing of my grandparents' possessions.

Then in 1952 when my mother died, I found among her letters that grandfather had sent the book, *My Ántonia*, to a writer friend in Czechoslovakia, and had suggested that he translate it into the Czech language.

At that time, Mother was in Prague so she went to see Grandpa's friend. He was quite ill, and died a short-time after that visit.

P.S. My mother was Dr. Olga Stastny, the second daughter of Teresa and Frank J. Sadilek.

Handwritten essay, 22 May 1982. A revised and shortened version of this essay was published in *A Flowering: A Festival. "Writing and Storytelling Festival for Older Nebraskans,"* University of Nebraska–Lincoln Division of Continuing Studies in cooperation with Nebraska Commission on Aging, vol. 3, 1983.

In the Family

Cather's parents and siblings were intelligent and multi-talented, fluent readers and writers, responsible and friendly neighbors, and constant correspondents. Evidence of this appears in testimonies by their professional colleagues and in their own letters and memoirs. They studied classical literature, read contemporary fiction, frequently were mentioned in the public press, taught at various levels, participated in community affairs, managed banks, investments, and oil companies, all the while they maintained a lively correspondence.[1]

Charles Cather's letters appear to flow strongly and gracefully from his pen, but although quite fluent, they do not reveal the vivacity about people and life around him as do Virginia Cather's letters. The latter suffer occasionally from mechanical errors (Cather was reportedly a poor speller herself), but the language resounds with local idiom and lively emotional involvement in life.[2] Apparently, Willa Cather inherited her writing ability in a wonderful combination from both her father and her mother.

ANN ZUROSKY

Like journalists in Nebraska, Illinois, and New York, Ann Zurosky played a role in keeping Cather's name before the public.[1] In Pittsburgh, Zurosky interviewed Helen Cather Southwick, daughter of James Cather and niece of Willa Cather. Southwick adds details to a portrait of Cather that only an intimate would know and remark, giving readers a more informal view of the relationship Cather had with Red Cloud and with her family after she became famous.

Willa Cather and niece Helen Louise Cather. Courtesy of the Nebraska State Historical Society, Willa Cather Pioneer Memorial Collection.

Author Still Lives in Vivid Memory

Without an invitation from "Aunt Willa" no one, not even a godchild and loved niece, intruded on the privacy Willa Cather demanded while she was writing.

These personal glimpses of the famous author who started her literary career in Pittsburgh more than a half century ago are vivid to Mrs. Philip L. Southwick of Fox Chapel.

Mrs. Southwick is the former Helen Louise Cather, god-child and niece of the late Miss Cather.

Although Miss Cather lived in Pittsburgh only ten years, from 1896 to 1906, this "city of dreadful dirt" made a lasting impression. The city and its people were recreated later in such stories as "A Golden Slipper," "Paul's Case," and "Double Birthday."

"She frequently talked of Pittsburgh and always wanted to come back more often," her niece recalled. Before World War I Miss Cather would make quick trips to visit friends and her brother, Jack, who was a student at Carnegie Institute of Technology.

But in later years she became too busy and the promised visit to see her niece and Dr. Southwick, who had just moved to Pittsburgh in 1946, never took place. She died April 24, 1947. . . .

Mrs. Southwick remembers her aunt as a short, almost stocky woman, with dark brown hair and bright blue eyes.

"Aunt Willa wasn't particularly conscious of high style, but she loved lovely fabrics, furs, and beautiful hats, which she had made especially by Bergdorf Goodman," Mrs. Southwick said.

When Helen Louise was a youngster of about six, summers meant visiting her grandparents in Red Cloud, Nebraska. She still remembers the summerhouse in the garden that "Aunt Willa" used as a workshop.

"It was quite an honor to be invited in there," she mused. "Aunt Willa liked order, and her large walnut desk was never cluttered." The room, with windows on all sides, was furnished very simply with big handmade chairs and a huge couch covered with a colored throw.

"And there were bachelor buttons growing outside the door," her niece laughed. "I always remember those."

Miss Cather always was a bit formal and, her niece recalled, "did not have a strong sense of humor, but she was kind and self-disciplined, with great strength of character." She was impartial with visiting nieces and nephews, introducing all of them to books at every opportunity.

During the many years Miss Cather lived in New York and produced a dozen books, it was her custom every Friday afternoon to welcome friends for tea. Over the years, many Pittsburghers visiting in New York stopped at her home on Park Avenue for this Friday visiting period.

Mrs. Southwick now has the lovely tea service that her aunt used, along with some fine pieces of jewelry and many first editions.

Pittsburgh Press, 22 Apr. 1959, 44.

HELEN C. SOUTHWICK

Until Cather died, Helen Cather Southwick (1918–   ) visited with her aunt Willa often in Red Cloud, in New York City, and later in Grand Manan. Today, Southwick owns the cabin Cather had built for summers on Grand Manan Island. Southwick is also related through her mother to the Silas Garber family of which the most famous to Cather readers is the wife of Silas, Lyra Garber, inspiration for Marian Forrester in *The Lost Lady* (Bennett, "What Happened" 619). Southwick has had a full intellectual and social life and has been a careful but generous friend of scholars who study her aunt's works. She has especially assisted in maintaining Cather's reputation in Pittsburgh where Cather lived for ten years and where Southwick spent much of her adult life. Like the other Cathers, Southwick also writes well.[1]

Willa Cather's Early Career: Origins of a Legend

In April 1978 the lead article in this magazine was "History's Unweeded Garden: Common Errors in Western Pennsylvania History" by George Swetnam. In it he showed how errors that find their way into print tend to be repeated and soon become accepted as facts. More recently, in 1980, Norman Mailer was awarded the Pulitzer Prize for fiction for his book, *The Executioner's Song.* Asked why he called it a novel, he replied that all biography is in some degree fictitious.[1] The shortcomings of historical and biographical research which these authors bring to our attention could scarcely be better exemplified than by the fictionalized portrait of the youthful Willa Cather that has emerged in recent years, based largely on a succession of reinterpretations of some recollections of Mrs. Elizabeth Moorhead Vermorcken, who wrote under her maiden name, Elizabeth Moorhead. She was one of the first writers to provide a written account of Willa Cather's life in Pittsburgh. In 1950 the University of Pittsburgh Press published her short and charming reminiscence *These Too Were Here: Louise Homer and Willa Cather.* However, by the time she wrote her book, some forty or fifty years after the fact, her memories had become so confused and so blended with hearsay and fantasy that a highly romanticized story emerged.

Vermorcken's color-enhanced version of Cather's life in Pittsburgh has had a great appeal for later biographers, who have usually accepted it without question. Although she was doing for Willa Cather what Parson Weems had done for George Washington, the largely mythical character of Vermorcken's contribution escaped recognition. Interestingly enough, the Homer and Cather sketches were among seven sketches in a manuscript that Vermorcken submitted to the University of Pittsburgh Press. Only the two were selected for publication because a staff editor and an outside reader felt that the others were overly sentimental and that some of them were not entirely factual.[2] In particular, one on Walter McClintock, a naturalist, contained invented dialogue and imagined scenes. The fictionalized aspects of the Willa Cather sketch, on the other hand, were not at all apparent. Vermorcken's sketch is well written and interesting and with its publication, the author gained recognition as something of an authority on Willa Cather's Pittsburgh years.

Elizabeth Moorhead Vermorcken was born in Pittsburgh shortly after the end of the Civil War. Her family connections on both sides contained persons of distinction. Her grandfather, James Kennedy Moorhead, was a successful industrialist and a member of Congress. In 1942 she wrote, "His grandchildren are scattered, and today not one of his descendants by the name of Moorhead remains in Pittsburgh. He was the great doorpost of the house and after his death the family began to fall apart and was never what it had been."[3] She was bright and eager for education at a time when not many women were being educated. She longed to go to college but says she was sent "to an expensive boarding-school in one of the most beautiful suburbs of Philadelphia where I was happy enough but obtained nothing that could possibly be considered education."[4] After her graduation, she spent a winter in Paris, where she learned to speak French. In 1891, when she was about twenty-five, she married Frederick Vermorcken, an impoverished Belgian artist, but the marriage was not a happy one. By the winter of 1894–1895, it had ended and she was back in Pittsburgh.[5] Very little is recorded about her life between this time and 1910, when she began an eighteen-year teaching career at Carnegie Technical Schools, now Carnegie-Mellon University, except for the fact that she spent part or all of the time in New York writing articles and short stories that were published in some of the leading magazines of the time. After her retirement from teaching in 1928, she wrote three novels with Pittsburgh backgrounds. Then, during the depression of the 1930s, having lost her house in Pittsburgh and a good deal of her money, she went to Italy to live in Florence. There she began a book, which she called *Whirling Spindle*, about her forebears, her family, and her friends in Pittsburgh and Philadelphia. She completed it in Pittsburgh when she returned here following Italy's entry into World War II, and it was published by the University of Pittsburgh Press in 1942, eight years before the publication of *These Too Were Here*. She died in Pittsburgh on June 2, 1955, at the age of eighty-nine.

The errors in Willa Cather biographies attributable to Vermorcken would not be of much significance except for the fact that some of them have been used to attribute Lesbian overtones to Cather friendships. These errors are the allegations that Isabelle McClung threatened to leave home unless her parents invited Cather to live at their house, that the two friends shared a bedroom, and that they spent nearly all their evenings reading together, away from the rest of the family.

The allegation of McClung's threat to leave home does not appear in Vermorcken's book, but in *Willa Cather: A Critical Biography* by E. K. Brown and Leon Edel, published without documentation in 1953.[6] There is no doubt that the story came from Vermorcken. She told it to me before the book by Brown and Edel was published, and she said she was the only one who knew it. She also told me that E. K. Brown had consulted her when he was in Pittsburgh doing research. Professor Brown died before he had finished writing his book, and his friend Leon Edel was asked to complete the unfinished chapters so that the book could be published. Edel was engaged at the time on his definitive biography of Henry James, the first volume of which was also published in 1953, and thus was not able to undertake the task of organizing Brown's source notes. As a result, the book was published without footnotes. However, as it was considered an official biography, other writers have relied on its authority.

Dorothy Goodfellow, the Pittsburgh poet and writer, recalls hearing George Seibel say it was actually Judge Samuel A. McClung, Isabelle's father, who first suggested that Willa live at their house so that she could help Isabelle in her study of languages, especially French—a language that Cather had been reading and speaking with the Seibels.[7] Cather's friendship with George Seibel and his wife, Helen is well documented. Dorothy Goodfellow and her late husband, Donald, met the Seibels in the late 1930s and shared a close friendship with them as long as the Seibels lived. In 1963 Helen Seibel was emphatic in her statement to Dr. Kathleen Byrne, a Cather biographer, that she had never heard of any opposition in the McClung family to Cather's living with them and said she was certain there was none. She pointed out that Cather would never have gone there if there had been, because she had too much pride to stay where she was not wanted.[8]

In 1970 James Woodress published his book, *Willa Cather: Her Life and Art*. He quoted Vermorcken's statement that Cather and McClung read together "evening after evening" in "the bedroom they shared"[9] and Brown and Edel's account of McClung's threat to leave home. He attributed the latter story to Edith Lewis, because he thought she had been Brown's and Edel's chief source of such information. Lewis, however, has published as a book the notes she made for Brown. In the book, which she called *Willa Cather Living*, she says that "Isabelle apparently had no difficulty in persuading her father and mother to invite Willa Cather to become a member of the McClung household. Mrs. McClung was naturally kindly and welcoming to everyone. And even the stern judge seems to have taken a great liking to Willa Cather from the first, and to have unbent toward her as he did to few people. She found him always a kind and considerate friend."[10] Woodress characterized Cather's friendship with Isabelle as "the one great romance of her life" and "a great love that lasted a lifetime."[11] He did not attempt to define what he meant by the terms "great romance" or "great love," but the book was widely read and influential, and it was after its publication that others felt free to suggest a Lesbian relationship. However, in response to a question on the Lesbian inference at a national conference on Willa Cather, Woodress disavowed any intention on his own part to suggest a Lesbian relationship, saying that Cather was too much involved with her art and work to invest any time and energy in sex of any kind.[12]

Cather's friendship with McClung and her family began at least as early as 1899.[13] In the fall of that year she had been their guest at their house at 1176 Murray Hill Avenue for a short time after she returned from her summer vacation in Nebraska. A little more than a year later, she spent the winter (1900–1901) in Washington DC, translating French documents and letters relating to the Paris International Exposition of 1900 and assisting her cousin, James Howard Gore, juror-in-chief of the exposition, in the preparation of the jury's report to the United States govermnent.[14] The report was published by the government in 1901 in six volumes, two of which bear the name of Gore as author. It is probable that those volumes were largely the work of Cather, as Gore was occupied by the responsibilities of his professorship in mathematics at the Columbian (now George Washington) University.

Shortly after the report was completed, Cather was offered both a job and a home back in Pittsburgh. The Central High School was in need of a teacher to finish the year. According to the *High School Journal*, Miss Heard, a recent graduate of Vassar, who had herself been hired as a replacement in January, had resigned because of failing health.[15] There has been considerable speculation as to how Cather got the job. It is quite possible that Judge McClung suggested her as a candidate. He may, indeed, have been asked to help recruit a person who could step into the position at that time in the school year. B. H. Patterson, who seems to have been a ranking member of the English department (he held the chair of belles lettres), and who himself was leaving at the end of the year, was the judge's fellow alumnus of Washington and Jefferson College.[16] The judge took a "deep interest" in the college and its alumni. He also had a "keen and helpful interest in civic affairs"[17] and may have been acquainted with some of the members of the Board of Education who lived in the East End not far from Murray Hill Avenue.[18]

In the "Changes in the Faculty" notes of the Easter 1901 issue of the *High School Journal*, it was noted that "Miss Cather, another new teacher, has now taken Miss Heard's place in Room 19 as teacher of Latin, Algebra and Composition. Miss Cather is a graduate of the University of Nebraska, '95, and has been engaged in literary work for Pittsburgh newspapers and is an accomplished linguist." There had been no evidence that she taught algebra until Byrne and Snyder reported the recollections of Frances Kelly, a former student at Central High School.[19] The fact that she did teach algebra explains why Cather had to work very hard, lost twenty pounds in not much more than three months, and returned to Nebraska in a state of exhaustion as soon as school was out.[20] It had been assumed that she had forgotten so much Latin that she had a struggle with that subject. But Latin had been one of her enthusiasms, she had read and studied the language and literature with facility and pleasure, and she had a solid background in it. On the other hand, she had always had trouble with mathematics and her background in that discipline was thin.[21] One wonders why she would take on such a difficult task when she had become fairly well known as a journalist. A possible explanation is that she knew there was to be an opening in the English department the following year and believed, or was told, that being on the faculty would put her in line for that position, which she did get.

At about the same time the March vacancy at the Central High School occurred, the McClungs were moving into a new house. On March 1, 1901, the house on the corner of Murray Hill Avenue and Fair Oaks Street was deeded to S. A. McClung by John Elder, a contractor, of 501 Shady Avenue. It was given the number 1180, being just next door to the house at 1176 Murray Hill Avenue, where the McClungs had been living since they moved to the East End from Allegheny City in 1895. Cather must have moved into the new house at about the same time the McClung family did. She was given a room on the third floor and a separate room for a study. Elsie Cather, her youngest sister, after reading Vermorcken's book, said that the statement that Cather shared McClung's room was in error. Elsie recalled that she had spent a school holiday in Pittsburgh as a guest of the McClungs when she was a student at Smith College (1910–1912) and had stayed in the room on the third floor that had been Cather's when she lived in the house and which was kept for her to use whenever she came to Pittsburgh. Elsie remembered being shown about the house and seeing McClung's room on the second floor. At that time Cather's books were still in her third-floor study, for she had no place for them in New York until she moved into a spacious apartment on Bank Street in the winter of 1912.[22]

People in Pittsburgh who know the former McClung house have always been puzzled by Vermorcken's description of the window which "gave on a downward slope across gardens and shaded streets towards the Monongahela River and green hills rising beyond."[23] The river is more than two miles away, and because of the topography, neither it nor the green hills beyond can be seen from any window of the house. This description is an example of Vermorcken's romantic tendency to disregard facts in order to achieve a dramatic effect.

It is doubtful she knew anything about the living arrangements in the house. She says that McClung fitted up a corner of the attic where Cather could write.[24] The house has no attic, but as Elsie remembered, a finished third floor with separate bedrooms and a bathroom. Though other writers have described the house as large, as indeed it is, Vermorcken told me that there was not a separate bedroom available for Cather, and thus it was necessary for her to share McClung's room. Elsie Cather told me that she was sure her sister would never have accepted the McClungs' invitation, in spite of their kindness to her and their beautiful house, if she could not have had a room of her own. Privacy was always important to her. She had had her own little attic room in Red Cloud, and even in college she never had a roommate. It is interesting to note that Brown and Edel, who cite Vermorcken as a source, do not say that McClung shared her room with Cather. Professor Brown had gone to Nebraska to do research, and while he was there, he had had several long talks with Elsie Cather, who was probably his primary source on Cather family history and on Cather's life before she went to New York.

Vermorcken is also indulging her fondness for romance in her description of Cather and Isabelle McClung spending "evening after evening" reading novels together. As Byrne and Snyder recognized, most of Cather's evenings would have had to be "devoted to the work she brought home from school [and] preparation for the next day's classes. . . ."[25] Having had teaching careers themselves, Byrne and Snyder take a realistic view and say that "Whenever they could, she and Isabelle would vanish shortly after dinner and retire upstairs to read Flaubert, Tolstoy, Balzac, and Turgenev and to share their responses."[26] In addition to her full-time teaching, Cather was doing an impressive amount of writing: poetry, short stories, newspaper articles and probably after 1903, editorial work for her future employer, S. S. McClure. Her first two books, *April Twilights* (poetry) and *The Troll Garden* (short stories) were written at the McClung house, as was a novel that she destroyed because it did not meet her standards.[27] Cather had a number of other good friends and many acquaintances in Pittsburgh.[28] She had been living in the city for nearly five years before she became a member of the McClung household. McClung, who had always lived in the twin cities, as Allegheny and Pittsburgh were then called, was involved in artistic, cultural, intellectual, and civic activities, and she had many friends.[29] Vermorcken, who herself says that "Isabelle was distinctly an individual in her own right,"[30] does not say that McClung and Cather spent all their leisure time together, but as she mentions no friends other than herself, she creates that impression.

The indications are that Vermorcken knew Cather and McClung only slightly, and not in 1905 and 1906 as she says but probably in 1914 or 1915 when Cather was in Pittsburgh working on her novel, *The Song of the Lark*. Most of that book was written at the McClung house, and it was dedicated to Isabelle in appreciation. Jack, Cather's youngest brother, was a student at Carnegie Tech in those years. It could have been through him that Vermorcken, who was one of his teachers, met Cather and McClung. Though she says she met them in the spring of 1905 and saw them frequently during the summer, it has now been established that Cather spent the summer of 1905 in Nebraska.[31] I can find no evidence that Vermorcken herself was in Pittsburgh in 1905. The biographical note on the cover of *These Too Were Here* says that she returned to Pittsburgh from New York in 1910 and began her teaching career that year. The faculty records at Carnegie-Mellon University concur. She gave the same date to Dorothy Goodfellow, who wrote an introduction to *Pittsburgh Portraits*, and to George Swetnam in an interview published in the *Pittsburgh Press* on April 26, 1953.

The fact is that *These Too Were Here* places a number of other events in 1905 that must have occurred several years later. There is a description of teas that McClung gave on Sunday afternoons for her friends and neighbors, and the guests she mentions (none by name) indicate a time later than 1905.[32] Some of them were said to have been members of the faculties of the departments of drama and music at Carnegie Tech. Byrne and Snyder have pointed out that the Carnegie Technical Schools (the forerunner of Carnegie-Mellon University) did not open until October 1905 and had no departments of drama or music at that time. In 1912 the name was changed to Carnegie Institute of Technology and the music department, among others, was added. The drama department, the first in the nation, was established in 1914.[33]

Members of the Dante Alighieri Society were also said to have been guests at those teas. Through a letter that McClung wrote to Cather's mother[34] and my own correspondence with the Dante Alighieri Society in Rome, I have learned that Isabelle McClung herself was instrumental in organizing the first Dante Society in Pittsburgh, but this did not occur until 1910. She told Cather's mother that she had had to write more than sixty letters in connection with the enterprise. The ones which she wrote to the headquarters of the Dante Alighieri Society in Rome are still preserved in the archives there and are said to be in almost perfect Italian.[35]

Another anachronism in Vermorcken's story concerns her account of Cather's first meeting with S. S. McClure, the editor and publisher of McClure's Magazine. She says that he returned from a trip to Europe in 1906 and found on his desk, wrapped to be returned, a rejected manuscript from an unknown writer. He unwrapped and read it, and was so impressed with the writing that he made a trip to Pittsburgh to meet the author and offer a position on his magazine.[36] Actually, by 1906 Cather had known McClure for three years. In her introduction to *April Twilights* (1903), which she edited for the University of Nebraska Press, Bernice Slote reported that the Nebraska State Journal of May 11, 1903, had printed a news item from a New York paper which said, "Miss Willa Cather of Pittsburg was in the city this week. She was summoned by the McClure people who of late have taken a lively interest in her literary work."[37] Bernice Slote, who has been engaged in Cather research for many years, believes that Cather did occasional jobs for McClure between that meeting in 1903 and the time she went to New York in 1906.

Vermorcken goes on to say that Cather accepted McClure's offer of a position, and at the end of the school year resigned from her teaching post and went to New York. Actually, she left Pittsburgh in the middle of the second semester. She seems to have taken a leave of absence at the time of the Easter vacation and gone to *McClure's Magazine* on a special assignment. An item in the March 1906 issue of the Allegheny High School student publication, the *Wah Hoo*, says, " When we return from our April vacation, we shall fail to see Miss Cather; but though the school will miss her very much, we feel relieved in knowing that next September she will again be able to take her classes."

Several of the key members of the editorial staff left *McClure's Magazine* on May 10, 1906, because of a dispute with the management.[38] Apparently as a result, Cather was offered a post as a permanent member of the staff. She must have made her decision to accept, and resigned from Allegheny High School by the end of the month. The June 1906 issue of the *Wah Hoo* printed her farewell letter, prefaced in the typically sentimental style of the period: "The following letter has been sent by Miss Cather to her reporting class in 307, and because we think everyone would like to hear from her, especially those who have known her at any time of their course, with the permission of the class, we publish it. We are truly sorry to hear that Miss Cather will not return, and we count it the saddest event of our school year. We, however, would rather grieve at her departure than not to have known her at all, for we feel that we have gained by being near her. We are proud of her success, and as friends we wish her much happiness, the fulfillment of her desires, and a splendid future." The letter was dated June 2, more than three weeks before the end of the school year. In it she said, "A number of my pupils . . . asked me, when I came away, whether I should be with you next year. At that time I fully expected to be. The changes in my plans which will prevent my doing so have been sudden and unforeseen."[39]

Cather's friendship with Isabelle McClung and her family continued after she moved to New York.[40] She frequently returned to Pittsburgh during the years 1906–1915 to write in the quiet of the study on the third floor. In 1912 she stopped over on her way to the Southwest. When she arrived in Pittsburgh, she found that Mrs. McClung had become ill, so she postponed her trip in order to be of help.[41] Mrs. McClung died the following year, but Cather's friendship with the rest of the family continued. Late in 1916 she wrote to her sister Elsie that several friends from Pittsburgh who were in New York for the holidays had been to tea at her apartment. Among them was Alfred McClung, Isabelle's brother.[42] At the time of Isabelle's death in 1938, Cather and Edith McClung Sawyer, Isabelle's sister, were in touch with each other, and the friendly and sympathetic letters Cather wrote to Sawyer are still in the possession of the McClung family.

In writing of Cather's early New York years, Vermorcken says that she visited her frequently in her apartment on Bank Street. Cather did not live there until 1912 and she left that apartment in 1927. Since Vermorcken was teaching at Carnegie Tech from 1910 through 1928, it is hard to see how the visits to the Bank Street apartment could have been frequent. Certainly she could not have been living in New York, as she seems to imply. Apparently she had been in the apartment, however, as she mentions a copy of a portrait of George Sand above the mantel in the living room and wonders "why Willa Cather had chosen this particular novelist to preside over her hearthstone." [43] In point of fact, it was not a copy, but an original etching by the French artist, Thomas Couture, and Edith Lewis says that it was chosen "not because she particularly admired George Sand but because she liked the etching." [44] Vermorcken does not mention having met Edith Lewis, as she surely would have done if she had made frequent visits to the apartment.

Cather and Lewis rented that apartment together; by combining their resources, they were able to afford a larger and more comfortable place to live than either could have afforded otherwise. Cather was leaving *McClure's Magazine* at that time, hoping to be able to make a living by writing, and she needed space in which to work. At first she did not earn enough money to meet her expenses, but she had lived frugally and saved her money, so she had a fund to draw on. [45] Brown and Edel say, "During the early years in Bank Street the apartment was often full of her friends. She was not so pressed for time as she had been; and the fatigue that often settled on her in later years was still a rare visitation. For a while she was at home to her friends on Friday afternoons: people from Nebraska and Pittsburgh, people she had met at McClure's, stage people, musicians, writers." [46] Vermorcken may have attended some of those Friday teas, perhaps during Easter or Christmas holidays, as the teas were not held in the summer months. Maybe she was one of the Pittsburgh friends who were there in December 1916 along with Alfred McClung.

Since close scrutiny tends to discredit much of Vermorcken's testimony, the question arises as to whether less equivocal evidence has been cited in support of the supposition that Willa Cather may have had a Lesbian involvement. The answer is that it has not. It is true that Sergeant and Woodress have portrayed Cather as being distressed about Isabelle Mc-Clung's marriage to Jan Hambourg, a violinist, but both of these authors were aware that, as Cather had said, [47] the distress owed much of its origin to her knowledge that the McClung house would be sold and she could no longer retreat to the study at the house at those times when she wished to focus all her attention on a novel in progress. Perhaps because of the fact that as a child she had been uprooted from the original Cather home in Virginia, she became emotionally attached to most of the houses in which she lived and was saddened by their being torn down or sold. She was, in fact, greatly distressed during the last few years of her life when her parents' last home in Red Cloud, the house where she had visited them many times in the summer and at the Christmas holidays, was sold by her sister Elsie in 1941. Such feelings had been a central theme in *The Professor's House.*

McClung's marriage did not by any means end her friendship with Cather, who always remained in close touch with the Hambourgs. During the early years of their marriage they lived in New York, and Cather saw them often. She was their guest for Christmas Eve dinner the first year they were there, and they gave her two fine Russian candelabra as a Christmas gift.[48] In 1920, when she was in France, they traveled from their home in Toronto and took her on a tour of the battlefields of the First World War, where they helped her find the grave of her cousin, Lieutenant G. P. Cather, the prototype of Claude in *One of Ours.*[49] Later they traveled together through southern France and spent some time in Cavaliere, a small fishing village on the Mediterranean coast. In a letter that Cather wrote to her mother from there, she said that Jan Hambourg was a fine person to travel with and mentioned his patience and good nature.[50]

It is also true that much significance has been read into Elizabeth Sergeant's account of Cather's decision to destroy letters she had written to Isabelle which Jan returned to her after Isabelle's death in 1938. Since Cather had asked all her relatives and friends to destroy the letters she wrote to them, however, there is no reason to assign any special importance to the destruction of her letters to Isabelle. She wished all of her letters to be destroyed and added a clause to her will prohibiting their publication, not only to preserve her privacy, but also to keep some of her hastily composed writing out of print. As Leon Edel said, "To understand the art of Willa Cather . . . is to understand why she decided her letters should not to be published. She belonged to the addicted 'revisionists' of art, and since she could not have the re-editing of her correspondence—moreover, since that correspondence was unrelated to her work except perhaps as furnishing occasional marginal comments on it—she imposed the testamentary restrictions."[51]

Many of her letters survived, however. Among these are some to Elizabeth Sergeant which expressed rather extravagant admiration for the voice, character, and physical attractions of a young man from Vera Cruz, Mexico, whom she met in Arizona in 1912.[52] To the best of my knowledge she never wrote a comparable account of an attraction felt for any woman.

NOTES

1. Interview with Norman Mailer on the "Dick Cavett Show."

2. The material on file at the University of Pittsburgh Press was made available to me through the courtesy of the director, Frederick A. Hetzel. The subjects of the five other sketches in the Vermorcken manuscript were: Andrey Avinoff, John A. Brashear, Helen Esquerre, Harold Geoghegan, and Walter McClintock. They were later published by the Boxwood Press (1955) under the title, *Pittsburgh Portraits*.

3. Elizabeth Moorhead, *Whirling Spindle: The Story of a Pittsburgh Family* (Pittsburgh, 1942), 221.

4. *Ibid.*, 287.

5. *Ibid.*, 260–61. Vermorcken recalled attending a concert by Ethelbert Nevin and that shortly before or after the concert, he had given a recital at a dinner party at the house of her cousins, the McClellands. The chronology in John Tasker Howard, *Ethelbert Nevin* (New York, 1935), gives December 21, 1894, as the date of the concert and January 3, 1895, as the date of the recital at the home of the McClellands.

6. E. K. Brown and Leon Edel, *Willa Cather: A Critical Biography* (New York, 1953), 97.

7. Statement at the Cather Circle dinner, Dec. 7, 1980.

8. Kathleen D. Byrne and Richard C. Snyder, *Chrysalis: Willa Cather in Pittsburgh, 1896–1906* (Pittsburgh, 1980), 42.

9. Elizabeth Moorhead, *These Too Were Here: Louise Homer and Willa Cather* (Pittsburgh, 1950), 49.

10. Edith Lewis, *Willa Cather: A Personal Record* (New York, 1953), 53. John W. Jordan, *Encyclopedia of Pennsylvania Biography* (New York, 1914), 1 : 167, describes Judge McClung as "a man of widest reading, a brilliant writer, an impressive speaker. . . . Himself a steadfast friend, he possesses the faculty of inspiring in others the most loyal attachment."

11. James Woodress, *Willa Cather: Her Life and Art* (New York, 1970), 86, 91. *Roget's Thesaurus* lists friendship, liking, and admiration among the synonyms for love.

12. Conference held in Hastings and Red Cloud, Nebraska, June 14–20, 1981.

13. Woodress, *Willa Cather*, 92.

14. *Webster County Argus* (Nebraska), Nov. 23, 1900. Reprinted in *the Red Cloud Commercial Advertiser* (Nebraska), Nov. 19, 1930.

15. *High School Journal* (Pittsburgh), Jan. 1901, 133, Easter 1901, 194. The teacher was probably Miss Gertrude Heard of Mount Washington, who graduated from Vassar in 1900.

16. *Ibid.*, Oct. 1901. 12.

17. Jordan, *Pennsylvania Biography*, 1: 167.

18. Charles Reisfar, Jr., secretary of the Board of Education, lived at 5814 Howe Street; board member David R. Torrance at 5604 Baum Boulevard and Samuel Andrews. The superintendent of schools, lived across Baum Boulevard, at 314 Stratford Avenue.

19. Byrne and Snyder, *Chrysalis*, 58.

20. Cather to George and Helen Seibel, July 17, 1901, cited by Mildred R. Bennett in her introduction to *Willa Cather's Collected Short Fiction, 1892–1912* (Lincoln NE, 1965), xxii.

21. Mildred R. Bennett, *The World of Willa Cather*, 2nd ed. Rev. (Lincoln NE, 1961), 214, 257.

22. Cather to Elsie Cather, no date, but internal evidence establishes it as December 1912.

23. Moorhead, *These Too Were Here*, 49–50. Woodress, using Vermorcken as his source, says, in *Willa Cather*, 92, "The McClungs lived at 1180 Murray Hill Avenue in a fashionable East End residential area that overlooked the Monongahela River."

24. Moorhead, *These Too Were Here*, 49.

25. Byrne and Snyder, *Chrysalis*, 49.

26. *Ibid.*

27. Bernice Slote, "Willa Cather as a Regional Writer," *Kansas Quarterly* 2 (Spring 1970): 13. See also, Alice Booth, "America's Twelve Greatest Women: Willa Cather," *Good Housekeeping*, Sept. 1931, 35.

28. See Byrne and Snyder, *Chrysalis*, for information on some of Cather's friends in Pittsburgh.

29. The earliest records of the Tuesday Musical and the Civic Club of Allegheny County show Isabelle McClung as a member of those organizations. Willa Cather also belonged to the Tuesday Musical from 1903–1906.

30. Moorhead, *These Too Were Here*, 50.

31. Slote, "Cather as a Regional Writer," 13.

32. Moorhead, *These Too Were Here*, 51.

33. Byrne and Snyder, *Chrysalis*, 105, n. 59.

34. Isabelle McClung to Mrs. Charles F. Cather and Elsie Cather, Feb. 1. No year, but internal evidence indicates 1910.

35. Renato Casarotto to Helen Southwick, Aug. 12, 1980.

36. Moorhead, *These Too Were Here*, 52.

37. Bernice Slote, introduction to *April Twilights* (1903): *Poems by Willa Cather* (Lincoln, Neb., 1962), xx.

38. Woodress, *Willa Cather*, 120. Quoted from Peter Lyon, *Success Story: The Life and Times of S. S. McClure* (New York, 1963).

39. *Wah Hoo* (Allegheny High School), June 1906. The text of the letter can be found in Byrne and Snyder, *Chrysalis*, 63. Willa Cather wished her students success in their coming examinations. The graduation ceremonies were held on June 26 that year but there were a few days of school after that.

40. Ever since Cather's family moved to Red Cloud, Nebraska, when she was ten years old, her important and lasting friendships had been largely with families. The first, and one of the best known, was with the Miner family which became the Harling family in *My Ántonia* (discussed in detail in Bennett, *World of Cather*). When she was in college, her friendships were with the Pound, Westermann, Gere and Canfield families. See Brown and Edel, *Cather*, 64, for Dorothy Canfield Fisher's recollection of her family's friendship with Cather. In later years she had a warm friendship with the members of the Menuhin family, whom she met through Jan and Isabelle Hambourg. In 1980 Yehudi Menuhin wrote "An Appreciation of Willa Cather" which appeared in *The Art of Willa Cather*, a publication printed by the Alderman Library of the University of Virginia in connection with an exhibition of Cather books. In it he said, "She was a person whom many could share, and perhaps the only one we five as a family, my parents and sisters and I actually did share."

41. Elizabeth Shepley Sergeant, *Willa Cather: A Memoir* (New York, 1953), 78.

42. Cather to Elsie Cather, Dec. 30. No year, but internal evidence establishes it as 1916. Isabelle's brother was named Samuel Alfred McClung, Jr., and was called Alfred by the family.

43. Moorhead, *These Too Were Here*, 56.

44. Lewis, *Willa Cather*, 89. Thomas Couture (1815–1879) was a French artist who is best known as the teacher of Manet and Puvis de Chavennes.

45. *Ibid.*, 84–85.

46. Brown and Edel, *Cather*, 181.

47. Woodress. *Willa Cather*, 173, tells of a Christmas letter Cather wrote to her Aunt Franc from the McClung house in 1915 in which she expressed her sadness in the knowledge that it would he her last Christmas in the house. Judge McClung had died in November, and Isabelle, who had inherited the house, was to be married in early April and leave Pittsburgh. In January 1915 Cather's friend Annie Fields, of 148 Charles Street in Boston, had died, and soon afterward, according to Barbara Rotundo [*American Heritage* 22 (Feb. 1971): 15], the house was torn down. Willa Cather's feeling for that house is indicated in her essay "148 Charles Street" in her book, *Not Under Forty* (New York, 1936). The death of Mrs. Fields and the destruction of her house would have made Cather especially vulnerable to the death of Judge McClung and the closing of his house.

48. Letter cited in footnote 42.

49. Lewis, *Willa Cather,* 120–21.

50. Cather to Mrs. Charles F. Cather, Aug. 12, 1920.

51. Editor's foreword to Brown and Edel, *Cather,* xxiii.

52. Sergeant, *Willa Cather,* 80–81.

Western Pennsylvania Historical Magazine 65, no.2 (1982): 85–98.

As a Mentor

Just as Cather seemed gifted in finding mentors as she was growing up and becoming a writer, she appeared gifted in mentoring others. Dorothy Canfield Fisher, Elizabeth Sergeant, and Fanny Butcher have all indicated that Cather provided important guidance and encouragement to them at some time in their lives. A number of Cather's students in Pittsburgh also considered her teaching and presence to be an important influence in their lives, whether or not they maintained their relationship with her.

The next reminiscences reveal individual, special relationships that two artists enjoyed with Cather. Grant Reynard credits Cather with teaching him a memorable, life-changing lesson in an hour:

> She said, "Above all things
> That in creating, we shall have an urgent, great desire.
> Life seen and lived and felt, desire to write it,
> To sculpture it, paint it, or to make a song." (Reynard 90)

After that, Reynard took his passion into various media and felt himself change from a man vying for rewards into the artist he felt he was.

Yehudi Menuhin's relationship with Cather was built on deep affinities, involved his entire family, and was mutually satisfying, giving Cather, some friends remarked, the family she never had.

GRANT REYNARD

Grant Reynard's (1887–1968) experience as a pupil of Cather's was not a formal one. Nevertheless, he began to learn a very important lesson from her about his own artistic self, much as she had learned about herself from Sarah Orne Jewett. Reynard and Cather were both at the MacDowell Writers' Colony in Peterborough, New Hampshire, the summer of 1926 as Cather was finishing *Death Comes for the Archbishop.* Cather was not fond of the kind of communal living a writer's colony provided, and it was the only time she ever resided at one. It was a fortunate event for Reynard.

Reynard's parents were musicians, and he studied piano as a youth, but drawing the figures he saw on the town streets was his passion. He said he did not find out how hard it was to draw until he studied in Chicago. There, he worked his way through the Chicago Academy of Fine Arts, then went off east to become an illustrator for the many popular magazines of the era. He did well; however, like Cather, he didn't feel he had "hit his home stretch" until he turned his talents to his own backyard.

Today, Reynard's paintings hang in museums throughout the United States, including the Metropolitan Museum of Art in New York, the Philadelphia Museum of Art, and the Museum of Nebraska Art at Kearney. The largest collection, however, is in the Stuhr Museum of the Prairie Pioneer in Grand Island, Nebraska, Reynard's birthplace.

Willa Cather's Advice to a Young Artist

Although I knew that Willa Cather was a distinguished writer identified with my home state, Nebraska, I had never read one of her books. It had never entered my young mind that I should ever meet her. Certainly I could not foresee that a short visit with her would prove a decisive turning point in the direction of my life and career as an artist.

In my early Nebraska years I developed a yen to draw, copied pictures by Charles Dana Gibson, took a twelve-lessons-and-you-may-be-famous correspondence course via an ad in the Sunday *Chicago Tribune.* This led to art school in Chicago and further study under Harvey Dunn, who ran a school for hopeful illustrators in New Jersey. I soon landed a steady job with the *Saturday Evening Post* and married Gwen, a lovely redhead from California. All this promised an ideal life.

For a while it seemed exciting to see my illustrations come out in the *Post.* They sent me stories by their good writers, among them J. P. Marquand, Sophie Kerr, Thomas Beer, and Scott Fitzgerald. Then monotony, speed, and pressure robbed the work of freshness. A summer came when Gwen said, "We're going to tell the *Post* the race is off for a couple of months. We'll take to the road." So we packed the Model T, overloading her tired springs, and bumped off to Maine. But somehow the summer was wasted in searching the right beaches, the quaint shacks where we could eat and sleep. The ideal spot always over the hill, a place we hadn't discovered. My worrying about money which should be coming in, the summer consumed with travel and indecision, thinking "What ails you, man? Where's the art you should be making?"

In August I decided to give up and start home. Driving down through New Hampshire we came into the little village of Peterborough trying to find a spot for lunch. You know how it goes—"That looked like a good place we just passed. You never stop where I want to." We were beyond the southern edge of town when Gwen spied a sign reading COLONY TEA BARN and insisted that she would go no farther.

While we were waiting for our food in this interesting place my alert wife recalled having seen a nearby sign reading TO THE MACDOWELL COLONY, and insisted we must stop long enough to see what it was like. I said no art colony for me thank you, the joint is probably full of nutty people declaiming poetry and weaving garlands in the woods. A lady with good hearing at a nearby table assured us it was a wonderful place. What chance had I with a determined wife and this recommendation? Without waiting for dessert off we went to look it over.

We chugged up a winding road encircling a gentle hill, and at the top found a New England farmhouse with a sign labelled HILLCREST. Gwen took off ahead of me up the flower path, mounted the front porch, and gave the doorbell a vigorous push. A smiling little lady opened the door and invited us in. It was a smile we would never forget. She wore a black Mother Hubbard dress tightly buttoned at the neck, a long skirt covering all but the toes of her shoes. Heaven I hope has pardoned me, she was so simply dressed that I mistook her for the housekeeper. She ushered us into a cozy room, and we found that our hostess was Marion MacDowell, the widow of Edward MacDowell. We were suddenly in easy conversation with the wife of a man whose piano music I had practiced years before in Nebraska. On my telling her that, she said I had no doubt played MacDowell's "To A Wild Rose" and that she had rescued the manuscript of the well-known piece from a wastebasket in his cabin. We would want to see the cabin in the woods nearby.

Mrs. MacDowell visited with pleasant sympathy as though she had all afternoon to devote to us. Gwen told her of my frustration in searching for a place to paint, of our curiosity about the colony, and that we were on our way back to New Jersey in a final retreat. The conversation then took an unexpected turn. Our hostess suggested that if I would like to work at the colony they had an opening created by a young man from New York City who had found a large studio, comfortable living quarters, and good food too great a change from his garret down in the Village. He had packed and left the place on short notice. If after looking over the colony, the studio, the Men's Lodge, and Colony Hall, we decided I would like to come for the balance of the season she would see to it that the board invited me. I would be asked to give them three letters from persons well known in my profession; only these would be needed with her recommendation.

As we talked the porch bell rang, and Mrs. MacDowell limped out into the little hall to the open door. We couldn't see the visitor, but a woman's voice was saying that she must have her studio changed. She needed quiet in which to write, and voices declaiming in the woods beyond the stone wall near her studio disturbed her. "Uh-Oh," I said to myself, "they're weaving garlands in the woods! No colony for me."

However, when Mrs. MacDowell came back she explained the visitor's trouble. "That was Miss Willa Cather," she said. "Her first visit here at the colony and she is in the middle of a very important work. We usually keep the sounds of pianos out of hearing of other composers. The writers aren't such a problem, but there is a theater camp called Mariarden near the edge of our property and occasionally they do rehearse outside. I assured Miss Cather that she would be moved this afternoon. We do everything we can to make our colonists as happy as possible."

Before we left Mrs. MacDowell led us through a hall and into the music room, where a dark Steinway grand brought memories of the time my parents had taken me to a recital by Edward MacDowell in Los Angeles, on a trip out to visit my brother. I was a grade-school kid, and greatly impressed at hearing him play his own compositions. A somber bronze of the composer peered from a corner near the piano. Mrs. MacDowell guided us out a side door and through the lovely garden to our car. She used a cane and walked with a slightly labored step. Waving us off, she pointed up the road toward the studio. "Come by when you finish your tour and tell me how you like it."

Like it we did. The twenty-five studios of various colonists were scattered through the woods along shady lanes which wound toward Colony Hall, a large white building where genius dined at breakfast and dinner. So we were told by Emile and Mary, the friendly combination of caretaker, cook, and general welcomers. Mary said that coming through the woods we had passed celebrities at every turn. Edwin Arlington Robinson was writing "Tristram" back a ways to the right, and not far from his cabin we had passed a stone chapel-like studio donated by Mrs. John Alexander in honor of her husband, the well-known painter. Emile said a young man had left that studio the day before. It probably would be filled from a waiting list before the week was out.

They showed us the rambling cottage where the ladies of the colony lived. Mr. Robinson was the only colonist with quarters in Colony Hall, upstairs over the dining room. We would find the Men's Lodge on passing the library, down through the trees. Taking a road from the Lodge we would come to Hillcrest again.

As we stood on the back steps of Colony Hall saying goodbye to Emile and Mary, a brisk-gaited man came by to leave his lunch basket. I didn't know when I had seen so much joy of living in a man. He gave the immediate impression that his mind and body were charged with an electric energy. Words and thoughts and feelings were so compressed within him that they might burst their bonds any moment. As he stepped animatedly away Emile said, "There's a fine man. That's Mr. Wilder, Thornton Wilder." "Oh," Mary said, "they don't come foiner than that one, bless 'im."

Gwen was liking the place better all the time. I, too, found a weakening of some of my earlier objections. It had seemed too much of a paradise of genius with the great pines and the thrushes' songs echoing through the arched lanes of the woods, but by the time we got back to Mrs. MacDowell's front door I had agreed to take the jump from illustration to colony art. We left with that grand little lady saying goodbye, her kind benediction waving us on our Jersey way.

We were so excited by this sudden turn in our plans that we drove on into the night and arrived home at dawn. I got busy pronto asking friends to write those three letters, and within the week I started one bright morning for Peterborough, the car packed head high, big rolls of canvas, big brushes, enough paint to do a mural, my ambition rampant. Goodbye illustration, I was at last to be a Fine Art artist!

On my arrival at the colony I checked in at Colony Hall and Emile told me I was to work in the Alexander studio, the big studio for painters. I had arrived too late for dinner with the colonists, but Mary gave me some food before I went to my room in the Men's Lodge. The next morning I entered the dining room and found there were no assigned places. With chairs for twenty five colonists I might choose a place at any of the five tables with the exception of a seat at the table nearest the door. This was by mutual consent of the diners reserved for Edwin Arlington Robinson who, although he was the last man to have considered himself so, was the distinguished dean of the colony.

The place was bursting with celebrities with only a few younger members like myself who hadn't gained recognition. My timid entrance to the dining room was softened by an easy introduction to those at my table, and I soon felt at home in Colony Hall. I had taken a place near the door and without knowing it had seated myself next to Mr. Robinson. I found him a very quiet man with whom you had to open conversations, agreeable once you spoke, but somewhat forbidding to a newcomer like myself. He was tall and thin and quite able to cope with people and the world about him, but he gave me a notion that he needed protection. There was nothing of the Bohemian poet about him, immaculately dressed, almost antiseptic in his formality, his head and features sensitive and distinguished. As he slowly raised his head from contemplating his food, his eyes gave you the impression that he had been away for a few seconds and had to adjust back into the little world of the table. The people, the morning, everything had come upon him too soon and he hadn't quite become part of it all.

I had never known a poet, certainly not a great poet, but this man was everything I imagined a sensitive poet to be. I was feeling my way in an unfamiliar circle of celebrated characters, but somehow his calm, almost bashful quality proved reassuring to me. With E. A. you took it easy. His every way was a quiet way. He didn't speak much, but when he did all of us were alert for every word since his was never ordinary conversation. He was slow to start, but not from an inability to express himself once he got the words going. Sometimes when asked a question he would hesitate to answer. With a long artist's finger he rubbed his fine high forehead into puzzled wrinkles as though to press the thoughts into words and get them out. Over something humorous in the conversation his lips pursed into the start of a smile and his dark eyes sparkled, a boy's eyes over sudden enjoyment, but it was all an inner fun with him. He could never deliver a good laugh. He wanted to with all his soul, but just couldn't burst the bonds and liberate it.

I had picked a lively table that morning. Thornton Wilder was seated around the other side from Mr. Robinson, then Dorothy and DuBose Heyward. I sat neglecting my scrambled eggs and listening to the dialogue between E. A. and DuBose on the question of what food could be bought for a hungry poet to act as the best filler for the least money, say ten cents. Early in his career E. A. had found a can of baked beans did the job best. The Heywards spoke of the gullah folk down Charleston way and how gullahs just about lived on porgies. Thornton Wilder asked DuBose to give us a sample of gullah, and as he did E. A.'s eyes sparkled with delight over the fun he felt inside.

Because of the conversation I had overheard on Mrs. MacDowell's porch I was curious to have Willa Cather pointed out to me, and Mr. Robinson said she was facing us at the next table. I had heard her lusty laughter and thought her a woman who expressed herself with vigor and freedom. There was a youthful animation about her, outgoing in conversation. Her hair reminded me of a favorite aunt of mine in Nebraska. It was parted in the middle and drawn plainly above her well-shaped ears to a terminal knot at the back. My grandmother Bacon had also kept her hair that way, and at once I was taken back to the pioneer women of the West. The New Hampshire morning being cool she wore, over a white shirtwaist, a mannish short coat with a design on the cuffs and pockets, the sort cowboys might wear. It reminded me of Annie Oakley in Buffalo Bill's Wild West Show. Her eyebrows dark and straight, she had an ample nose and a firm, full mouth, the valley between the nose and mouth deeply indented and her chin a good one. All in all a forthright, gay, laughing person. Something about her facial structure recalled Russian women to me, the wives of workers on the Union Pacific railroad back home. I wondered what she would say to me when she found that I was born out in her country.

After breakfast I unloaded my equipment at the studio. No wonder the place had overpowered my predecessor; it was a size for mural painters. I felt it a vacant church and the scale convinced me I must work in a size to match it. Without taking time to plan much I decided to do a series far removed from my illustrations, compositions on the artiest subject I could quickly think up—nude ladies romping in the woods with goats. The trees for these paintings were everywhere outside the studio, and I had brought a portfolio of figure drawings which I hoped to make use of eventually. My idea was to get as far away as I could from the work I had done for magazines.

I tried at once to outdo the painter Arthur B. Davies, a member of The Eight, who also painted nudes and goats in outdoor settings. Feeling that I had been too conventional in doing the required pretty girls for the magazines I would have my gals run wild in the woods and add goats for Dionysian abandon, all of which should prove very effective. Off on a new attack at art, I certainly wasn't identified with the paintings which came vigorously off my flying brushes. We had a few goats in Nebraska, but no nude ladies romping in the woods.

After devoting eight dedicated hours a day for several weeks I had the walls of the Alexander studio profanely covered with productions intended to rival Rubens, and especially recalling to mind the pulchritude if not the solidity of his second wife. This work, I thought, was either great or terrible, but there was no doubt that I had gone Fine Art with an abandon, inspired by the New Hampshire air and my colony associates. I was vigorously on an art-for-art's-sake spree.

During these working weeks I had talked with Miss Cather a number of times in the dining hall. She had discovered that I was a Nebraskan and a painter, but had never asked about what sort of art I did. She told of her great admiration for line in graphic work, of the spare beauty of line drawing which enclosed form. W. T. Benda, the illustrator, had done a book of hers, *My Ántonia*, in line. In one of these table conversations she told me that she needed a quiet place to write: that noise was a great enemy. She spent a part of the year lying fallow (like farm land in the West) gaining ideas and inspiration from life itself.

I was a bit in awe of her and much impressed that she was a celebrity. It never occurred to me that she would be the least bit interested in my career. However, one morning at breakfast toward the close of the season she told me that on finding I was a fellow countryman she was curious to see my painting. Might she come by one afternoon at the close of our working hours and visit my studio? I was surprised and delighted, and we agreed on a convenient hour for her to come that afternoon. I hurried to the studio immediately after breakfast and worked throughout the day sweeping the place, preparing to give her tea, and adjusting my big canvases in the best possible light around the walls.

Promptly at five Miss Cather arrived. She came in with that pleasant way she had of forthrightly greeting people, put her empty lunch basket on a chair near the door, and promptly began a tour of the studio. She looked hurriedly over the canvases and made no comment on my goats and unadorned ladies.

Finishing her tour of the walls, she came at my invitation to have a cup of tea and the store cookies I had bought for the occasion. Before sitting down, she sorted over some small drawings of the woods and Mt. Monadnock and said she liked them.

Without a word of comment on my paintings she sat at tea and talked entirely about herself for the rest of the visit. I thought, "Well, I suppose writers are like this, wrapped up in themselves." I listened, however, to every word in spite of my disappointment at her failure to praise my work. It wasn't until she left my studio that I realized that the talk about herself was directed straight at me.

She told of coming as a child from her birthplace in Virginia along with her family out onto the great prairies of Nebraska and to the little town of Red Cloud. She talked of how a Bohemian hired girl had befriended her. Willa Cather grew up in this rolling prairie land, went to the University of Nebraska, later to Pittsburgh and an editorial assignment, then to New York and a better job with *McClure's Magazine.* She was fascinated with city life—the gaiety, the parties, the opera. She said her stories and poems reflected her desire to do *fine* writing, and they won some acclaim.

"However," she said, "it wasn't until I suddenly thought of my youth in a great wave of nostalgia for the early Nebraska days that my work took on a new dimension. I remembered with deep feeling my homeland and the Bohemian hired girl—who had been so kind to me. It was as though I had turned up the corner of a rarely beautiful rug and looked at the warp of the dusty back of it. Something happened within me, a sweeping surge of feeling for Nebraska, and I wrote *My Ántonia,* a book that came through on so great a wave of desire that the story *must* be written. It came and grew as nature does from inside out.

"The crux of this whole art experience is in that word *desire*—an urgent need to *recreate* a vital life experience which wells up within and must find release in the writing.

"*My Ántonia* came that way, born of feeling and memory, flooding the pages. It was wonderfully received and later translated into other languages, a solid success.

"At the time of creation," she continued, "a writer must not think of a work's future, of critics, publishers, or prizes. The painter must not think of art dealers, awards to be won, membership in academies; nor the composer worry about performances, Carnegie Hall, the approbation of conductors. The important thing is that the book be written, the picture be painted, the symphony burst forth, the song sing its way into life from the heart of the artist."

Miss Cather thanked me for my tea, and after she left I sat in a state of shock, there in the hollow shadows of the studio amid the ruins of my goats and phoney women. I felt that everything about me was thin, trumped up. For the remainder of my stay at the colony I could not paint at all. In half an hour a distinguished writer had left me and my summer's work in utter shambles. I wanted to begin again, but how could I paint in a void without a subject. I took down the goat women on which I had wasted canvas and paint, packed my stuff and suitcase into the old Model T, and took off for New Jersey. I had not spoken to any colonist or to Mrs. MacDowell about my art debacle, and that great lady told me that, if I wanted to, I might return another summer. That fall and through the winter and spring I went back to illustration, but nothing seemed to click. I was in a deep valley after a sky ride.

The following summer, on the board's invitation, I returned to the colony but this time without the big canvases. Instead I took a couple of drawing pads, some water colors, a minimum of material, and asked Mrs. MacDowell if I might have one of the smaller studios. My creative life was at a standstill. No matter how I tried I could not find a subject. I was stopped. The urge, talent, call it what you will, had left me. There in that ideal creative place I could not work. After several weeks of this vacant feeling I went to Mrs. MacDowell and told her I knew she was not running a summer resort, that I could not get started and had come to tell her I was leaving the colony. "Oh now," she said, "I understand this sort of thing. Remember I had an artist husband. You must take another week here. Don't try to work; walk these woods, look at Monadnock through the trees. Just loaf. I'm sure you will find I am right about your not leaving the colony."

What a wise and lovely person she was. I did as she had advised me. I spent a few days given up to loafing, listened to sounds of the forest, to the cool loveliness of a thrush's song at sunset in the wilderness of great pines, a sounding board of beauty made for poets. One evening, so full of intoxication only the great woods can give, things began to come through, filling my empty head and heart. I thought of Willa Cather's visit, and of how I had sought to do *fine* art. Suddenly my search for a motive was over. The far sound of a dog barking down in the village of Peterborough brought back my home town in a nostalgic chain of memories—Grand Island, Nebraska, and our house on Third Street; practicing piano on a spring afternoon, and the sound of kids down the block playing one-o-cat and kick-the-can. The wave of subjects overwhelmed me.

The question was where to start: the town characters, the Methodist church across our street where kids climbed into the bell tower and bombarded the enemy with ripe tomatoes; the Elks Club where I had set pins in the bowling alley; the Fourth of July, Circus Day, the Opera House, my Uncle Bryan's Keeley Cure for drunks; the German dances down at Sand Krog, the Koehler Hotel across from the U.P. station where Buffalo Bill got tight the day of his Wild West show and had to be tied to his horse! Subjects—there were so many that a lifetime could not be long enough to turn them into art.

The next morning in my studio I began making drawings from memory—more felt than remembered. I spent part of the days doing water colors of the woods and village. Everywhere there were wonderful places and people asking to be drawn and painted, both there in New Hampshire and far out in my native Nebraska, endless opportunities. Mrs. MacDowell was delighted at the news that I had "gotten going" as she put it.

Willa Cather did not return to the colony that year. It was my great good fortune to have had my talk with her the year before. She never came back to the colony. I think the place was not suited to her particular temperament. I heard later that she had an apartment down in Greenwich Village and had rented the floor above so that noise would not disturb her writing.

I was sure that next to the measure of vision the good Lord had given to me nothing greater could have happened to me than my meeting with this distinguished woman. False ambitions and the race for position in art dropped away. The following winter I resigned from an art club in New York where I had been involved in logrolling, politics, working for prizes, and other things which I could tolerate no longer. I quit pushing for success, left off speculating and theorizing about *how* to be an artist, and painted freely with excitement and joy my vital impressions, versions, and memories of people and places near and far.

The following summer at the colony, working on my drawings of Nebraska, I felt that graphic art did not fully express what I had to say and began to write down some of my memories of people and places. I was back in Grand Island and got so excited there were days when I forgot to eat my lunch, delivered to the studio in a basket.

The news leaked out that I, an artist, was writing, and one evening after dinner I was asked by a small group to let them hear what I had done. Although a bad reader, I stumbled through a few of these word sketches at a private little assembly in the library. When I finished they spoke with approval and some astonishment at what I had done in their medium, and DuBose Heyward, a kind and gentle man who was writing *Porgy* at the colony that year, said he hoped an editor would never edit the writing. I asked for advice and again DuBose was first to say he felt I might slow my pace a bit, take time to write my artist's observations into the pieces, the color and details that I as an artist saw. He felt this would not slow down my German dances and circus parades. I greatly valued and used his advice, and was much encouraged that so fine a writer had taken time to give me his ideas.

He had mentioned editors, but I was afraid to show my writing to critical editors, and back home put the manuscripts in an abandoned icebox which stood in a corner of my studio. Some time later I got them out and on rereading decided to try marketing the stories and drawings together.

Loathing the peddling job, I took them around to several magazines.

Editors who liked the drawings didn't go for the stories. About to give up I sent them to *Scribner's Magazine* and received word that they no longer used illustrations in the magazine, but liked my writing and would use five of the little stories under a collective title in a coming issue. I decided on a title, *West of Omaha*, which they used on publication.

Later I had a letter from the editor asking if *Scribner's* might use my *West of Omaha* in a collection of the work of young writers, *Life in the United States*. I hoped Willa Cather might like my written sketches should she ever see them.

I kept track of Miss Cather through book reviews, read what she wrote with great delight, and tried to think how I might let her know how deeply grateful I was. Letters I composed seemed clumsy. Time sped by, and remembering how she valued privacy, I discarded impulses to contact her. I would not in any way spoil our short acquaintance and its tremendous meaning to me with a fumble of some sort. I saw her some years later coming down the grand stairs at the Metropolitan between acts of *La Bohème* with her publisher, Alfred Knopf. It hardly seemed the time or place to interrupt their animated conversation.

Later on a lecture tour I came into Nebraska from Kansas, and near her old home town of Red Cloud crossed the Republican River. I remembered how Lucy Gayheart, the heroine of one of her novels, had returned to her homeland and a little Nebraska town, a sad and disappointed woman after a time of early success and adulation as a promising pianist in Chicago. In the book she had gone down to another river, the Platte, one winter evening at sunset, had put on her skates and gone onto the ice alone. As she glided silently around the curves of snowy hills, thin ice cracked and the river swallowed Lucy Gayheart into its dark waters.

I was in a nostalgic mood coming into Red Cloud, and inquired about the home where Willa Cather had returned over the years to visit with her folks. Locating the place, I found it a replica of thousands of little white houses in western towns. The summer had been dry, the trees were parched, and the grass was dead, but as I sat in my car working on a water color the dusk deepened and a mood came into my picture, the feel of the old house with its ornamented porch running around the side, the time of evening, an intangible haunting quality enfolding the commonplace subject.

When I got back to New Jersey I found that something Willa Cather put into her writing had come into my painting. I would give it to her, the perfect way to say to her in paint what I could not do so well in any other way. I inquired of her publishers and found that she was not in New York, but

I might write to her secretary. She replied that Miss Cather on her return would be glad to see me, and was sure my painting would please her.

Some weeks went by and I had no word. Gwen and I had gone to Denver, where I wanted to paint mountains. We were visiting with old friends and at breakfast I opened the morning paper to see what was wrong with the world. Turning a page I found with a shock of recognition a photograph of Willa Cather. The type heading read "Willa Cather, Noted Writer, Dead." I could hardly believe that this inevitable last line had been written for my benefactor, that now she could never see the painting of her family home in Red Cloud, nor know the gratitude I owed her.

Turning back to the paper and its photograph of a sad elderly woman so like one of her pioneers, I recalled that first morning at the colony, her robust laughter and the zest for life in her radiant face. I thought of the little girl who had come so early from Virginia and had called the prairies her homeland; the many years between those Nebraska days and our meeting at the colony.

Then I recalled her great kindness to me, a fellow Westerner mixed up in arty ambitions, and how in a half hour's conversation she had, in telling of herself, revealed to me my need of that activating force in art, the creative spark of desire.

Prairie Schooner 46, no. 2 (1972): 111–24.

YEHUDI MENUHIN

Willa Cather often became a friend of a family: the Miners, the Canfields, the Seibels, the Knopfs, and the Menuhins. Yehudi Menuhin (1916–1999) may have been the most famous and perhaps her favorite Menuhin, but she enjoyed Marutha, Hephzibah, Yaltah, and the next generation, too. In a lively letter to E. K. Brown in 1947, Cather tells about a whirlwind, yet relaxed, visit she had just had with Hephzibah, her husband, and two children and Yehudi and his two children. Although they spent only a short morning together before the group sailed to London, where Hephzibah and Yehudi were to give a series of concerts, the day after the visit Cather could still feel intensely the reverberations of their presence and friendship throughout the apartment. The enjoyment was mutual, for Yehudi said that his friendship with Cather was the greatest debt he owed Jan and Isabelle Hambourg, whom he often visited when he was in Europe (Menuhin 77–78).

Since Cather's death, the Menuhins have given many concerts dedicated to her memory.

From Unfinished Journey

The Ansonia Hotel apartment being too small for parties, my mother's entertaining had to be select rather than lavish, but there were some friends who came frequently. Of them all the most beloved was Willa Cather, to whom Jan and Isabelle Hambourg had introduced us in 1930. From the outset there was between us a family closeness which we children accommodated with the title "aunt" while Mammina [his mother], always drawn to the utterly authentic, embraced her as a sister. I don't know if each ever knew that the other had created scandals, half a world apart, by wearing her hair shingled in adolescence, but it appeared to have predestined them for sisterhood (their confidences must have been fascinating; sadly I never overheard them). As if to enshrine that relationship and make it immortal, perfect and inalienably hers, Mammina when Aunt Willa died, burned her letters.

Willa Cather was the embodiment of America—but an America which has long ago disappeared. Her books, as everyone knows, describe a country still overwhelmingly natural, a way of life still rural, lived by settlers lately arrived from Europe whose traditions were all the more precious for their transplantation to a strange land. Only recently has the United States become a society of abstractions; no doubt the abstraction of the pursuit of happiness existed then, but happiness itself had not become an abstraction and was still rooted in the earth, as Aunt Willa was herself. She had an eye and an ear for the aesthetic wonders of nature, the fall of light on a landscape, the rustle of trees, and a realistic, penetrating, compassionate understanding of the human animal in his setting. The people she wrote about grew out of and belonged to their environment, whether the Middle West, New Mexico, or Quebec, and it is this which makes her work so American of its period. It is not too much to say that she revealed a face of America to us youngsters who were growing up among adults largely born abroad. Her mannish figure and country tweediness, her let's-lay-it-on-the-table manners and unconcealed blue eyes, her rosy skin and energetic demeanor bespoke a phenomenon as strangely comforting to us all as it was foreign, something in the grain like Christian Temperance or the Girl Scout movement. In reminiscences a quarter of a century old she provided historical perspectives to my lament for New York, resurrecting a Manhattan where whole houses belonged to single families, the breadwinners of which walked or rode to Wall Street, tipping their hats to acquaintances met en route. Even by the 1930s the thought of knowing one's neighbors on Fifth Avenue was absurd.

She was a rock of strength and sweetness. Ever since coming east she had reserved time during the week for walking in Central Park, which was to her native Nebraska as a nosegay to an interminable prairie. Her favorite walk was around the reservoir in the park, where contact with the earth renewed her sense of belonging in a metropolis in which so much conspired to alienation. Park veterans ourselves, my sisters and I often joined her, taking turns at the honor of walking by her side. When I had the opportunity I saw her very frequently, not only in New York but in Los Angeles, where sometimes a tour delivered me when she was visiting relatives there. At one period I had particular cause to lean on her: in the unhappiness of my first marriage Aunt Willa was someone to be utterly trusted. One could tell her everything in one's heart: it would never be misused, never turned against one, never cause her to alter her regard. In those days she and I took many a walk around the reservoir. Her strength had a patience and evenness which did not preclude a certain severity. There were abuses and vulgarities she refused to tolerate, such as exposure in newspapers or on radio. She had a contempt for anything too much owned or determined by mobs, reserving admiration for high individual endeavor, withdrawing more and more from society even as she drew closer to us. The outside world became increasingly obscure for her, as on the fogbound island of Grand Manan in the Bay of Fundy, where she built a summer cottage. But indoors life burned bright, with parties and birthday luncheons, excursions to the Metropolitan Opera, baskets of flowers and orange trees arriving in snowstorms, and always books and walks in Central Park.

She adored what she felt had not been her birthright—the old, the European, the multilayered, and above all music. But her reverence did not cause her to stray into the self-doubt which some Americans used to show when confronting Europe. Early in 1936, on the point of returning to California, I must have expressed some uncertainties about the future, for in reply I received these words (words which, it must be said, have since been overtaken by time):

Yes, my dear boy, you *are* confronting a problem. But it is the problem which every American artist confronts. If we remain always in our own land we miss the companionship of seasoned and disciplined minds. Here there are no standards of taste, and no responses to art *except emotional* ones.

On the other hand, if we adopt Europe altogether, we lose that sense of *belonging* which is so important, and we lose part of our reality. I know a few very talented young writers who at the age of twenty-one or two decided that they would be French. They went abroad to live, and have never amounted to anything since. They can't be *really* French, you see, so they are just unconscious impostors. The things his own country makes him feel (the earth, the sky, the slang in the streets) are about the best capital a writer has to draw upon. A musician is much less restricted. The very nature of your work means "pack your kit." You, Yehudi, will simply have to do both things and live two lives. But I think you must spend your vacations in your own country when possible.

Her friend and biographer Elizabeth Shepley Sergeant wrote that she "made a story" of us Menuhins "as if she had at last, by proxy, a family exactly to her taste. Not at all like her beloved father's family with its pioneer tradition; in this brilliant Jewish milieu, erudition and art were primary, and everything else of secondary importance." When this passage is considered in the light of a remark uttered by Harsányi in *The Song of the Lark,* "Every artist makes himself born," it becomes apparent that creating fiction and merging with us celebrated a single impulse, that we who had found our American author gave our author her European novel.

If so, she returned our gift in kind and overmeasure, sharing her perception of European literature, making us presents of the German poets, taking us by the hand through Shakespeare's plays. In our apartment there was a little room, nobody's property in particular, small enough to be cozy, and furnished with a table around which Aunt Willa, Hephzibah, Yaltah, myself and often Aunt Willa's companion, Edith Lewis, gathered for Shakespearean readings, each taking several parts, and Aunt Willa commenting on the language and situations in such a way as to draw us into her own pleasure and excitement. She herself ferreted through secondhand bookshops to procure us copies of the plays. As originally chartered, the reading circle did not include me since I was often away on tour; but when present, I pressed for membership and was granted it. Her favorite author was Flaubert and her own style had his economy and elegance. She would polish her prose until it shone like a jewel.

Thus, representing America and presenting us with the values of Europe, Aunt Willa possessed the unity in diversity which underlay all my life. I had by now seen many other Americas than my own, but at a remove; the real discoveries were yet to come and in consequence were launched from a base as much European as American. Long before we saw Europe, we were conscious of it: it formed our parents, it gave us the books we read, it was the fount of music. Languages and travel confirmed the tendency, never excluding the United States but complementing it with a wide circle of attachments. The twice-yearly transatlantic crossings of adolescence did not split my life in half; rather they linked my double heritage into a seamless whole. . . .

When Rosalie had gone, I wrote to my favorite confidante, Aunt Willa, to tell her of my loss. With a truly auntlike combination of sympathy, moral stiffening and humor, she remarked in reply, "A little heartache is a good companion for a young man on his holiday," then took the opportunity to give me some serious advice on the choice of a wife—advice which in retrospect might be thought prophetic:

> You will need fundamental honesty in a wife more than anything else, I think. By honesty I mean the knowledge that two and two make four and can never be sighed or dreamed into making five. Also the knowledge that real love is not so much admiration as it is the drive to help and to make life easy for the other person. If the man is a man with a career before him, she must have good sense and stamina as well as charm. . . . But I doubt if you will marry an American at all. I rather think you will need a girl with a more disciplined nature than our girls are likely to have. . . .
>
> Fortune has always been good to you, my boy, and I rather suspect her crowning favor will be a girl like that: slight, heroic, delicate, unconquerable (sounds as if I were describing Marutha, doesn't it!). Well, like enough you will marry someone much your mother's type.

New York: Knopf, 1977. 128–31, 144–45.

In a Spiritual Community

The Cathers attended the Baptist church when Cather was a child, but Elsie Cather joined the Grace Episcopal Church in Red Cloud in 1907, when she was seventeen.[1] Cather was then going through her years of skepticism. However, in 1922, Cather, her mother, and her father joined the same congregation. By that time, many Cathers had also joined Grace Church. Cather's reading had always taken her into the byroads of faith. She found *The Varieties of Religious Experience* by Henry James, for instance, well worth studying.

The selections that follow are not reminiscences but eulogies; however, it seemed important not only to make the documents available to a wider audience but also, in the context of people's memories of Cather, to recall that she engaged in religious thinking throughout her life and works.

The final article, a tribute by a Nebraska journalist who visited Cather's gravesite in Jaffrey, New Hampshire, draws into one view the Nebraska and the Jaffrey that Cather had loved. It seems appropriate, too, that the last article circles readers back to the first, both by Nebraska journalists.

GEORGE ALLEN BEECHER

Cather's ideal pastor seemed to be Bishop George Beecher (1868–1951), who had received her into membership at Grace Church. He appeared physically, mentally, and spiritually to be of the same cast of her Bishops in *Death Comes for the Archbishop*. Beecher was a much beloved "missionary Bishop" in western Nebraska. In many ways, he was a life-sized combination of Bishop Latour and Father Vaillant. Beecher and Cather enjoyed a warm intellectual relationship until the end of her life.

On 2 November 1947, the *Commercial Advertiser* reported that the All Souls Day service at Grace Episcopal Church was "especially impressive . . . including as it did a memorial service for Miss Willa Cather." Dean Winfield R. Post of Hastings Pro Cathedral led the service and Bishop Beecher gave the memorial sermon. On the altar table was "a beautiful brass cross used for the first time at this service" graced by bronze chrysanthemums, a gift from Elsie Cather. Afterward, "the Guild served a buffet supper at the home of one of the parishioners."

From A Bishop of the Great Plains

WILLA CATHER

December 7, 1876–April 24, 1947

Willa Cather and the members of her family worshipped God for many years in Grace Episcopal Church, Red Cloud (named after the Sioux Indian warrior), Nebraska; and there on December 27, 1922, I confirmed her and her father and mother. It was the very year she received the Pulitzer Prize for her novel, *One of Ours*, the story of a Western boy in World War I.

Almost twenty-five years later, on Sunday afternoon, November 2, 1947, in this same little church, it was my privilege, though a sad one, to hold a memorial service in Miss Cather's honor, attended by a group of her friends and neighbors who had known Miss Cather, and longed to express their love and appreciation of her.

The substance of my remarks at this quiet and peaceful service, held during the octave of All Saints Day, was somewhat as follows:

I have chosen for my text the eighth verse of the fifth chapter of the Gospel according to St. Matthew, which is part of our Lord's Sermon on the Mount, *Blessed are the pure in heart, for they shall see God.*

What thought could better express the life and character of Willa Cather than that expressed in this beatitude. To us who knew her, many from the days of her early childhood, her influence has been felt not only in the fascination of her literary productions, but in the simplicity and priceless beauty of her personality and Christian character.

Born and reared in the environment and culture of a Christian home, where religion was recognized as the basis of the marriage vows and expressed in the daily habits of that home, she absorbed those qualities of purity and poise, which, through the years, became the inspiration of her happy and useful life. Everyone present who knew her will agree that she lived up to her baptismal vows as a *member of Christ, the child of God, and an inheritor of the kingdom of heaven.*

Coming to Red Cloud as an eight-year old girl, she traveled by pony from neighbor to neighbor, "soaking in the pleasant flavor of alien ways." Using her own words, "I grew fond of some of the immigrants, particularly the old women, who used to tell me of their home country. I have never found any intellectual excitement more intense than I used to feel when I spent a morning with one of these pioneer women at her baking or butter making. I used to ride home in the most unusual state of excitement."

After being graduated from the high school here in Red Cloud, Miss Cather attended the University of Nebraska, where she supported herself in part by working as a reporter. Following her graduation in 1895, she taught English in the high school of Allegheny, Pennsylvania, and served on the staff of the Pittsburgh *Daily Leader*, 1898–1901.

Her first book was in verse, *April Twilights* (1903); and her first volume of stories, *The Troll Garden* (1905), led to her appointment as associate editor of *McClure's Magazine*, from 1905 to 1912. This brought her into contact, not only in New York and London but on the Continent, with some of the leading literary figures of the time.

At this point in her career, she had the natural desire to return to her home town, and had the good judgment to do so. She renewed her friendship with the country people of her youth. She loved the prairie breezes, the dust of the winding trails, the golden sunsets, the fading horizons with the happy anticipation of the promised days ahead. In other words, it was home.

With the publication in 1913 of *O Pioneers!*, there began that series of novels from her pen upon which her fame chiefly rests. In the concluding words of *The Song of the Lark*, concerned with Thea Kronborg, Miss Cather said, "This story attempts to deal only with the simple and concrete beginnings which color and accent an artist's work, and to give some account of how a Moonstone girl found her way out of a vague, easy-going world into a life of disciplined endeavor. Any account of the loyalty of young hearts to some exalted ideal, and the passion with which they strive, will always, in some of us, rekindle generous emotions."

Whether consciously autobiographical or not, this passage epitomizes one phase of Miss Cather's life. She certainly "found her way out of a vague, easy-going world into a life of disciplined endeavor"; and she certainly had loyalty to an "exalted ideal," and strove towards it with passion.

I shall not attempt to review any of her books, but the opinion of such a noted critic as Dr. Henry Seidel Canby is not out of place: "With it [*O Pioneers!*] she put herself in the forefront of those who had begun to realize the importance of pioneer life in America. *My Ántonia* (1918) was another book with the same general background, which established her reputation as a novelist of unusual depth and power of beauty, who could see deep currents

of emotion running in those Main Streets which [others were] to satirize for their decline into dullness. . . . Among the writers who have deepened and refined the study of American character, Willa Cather is perhaps preeminent. . . . She is perhaps closer to essential Americanism than any other contemporary writer. . . . She comes closest in American literature of this period to the classic ideal of balance, insight, restraint."

I once asked her how she felt after she had finished a story and submitted it for publication. Her reply was, as I remember it, "Well, I feel as though I had launched a part of my soul in a boat, and stood upon the shore long enough to watch it disappear into the open sea."

It is right that in some measure we record the recognition of Willa Cather's well merited honors. In 1931, Princeton University for the first time in its history of one hundred and eighty-four years, bestowed upon Miss Cather the honorary degree of Doctor of Letters, never before having bestowed it upon a woman. She also received the same degree from the Universities of Nebraska, Michigan, Columbia, and Yale. The University of California conferred upon her the honorary degree of Doctor of Laws. In 1933, she won the *Prix Femina Americain*, awarded in France for *Shadows on the Rock*. She was a member of the American Academy of Arts and Letters; and in 1944, the National Institute of Arts and Letters gave her a gold medal, its highest award, in recognition, not of any particular book, but of her great achievement in letters.

Among the many friends gathered together that day in tribute to the memory of Willa Cather, was her secretary, Miss Edith Lewis. In a letter I received from her shortly after the service, Miss Lewis wrote, "Could you, Bishop Beecher, send me the prayer that you made for Miss Cather at that service? I should like so much to add it sometimes to my thoughts and prayers for her. I know how much you and all her friends out there loved her. But sometimes I think that no one who did not see her every day, under all the trials and hard things of life, could know all the beauty and courage and steadfastness of her spirit; how generous she was in every thought and act; how loving and faithful to all her friends, and to everyone who needed her. One can say so little, and, besides, with you there is no need."

Surviving are two brothers, John E. Cather, of Whittier, California, and James Cather, of Long Beach, California; and two sisters, Mrs. Jessica Auld, of Palo Alto, California, and Miss Elsie Margaret Cather, of Lincoln, Nebraska, who was present that day, and shared with us the tribute to her beloved sister.

Blessed are the pure in heart: for they shall see God.
Philadelphia: *Church Historical Society*, 1950. 209–12.

ANDERS G. LUND JR.

Willa Cather died at home one afternoon from a massive cerebral hemorrhage. Her companion of the hour was her secretary, Sarah Bloom. A private funeral was held in New York City, attended by a few family and friends, then her brothers, James and John, and a few other relatives took the body to the old cemetery at Jaffrey, New Hampshire. Cather had asked to be buried there, east of Mount Monadnock, along a rock wall, at the end of the lane that leads directly from the classic, distinguished-looking, old Meeting House down to her gravesite. At that time, a gravesite service was held and the reading was from *The Book of Common Prayer.* One can imagine her enjoying the sonorous phrases of the King James Bible.

Since Cather belonged to no church in Jaffrey, the pastor of the local Presbyterian church, Anders G. Lund Sr., was asked to care for the service. He, in turn, asked his son, an ordained Episcopalian priest, to read the service. The Rev. Anders G. Lund Jr. served many different congregations in Connecticut, Massachusetts, and New York. His last known parish was St. John in South Salem, New York.

Death Comes for Willa Cather

In April, 1947, a New York Funeral Director whose name I do not recall phoned my father, the Rev. A. G. Lund, Sr., pastor of the First Congregational Church in Jaffrey Center, New Hampshire. He said that the famed novelist, Willa Cather, had died in New York, and according to her wishes would be buried in the Old Burying Ground at Jaffrey. She and her close friend Edith Lewis had for many years been summer visitors at nearby Shattuck Inn, and they had both become enamored of the quaint New England village at the foot of majestic Manadnock mountain. She had picked out a burial lot which had an unobstructed view of the mountain.

Miss Cather was an Episcopalian, and had said that she wished a priest would conduct the burial office from the Book of Common Prayer. My father called me, at that time rector of St. Thomas Church, Brooklyn, and I of course was delighted to have a share in such a memorable occasion. I learned that the service was planned for 2 P.M. on Saturday.

Not many local people had heard of the service, but I recall that some twelve or thirteen people were at the graveside in addition to Miss Lewis and two other women from New York. Dr. and Mrs. Julius Seelye Bixler,

President of Colby College, were there; so were Professor and Mrs. Ernest Bernbaum, the literary scholar from the University of Illinois; Dr. Theodore A. Greene, pastor of the Congregational Church in New Britain; my father, mother, sister, and a few white-haired ladies.

It was a cold and foggy day, matching the somber occasion. Shortly before 2 o'clock a truck pulled up, carrying an enormous bronze casket which I was told cost $10,000. On it was a gold plate with the inscription, "Willa Cather." No pallbearers could lift such a great weight, and a crane lowered it to the grave site. There were no flowers. I read the Burial Office from *The Book of Common Prayer*, and used the two Psalms which Miss Cather had requested, Psalms 23 and 103. I thought of one of the themes in her great novels as I read these verses: "As for man, his days are like grass; he flourished like a flower of the field; for the wind passes over it, and is gone, and its place knows it no more. But the steadfast love of the Lord is from everlasting to everlasting upon those who fear him."

The awed and saddened little group quickly dispersed in the chilly afternoon.

Letter to L. Brent Bohlke. 6 Apr. 1983.

RICHARD C. HERMAN

Dick Herman (1928–), as his byline identifies him, is another of those keen, curious reporters that come from Nebraska. His writing and editing skills led him to the position of editorial page editor at the *Lincoln Journal*. Recently, he recalled the occasion for his story about Willa Cather's grave at Jaffrey: "We were on a vacation in New England, so of course, we stopped at Willa Cather's gravesite. I didn't go for the story, just out of curiosity of seeing the grave of a famous writer from Nebraska." Since a good journalist always carries a well-stocked camera, he took numerous pictures and, after enjoying the hospitality of a large inn in the Jaffrey area, promptly turned out a front-page spread for the *Lincoln Journal* Sunday supplement.[1]

Memories of Willa Cather Shared with New Hampshire

The man I hailed alongside the gravel roadway responded rather enigmatically. But he was correct, as it turned out.

"Shouldn't be difficult to find," he said when asked about the location. Very Yankee-like.

This is another of New England's ancient burying grounds. The titled slabs of grayish, weathered marble crowd together on a hillside slope. Some broken. Some flaked. Many unreadable. Americans of several centuries here. Hard bones in hard ground. Roots of the national family tree.

And yet . . . and yet . . . You almost automatically bear left at the entrance gate and walk parallel with the low wall of gathered heaped boulders, somehow directionally pulled or compelled. I really cannot describe the sensation.

And there it is in the very corner of the cemetery, in the angle of the granitic fence, a clear distance away from all the others, as if the isolation and space sought in life is maintained in death, the grave of Willa Cather.

Most Nebraskans may consider it unusual their state's most famed writer is buried almost 2,000 miles away from the ground she celebrated. For them, and others, the memory of Cather and her series of Nebraska-based books is permanently fused. Inseparable.

That Cather explored, in her illuminating art, other landscapes internal as well as external; that she never returned to Red Cloud in later years (after the 1930s); that the East was home and workshop for more than half-century prior to her death in 1947—well, those are subordinate shadows which still do not cover the central image.

But why Jaffrey, New Hampshire, a sort of a charming, elongated dot of a place, curved along mapled hills rather like Grant Wood saw Stone City?

The explanation has its beginning in 1917. Willa Cather was then in the creative process of writing a new book. It would be entitled *My Ántonia*. Friends from Pittsburgh had leased a house near Jaffrey for the summer. Cather followed, taking accommodation at a generously large and sprawling tourist hotel called the Shattuck Inn. This was an inn of good reputation throughout New England.

One may learn a good deal of those days from D. D. (Jack) Bean, a native whose sense of place in a devotion to the Jaffrey region fills any stranger with as much envy as delight. Bean relives his boyhood, when five hundred guests were fed and rested at the Shattuck Inn. Trains from Boston and points east disgorged guests summer and winter. The inn was a lively place.

Jack Bean is president of a matchbook manufacturing firm of international dimensions today. He stands behind his magnificent house (with great wooden exposed beams) and contentedly looks beyond his private tennis court to the distant woods. There is, he guarantees, no better spot on earth.

Willa Cather apparently came to have something of the same opinion.

Ed Shattuck and his wife operated the inn when Cather first registered. They catered to her desire for strict privacy and solitude. She was given rooms of her choice, on the inn's top floor.

Mrs. Pauline Ingrahm Medlyn, a jolly, brisk woman, well remembers Willa Cather. Mrs. Medlyn was one of the regular waitresses at the Shattuck Inn.

"Oh, she was a large woman who wore suits. She was very, very nice," says Mrs. Medlyn, beaming on many yesterdays. "For years and years, she was one of the favorite guests. Very quiet and very reserved. You never saw her get excited . . . She wrote her stories—do you know she wrote love stories and was never married?—looking out at Mt. Monadnock."

As a rule, Mrs. Medlyn recalls, Cather dined alone. Fools and intrusions were jointly insufferable, it seems. She habitually occupied a small table in the middle of the large dining room. "She liked the food," Mrs. Medlyn emphasized.

Being isolated on the upper floor had certain potential disadvantages. Mrs. Medlyn revealed Cather was "Very, very afraid of fire." Accordingly, the Shattucks directed construction of a rope ladder. It was put in Cather's room, available for emergency descent along the outside frame wall.

Come to Jaffrey today, and you'll find the Shattuck Inn. You'll find it quite vacant, a giant house from which sounds are absent.

After the deaths of the original proprietors, the rambling resort center was sold to a Roman Catholic order as a seminary. That was about twenty years ago. In 1972, however, the school was closed for lack of students, Bean reported. Then the inn was sold to New York interests.

But they have done nothing, New Englander Bean observed sadly. Not only is the paint peeling—that's offensive—but the businessman in Bean objects to an investment failing to produce a return.

The inn is but a fair walk to Old Jaffrey's green, to the Meeting House at the hill's crest—a steepled hall supposedly erected on the day of the Battle of Bunker Hill. Just beyond the Meeting House, with its restored horse barns, is the cemetery.

If all the trees were cleared, Cather's grave would directly face Mt. Monadnock and its 3,165 foot summit, a kind of Green Mountain sentry.

But [for] a visitor who, like Cather, may have known what it was to stand on a Nebraska divide, to feel the convergence of limitless land and limitless sky, to see the grass alive and running, the line of infinite sight extends beyond the regionally-known mountain and goes to the Plains, miles and miles away.

Sunday Journal and Star Magazine of Nebraska, 29 Dec. 1974, 1.

Willa Cather's gravesite in Jaffrey, New Hampshire. Courtesy of Fenna
Mandolang.

Chronology of Willa Cather's Works

Notes

INTRODUCTION

1. Unless otherwise noted, biographical details of Willa Cather's life throughout this volume can be found in Woodress.

2. WC, letter to Helen Louise Stevens Stowell, 31 Aug. 1888. Willa Cather Pioneer Memorial Archives, Red Cloud, Nebr.

3. Will Owen Jones Papers, Nebraska State Historical Society, Lincoln, series 3, vol. 2.

4. See, for instance, WC, letter to Carrie Miner Sherwood, 14 Dec. 1933, Willa Cather Pioneer Memorial Archives. Cather asks Sherwood to make specific purchases for one person and to deliver a check and some clothing to another. Cather also mentions taxes and interest to be paid for a friend.

5. WC, letter to Mr. Anderson, 24 Nov. 1922, New York Public Lib., New York.

A LIVELY APPRENTICESHIP

1. For a history of the *Red Cloud Republican*, see *Biographical and Historical Memoirs* 558.

2. WC, letter to Mrs. Stowell, 31 Aug. 1888, Willa Cather Pioneer Memorial Archives.

3. See Curtin for reprints of many of Cather's early professional articles. Copies of the college publications on which Cather worked are located at the University of Nebraska–Lincoln Libraries, Archives and Special Collections.

4. WC, letter to Sarah Orne Jewett, 17 Dec. 1908, Houghton Lib., Harvard University, Cambridge, Mass.

5. WC, letter to Dorothy Canfield Fisher, 2 Sept. 1916, Columbia Butler Lib., University of Virginia–Charlottesville.

A WRITER'S BEGINNINGS

1. See articles collected in the Will Owen Jones Papers.

ELIA W. PEATTIE

1. The following information is taken from the Elia W. Peattie website at *http://www.unk.edu/departments/english/George/peattie/ewpbio.htm.* The website was created by Judith Boss of the University of Nebraska at Omaha and Susanne George-Bloomfield of the University of Nebraska at Kearney.

WILL OWEN JONES

1. Will Owen Jones Papers.

LOUISE POUND

1. See the *Nebraskan*, 1 Nov. 1892: 18, 24.

2. See the Louise Pound memorial issue of *Western Folklore* 18.3 (July 1959) for a full treatment of Pound's professional life. See O'Brien (129) for Pound's athletic triumphs in many sports.

MARIEL GERE

1. See the Gere Family Papers, Nebraska State Historical Society, especially letters of 10 Oct. 1904 and 24 Apr. 1912 from Cather. In Gere's article, it is unclear that Cather began living with the McClungs in 1901.

GEORGE SWETNAM

1. Information about George Swetnam comes from Deasy; Hoover; and Miller.

ELLA FLEISHMAN

1. Inquiries at the *Omaha World-Herald* and the Omaha Historical Society did not provide any bibliographic information on Ella Fleishman. Neither did a search of numerous biographies for journalists. It is possible, of course, that Fleishman was a pseudonym.

MARJORIE WYMAN

1. Although a Marjorie Wyman graduated from Omaha Central High School in 1920, a search of the Omaha census records did not reveal a registration of her birth and death dates.

JUNE PROVINES

1. Eric Gillespie, correspondence, 15 Apr. 1997, Col. Robert R. McCormick Research Center, Wheaton, Ill.

P. I. W.

1. Correspondence with the director of the *Kansas City Star* Library did not reveal the identity of P. I. W., 8 Apr. 1997.

FORD MADOX FORD

1. WC, letter to Cyril Clemens, 30 Jan. 1937, University of Virginia Lib.

A LITERARY LIFE

1. See O'Connor for an account of the reviews.

ELIZABETH YATES

1. Katherine Savage, letter to L. Brent Bolhke, Oct. 1982.

REQUIRED READING

Yates's original notes follow the text on page 121.

DEAN TERRILL

1. Dean Terrill, telephone interview, 5 Sept. 2001.

TOM ALLAN

1. Tom Allan, telephone interview, 7 Sept. 2001.

MARJORIE SMITH

1. Janet Sherwood Crary and Marjorie Smith, telephone interviews, 13 July 2001 and 17 July 2001.

ELSA SKOCPOL

1. William J. Skocpol, e-mail to Sharon Hoover, 29 Sept. 2001.

IN THE FAMILY

1. See Bennett for a succinct presentation of the details of the lives of the children of Charles and Virginia Cather.

2. See Riley for examples of letters by Charles and Virginia Cather and by other Cather family members.

ANN ZUROSKY

1. Correspondence with the Carnegie Library in Pittsburgh, Pa., and with Helen Cather Southwick did not reveal any details about the identity of Ann Zurosky.

HELEN C. SOUTHWICK

1. Readers who seek more background information about the relationship between Willa Cather and Elizabeth Vermorcken will want to read the ten letters Cather wrote to Vermorcken between 1906 and 1944 that are housed at the Pierpont Morgan Library, New York.

WILLA CATHER'S EARLY CAREER: ORIGINS OF A LEGEND

Southwick's original notes follow the text on pages 167–70.

IN A SPIRITUAL COMMUNITY

1. These records can be found in the *Bates Record Book* at the Nebraska State Historical Society.

RICHARD C. HERMAN

1. Richard C. Herman, telephone interview, 5 Sept. 2001.

Bibliography

Acocella, Joan. *Willa Cather and the Politics of Criticism*. Lincoln: U of Nebraska P, 2000.

Bennett, Mildred R. "Friends of Willa Cather." *Willa Cather Pioneer Memorial Newsletter* 41, no. 1 (1997): 5–7.

———. "What Happened to the Rest of the Charles Cather Family?" *Nebraska History* 54, no. 4 (1973): 619–25.

———. "Willa Cather in Pittsburgh." *Prairie Schooner* 33, no. 1 (1959): 64.

———. *World of Willa Cather*. Lincoln: U of Nebraska P, 1961.

Biographical and Historical Memoirs of Adams Clay Webster and Nuckolls Counties Nebraska. N.p., n.d. Located in Lincoln at the Nebraska State Historical Society.

Bohlke, L. Brent. *Willa Cather in Person: Interviews, Speeches, and Letters*. Lincoln: U of Nebraska P, 1986.

Brown, E. K., with Leon Edel. *Willa Cather: A Critical Biography*. Lincoln: U of Nebraska P, 1953.

Brown, Marion Marsh, and Ruth Crone. *Only One Point of the Compass: Cather in the Northeast*. N.p.: Archer Editions, 1980.

Bruccoli, Matthew. " 'An Instance of Apparent Plagiarism': F. Scott Fitzgerald, Willa Cather, and the First *Gatsby* Manuscript." *Princeton University Library Chronicle* 39 (1978): 171–78.

Bynner, Witter. "Autobiography in the Shape of a Book Review." *Prose Pieces*. New York: Farrar, 1979. 158–67.

Byrne, Kathleen D. and Richard C. Snyder. *Chrysalis: Willa Cather in Pittsburgh 1896–1906*. Pittsburgh: Historical Society of Western Pennsylvania, 1980.

[Chase]. "Literature and Life of Present Day Discussed by Miss Chase." *Mankato Daily Free*, 25 Feb. 1929.

Curtin, William M., ed. *The World and the Parish: Willa Cather's Articles and Reviews, 1893–1902*. 2 vols. Lincoln: U of Nebraska P, 1970.

Deasy, Deborah. "Ghostly Tales from a Non-Believer." *Pittsburgh Tribune-Review*, 30 Oct. 1994, G1.

Edel, Leon. *The Age of the Archive*. Monday Evening Papers 7. Middletown, Conn.: Wesleyan U, Center for Advanced Studies, 1966.

Fitzgerald, F. Scott. *The Great Gatsby*. 1925. New York: Scribner, 1992.

Ford, Ford Madox (Hueffer). *Return to Yesterday*. New York: Liveright, 1932.

Foster, Joseph. *D. H. Lawrence in Taos*. Albuquerque: U of New Mexico P, 1972.

Greenslet, Ferris. *Under the Bridge: An Autobiography*. Boston: Houghton Mifflin, 1943.

Hoover, Bob. " 'Pittsylvania' Author Still Writing Local Folklore." *Pittsburgh Post-Gazette*, 23 Nov. 1991, 10.

Kvasnicka, Mellanee. "Education in the Parish/Preparation for the World: The Educational Tradition in the Life and Works of Willa Cather." *DAI* 58.2A (1997): 4272. U of Nebraska–Lincoln.

Lacy, Gerald M., ed. *D. H. Lawrence: Letters to Thomas and Adele Seltzer*. Santa Barbara: Black Sparrow, 1976.

Lee, Hermione. *Willa Cather: Double Lives*. New York: Pantheon, 1989.

Lewis, Edith. *Willa Cather Living: A Personal Record*. New York: Knopf, 1953.

Madigan, Mark J., ed. *Keeping Fires Night and Day: Selected Letters of Dorothy Canfield Fisher*. Columbia: U of Missouri P, 1993.

March, John. *A Reader's Companion to the Fiction of Willa Cather*. Ed. Marilyn Arnold. Westport, Conn.: Greenwood, 1993.

Menuhin, Yehudi. *Unfinished Journey*. New York: Knopf, 1976.

Miller, Donald. "George Swetnam's 'Pittsylvania.' " *Pittsburgh Post-Gazette*, 12 Jan. 1997, E10.

Moorhead, Elizabeth. *These Two Were Here: Louise Homer and Willa Cather*. Pittsburgh: Pittsburgh Press, 1950.

Mott, Frank Luther. *A History of American Magazines, 1885–1905*. Cambridge: Harvard UP, 1957.

Nehls, Edward. *D. H. Lawrence: A Composite Biography*. Vol. 2. 1919–25. Madison: U of Wisconsin P, 1958.

O'Brien, Sharon. *Willa Cather: The Emerging Voice*. New York: Oxford UP, 1987.

O'Connor, Margaret Anne, ed. *Willa Cather: The Contemporary Reviews*. New York: Cambridge UP, 2001.

Peattie, Elia W. "Newspaper Women of Nebraska." In *History of the Nebraska Press*

Association, ed. Henry Allen Brainerd. Book 2, 23–32. Lincoln: N.p., 1923. First published in the *Beaver City Nebraska Editor*. 1895.

Rascoe, Burton. "Contemporary Reminiscences: Willa Cather, Zoe Akins, Theodore Dreiser and Others." *Arts & Decoration* 20 (April 1924): 28 ff.

Red Cloud (Nebr.) Republican. Willa Cather Pioneer Memorial Archives.

Reynard, Grant. "Willa Cather." *The Colors of My Life: Memoirs of a Nebraska Artist*. Rev. Harry H. Hoffman. Kearney, Nebr.: Kearney State College, 1986. 89–91.

Riley, Paul D., ed. "Cather Family Letters." *Nebraska History* 54, no. 4 (1973): 585–618.

Rinehart, Mary Roberts. *My Story: A New Edition and Seventeen New Years*. New York: Rinehart, 1948.

Sergeant, Elizabeth Shepley. *Willa Cather: A Memoir*. New York: Lippincott, 1953.

Shively, James R. *Writings from Willa Cather's Campus Years*. Lincoln: U of Nebraska P, 1950.

Slote, Bernice, ed. *The Kingdom of Art: Willa Cather's First Principles and Critical Statements, 1893–1896*. Lincoln: U of Nebraska P, 1966.

Stout, Janis, ed. *A Calendar of the Letters of Willa Cather*. Lincoln: U of Nebraska P, 2002.

Tannen, Deborah. *You Just Don't Understand: Women and Men in Conversation*. New York: Ballantine, 1990.

Woodress, James. *Willa Cather: Her Life and Art*. Lincoln: U of Nebraska P, 1970.

———. *Willa Cather: A Literary Life*. Lincoln: U of Nebraska P, 1987.

Source Acknowledgments

Permission to reprint has been given as follows:

PART 1. A LIVELY APPRENTICESHIP

A Writer's Beginnings

Will Owen Jones. "More or Less Personal." Reprinted by permission of the *Lincoln Journal Star*.

"Modern Coed Lacks Fire, Laments Louise Pound" (unsigned). Reprinted by permission of the *Omaha World-Herald*.

Mariel Gere. "Friends of Willa Cather's Campus Years." Reprinted by permission of the *Lincoln Journal Star*.

George Swetnam. "Bill Cather's Buddy." Copyright, *Pittsburgh Post-Gazette*, all rights reserved. Reprinted with permission.

A Nebraska Legend Grows

Ella Fleishman. "Willa Cather, Former Nebraska Girl, Puts Prairie in Literature." Reprinted by permission of the *Omaha World-Herald*.

Marjorie Wyman. "Willa Cather, Novelist, Was Modern Flapper at Nebraska U Thirty Years Ago." Reprinted by permission of the *Lincoln Journal Star*.

John M. Thompson. "'Confessions' of a Reporter—Partial but Voluntary." Reprinted by permission of the *Lincoln Journal Star*.

June Provines. "This Gala World." Reprinted by permission of the Chicago Sun-Times Inc.

P. I. W. "The Home on the Nebraska Prairie Which Always Recalls Willa Cather." Reprinted by permission of the *Kansas City Star*.

A Pittsburgh Teacher

Alexander Woollcott. "Shouts and Murmurs and Contents Noted." Reprinted by permission; © 1932 by The New Yorker Magazine, Inc.

Fred Otte Jr. "The Willa Cather I Knew." Printed by permission of the University of Nebraska–Lincoln Libraries, Archives & Special Collections.

Phyllis Martin Hutchinson. "Reminiscences of Willa Cather as a Teacher." Copyright © the New York Public Library, Astor, Lenox, and Tilden Foundations. Reprinted by permission.

Jane Shaw. "Seventy-fifth Anniversary Tea Recalls Student Teas." Copyright, *Pittsburgh Post-Gazette*, all rights reserved. Reprinted with permission.

A New York City Journalist

Ford Madox Ford. From *Return to Yesterday*. Copyright 1932 by Ford Madox Ford, renewed © 1959 by Janice Ford Boala. Reprinted by permission of Liveright Publishing Corporation and Carcanet Press Limited.

Adela Rogers St. John. From *Some are Born Great*. Copyright © 1974 by Adela Rogers St. John. Reprinted by permission of Doubleday, a division of Random House, Inc.

Witter Bynner. "A Willa Cather Triptych." Reprinted by permission of the *New Mexico Quarterly*.

PART 2. A LITERARY LIFE

An Established Writer

Elizabeth Shepley Sergeant. "Willa Cather." Reprinted by permission of the Estate of Elizabeth Shepley Sergeant.

Thomas Beer. "Miss Cather." Copyright © 1925. Reprinted by permission of Alfred A. Knopf Inc.

Joseph Foster. From *D. H. Lawrence in Taos*. Copyright © 1972. Reprinted by permission of the University of New Mexico Press.

A Novelist

Dorothy Canfield Fisher. "Novelist Recalls Christmas in Blue-and-Gold Pittsburgh." Reprinted by permission of the *Chicago Tribune Magazine of Books*.

———. "Willa Cather, Daughter of the Frontier." Reprinted with permission of Whitney Communications.

Henry Seidel Canby. "A Reminiscence." Copyright © 1947 Saturday Review Magazine Co. Reprinted by permission.

Fanny Butcher. "Willa Cather." From *Many Lives—One Love*. Copyright © 1972 by Fanny Butcher. Reprinted by permission of HarperCollins Publishers, Inc.

The Legend Grows

Elizabeth Yates. "Required Reading." Copyright © 1955. Reprinted by permission of Elizabeth Yates.

Paul Horgan. From "In Search of the Archbishop." Reprinted by permission of *Catholic Historical Review*.

Truman Capote. From *Music for Chameleons*. Copyright © 1975, 1977, 1979, 1980 by Truman Capote. Reprinted by permission of Random House, Inc.

A Mature Professional

Lorna R. F. Birtwell. "Remembering Willa Cather." Reprinted by permission of the Young Women's Christian Association Interchange National Board.

Mary Ellen Chase. From "Five Literary Portraits." Reprinted from *The Massachusetts Review*, © 1962 The Massachusetts Review Inc.

Alfred A. Knopf. "Publishing Willa Cather." Copyright © 1964 The New York Public Library, Astor, Lenox, and Tilden Foundations. Reprinted by permission.

PART 3. FRIENDSHIPS

In the Neighborhood

Dean Terrill. "Willa, Carrie Shared Human Story." Reprinted by permission of the *Lincoln Journal Star*.

Tom Allan. "Memories of Cather Abound for Centenarian." Reprinted by permission of the *Omaha World-Herald*.

Marjorie Smith. "In Neighborhood, It Was Willie Cather." Reprinted by permission of the *Lincoln Journal Star*.

Elsa Skocpol. "Willa Cather in Wilbur." Handwritten essay, 22 May 1982. Used by permission of the Nebraska State Historical Society and William J. Skocpol.

In the Family

Ann Zurosky. "Author Still Lives in Vivid Memory." Copyright, *Pittsburgh Post-Gazette*, all rights reserved. Reprinted with permission.

Helen Cather Southwick. "Willa Cather's Early Career: Origins of a Legend." Copyright Historical Society of Western Pennsylvania, Pittsburgh. Reprinted by permission.

A Mentor

Grant Reynard. "Willa Cather's Advice to a Young Artist." Reprinted from *Prairie Schooner* by permission of the University of Nebraska Press. Copyright 1972 by the University of Nebraska Press.

Yehudi Menuhin. From *Unfinished Journey*. Copyright © 1976 by Yehudi Menuhin and Patrick Seale and Associates Ltd. Reprinted by permission of Alfred A. Knopf Inc. and Patrick Seale Books Ltd.

A Spiritual Community

Rt. Rev. George Allen Beecher. From *A Bishop of the Great Plains*. Reprinted with permission from *Anglican and Episcopal History/The Historical Magazine of the Protestant Episcopal Church*.

Letter from Reverend Anders G. Lund Jr. to L. Brent Bohlke, 6 April 1983. Quoted by permission of Reverend Anders G. Lund Jr.

Richard C. Herman. "Memories of Willa Cather Shared with New Hampshire." Reprinted by permission of the *Lincoln Journal Star*.

Index